ANASTASIA KIRBY LUNDQUIST

OUT FOR BLOOD

The pursuit of life for the wounded on the fighting fronts of World War II

ISBN: 1484022130
ISBN 13: 9781484022139

Library of Congress Control Number: 2013920289
CreateSpace Independent Publishing Platform
North Charleston, South Carolina

DEDICATION

This book is dedicated with love and gratitude to my family.
To my husband
Lieutenant Commander Henry W. Lundquist, USNR (Ret.)
1904–2003
To my son
Captain Carl I. Lundquist, USN (Ret.)
To my daughter
Marilyn K. L. Anderson
To my son
Captain Edward H. Lundquist, USN (Ret.)
To my brother
Staff Sergeant Charles F. Kirby Jr., USMC
1921–2010
and
To my parents
Charles F. and Lillian L. Kirby
1891–1961 1890–1990

CONTENTS

PART VII
THE ARMY AIR FORCES

PART VIII
V-J DAY

PART IX
THE END

AN EPILOGUE

ABOUT THE AUTHOR

INDEX

FOREWORD

World War II was a defining moment in history. Yet that war and its details continue to slip from our national memory. Fortunately, Anastasia Kirby Lundquist counters the problem with an extraordinary story that comes from the heart.

The events that Anastasia relates are based on her experiences in the wartime Red Cross Blood Donor Center of Boston, where she served as the assistant director for virtually the entire war. Her work there began right after Pearl Harbor and extended to shortly after V-J Day (January 1942–September 1945). Her late husband—then—Lt. Henry W. Lundquist, USNR—was assigned to the First Naval District Office in Boston, with collateral duty as blood donor officer for the headquarters. Before his sought-after sea duty assignment became a reality, Anastasia Kirby and Lieutenant Lundquist created and produced a radio show called *Life to the Front*, broadcast weekly over the Columbia Broadcasting System's New England network outlet WEEI. On June 11, 1944, Anastasia and her coproducer were married.

Against that background, Anastasia relates a story that is straightforward and honestly told. The main players of her narrative are the "unfamous" men and women who lived through—and won—the major geopolitical struggle of the twentieth century. To emphasize how different the era was, Anastasia points out that there was no television, no e-mail, and no dishwashers.

On the plus side, however, it was a time when *our entire nation* was committed to a unified effort that included not just one political party, or one age group, or a particular administration, or selected media. Yes, there were war profiteers, draft dodgers, and "war slackers," but they were very few, and they were shunned as outliers. There was in fact no area of the country, geographic or otherwise, where the blue stars indicating a family member in the military—or the gold star indicating a member killed in action—did not hang in its front windows.

That's the way it was during World War II, and there has not been a comparable national commitment since that war ended. That makes Anastasia's story of special historical importance.

The full commitment of Americans during World War II cut across virtually all economic, ethnic, and geographic groups in the country, and thus Anastasia's central theme about the phenomenon of volunteer blood donations is uniquely appropriate. There is also the profound symbolism wrapped up in the transfer of the blood—mostly in the form of plasma—from the veins of those "on the home front" to the veins of those on the globally dispersed combat zones of World War II. Anastasia puts it well: "[T]he most intimate gift of all, a person's own blood, was often the gift of life for many a casualty."

Anastasia's story is parenthetically a story about blood plasma, the amazingly effective product that became the central component of the medical treatment that saved the lives of many thousands of U.S. wounded during World War II. The Red Cross describes plasma as the "liquid portion of blood—a protein-salt solution in which red and white blood cells and platelets are suspended." Because plasma could be reduced to a powder, mass produced, and then reconstituted and administered within minutes after a battle wound occurred, it was a life saver for U.S. fighting forces in the North African, European, and Pacific combat theaters.

By reducing shock and hemorrhaging immediately after a battle wound, plasma became the critical first step in the coordinated, in-depth medical system that dealt with the issue of combat casualties in World War II. The famous news correspondent Ernie Pyle wrote about what the medical personnel in combat thought about plasma; he is quoted in *Out for Blood*:

> *The doctors asked me at least a dozen times to write about plasma. They say that plasma is absolutely magical...They cite case after case where a wounded man was all but dead and within a few minutes after a plasma injection would be sitting up and talking. These doctors knew.*

To establish the importance of plasma, *Out for Blood* relates many firsthand accounts from wounded servicemen. One of the on-scene accounts involves a U.S. Marine wounded on the landing beach at the Pacific island of Tarawa. Anastasia writes:

> *The Navy transferred another man from Tarawa to Chelsea Naval Hospital. He was Pfc. John Stryhardz, USMC, and he described the beach at Tarawa.... "When I came to, the doctor and another corpsman were working on me...but all I can remember was a bottle hanging from a rifle." It was plasma, of course, and he went on to explain the sensation. "It was as though I was rising—being lifted right up off the ground. The best thing I can compare it to is being out of breath, and all of a sudden getting your breath back. Half an hour later I was up on my elbow, leaning over on my side, smoking a cigarette, and looking around the beach." When I asked him what he saw, he explained, "Poles and rifles all over the place. It looked like a lot of beanpoles in a vegetable garden, only they all had bottles hanging from them and wounded Marines lying on the beach beside them."*

Among its numerous firsthand accounts, *Out for Blood* also includes a description of a dramatic meeting that resulted from the Boston blood donor program:

> *One day a young soldier came to the center to give blood as a payback...He [Pvt. Richard Harvey] pulled a little tag out of his pocket, wondering if we might be interested in it. He explained that he had taken it off a bottle of blood that he was being given in a hospital in England. It said "Boston Center" on it. Interested? We were excited! We wasted no time in tracing the serial number on the tag. We had not far to look. The donor, Mrs. Audrey Woodward, 23, worked around the corner from the Center as a secretary in the accounting department of Holtzer Cabot, a company that sent us many donors. To have a donor meet a recipient of her blood was a first for us and an only!*

Considered together the numerous combat experiences that Anastasia relates add up to a highly personal narrative that involved the Boston community of the time, including herself and her family. Hers is not a story about national celebrities or eminent political leaders. It's a story about mostly ordinary but deeply patriotic citizens and local organizations that had no misgivings about encouraging their employees to support the war effort by donating blood. As such Anastasia's verbal vignettes provide some often missing "connective tissue" of the World War Two epic.

The very personal, stream of consciousness manner of this story takes on the feeling of a one-on-one conversation with Anastasia, perhaps over a mug of coffee in her living room or kitchen. The resulting sense of authenticity multiplies the narrative's impact.

Vivid images describing horrific naval battles in the Atlantic and Pacific, the bloody amphibious assaults on D-Day, the grinding infantry assaults as the Allies fought their way up the Italian peninsula, air combat, and the bloody, island-by-island march through the Pacific islands leading towards Japan are all part of the first-hand images of World War II that Anastasia delivers with jolting impact.

Perhaps the most important aspect of *Out for Blood* is its instructive function as comparative history. As we read the stream of individual stories, it's hard to not compare the attitudes and spirit of Bostonians in World War II with our own times and national culture.

Best-selling author Ken Follett wrote, "World War II is the greatest drama in human history, the biggest war ever and a true battle of good and evil." Anastasia Kirby Lundquist has delivered a view of that drama that is a thought-provoking example of how Americans can unite when faced with an existential threat.

Rear Adm. Joseph Callo, USNR (Ret.)
Author of *John Paul Jones:*
America's First Sea Warrior and
five additional books

ACKNOWLEDGMENTS

Many people provided advice, assistance, and encouragement to write this book. It is an important story that has not been told, and I look at this effort as an opportunity to recognize the extraordinary privilege that was mine to work with those wonderful and generous donors, and those men whom I interviewed, from admirals to privates, and the military and broadcasting professionals who produced the award-winning *Life to the Front* programs each week during the war.

I am appreciative of my neighbor Danny Kutner, who when he needed a community service project to qualify for his Bar Mitzvah, chose to teach me how to use my computer, and to his parents, Lena and Bob Kutner; my grandson Tom Lundquist for scanning photos and documents and providing computer support; and Vin Chau, who helped me move beyond my word processor to a desktop computer.

I am grateful for the editorial assistance from Godson Peter Maloy, son-in-law Steve Anderson, longtime friend Esther Johnson, and Jennifer Babb, an intern from Emmanuel College, who researched information, facts, and figures.

My daughter Marilyn helped in gathering and scanning photos and illustrations and reviewing the manuscript.

I thank both of my sons, Carl and Ned, for their Navy and military expertise, as well as their careful examination of the many iterations of this manuscript. My son Ned excelled in his role of project manager and editorial supervisor. Through him, I am grateful for the careful editing of author Debra McKesson, Kim Perz, and Mike Sorohan, as well as the perspective of historian and author David McComb and the foreword by historian and author Rear Adm. Joseph Callo.

I thank my late brother, Bud, who provided his insight and recollection of his war years as a Marine. And I wish to especially recognize my late husband, Henry, who was with me in our feeling that this story should be told, and who was very involved in the writing before he died in 2003.

To the hundreds of people who helped promote and organize groups who gave blood, to the thousands of donors who helped us achieve our quotas each week, and to the men and women of the military and broadcasting industry in Boston who helped produce *Life to the Front*, I offer my profound thanks.

PREFACE

The book you are about to read is a true story of World War II. It is not a history book, although it is history. It is a human-interest story, connecting the home front with the fighting front in a very real and personal way.

The story begins stateside on December 7, 1941, after the Japanese attack on Pearl Harbor. It ends in Tokyo Bay aboard the USS *Missouri* on September 12, 1945, following the signing of the instrument of surrender. In between, it touches on people, places, and events of the war days. If only some are mentioned, it is because there were so many, too many to be contained in one nvolume but not too many to be forever remembered with warmth and respect by this author.

As assistant director of the wartime Red Cross Blood Donor Center of Boston, I helped keep alive the connection between the home front and the fighting fronts as part of my job.

Out for Blood is a story of pursuit, the ongoing quest for life for the wounded, and a search for blood donors. You'll read about the extraordinary generosity of those donors, the profound gratitude of the recipients, and the dramatic testimony of witnesses: comrades who stood by their fallen buddies, chaplains who ministered to the wounded, and doctors who linked the donors with the dying to produce more survivors than was thought possible.

Much has been written about the greatest generation but not about its greatest gift. While the people at home contributed to war bond drives, raised victory gardens, and collected scrap metal for the war effort, the most intimate gift all, a person's own blood, was often the gift of life for many a casualty. These gifts were given through the wartime American Red Cross Blood Donor Service for the exclusive use of the surgeons general of the Army and Navy wherever needed. "Wherever" meant Africa, Sicily, Italy, France, Belgium, Germany, on the Atlantic Ocean, the Mediterranean Sea, and in the Pacific on more islands and the seas around them than we knew existed. That's where these gifts were needed. That's where they were sent. And that's where they saved lives.

Most gifts from these donors were processed into plasma. Where plasma went in World War II was an adventure story in itself. It rode in donkey carts up through the hills of Sicily to a battalion cut off in the mountains. It was strapped to the backs of doctors parachuting onto the fields of Sicily ready to go to work together. It was stored in sick bays on all warships and, in special quantities, ready for lavish use on hospital ships.

You will read how it was stored under tarp-covered trees in jungle aid stations near the front lies. It hung from branches of those trees, dripping life into casualties lying on the ground where litter bearers had laid them. Plasma went ashore with a high priority at Anzio; it followed Marines off amphibious landing boats at Iwo Jima. That's where gifts of the greatest generation went.

Some of you may learn that you are alive today because the life of your father or grandfather was saved by one of these pints of plasma; if not you, someone somewhere! Any reader who has a connection with the "greatest generation" may wonder if that person gave blood and where in the wide war world it may have gone.

As you read this book, you will learn how shipments of whole blood came on the war scene in Europe in August 1943. The surgeons general of the Army and Navy requested one thousand pints a day of whole blood for Europe. The request was fulfilled immediately when Basil O'Connor, the national chairman of the American Red Cross, announced on August 22 that a shipment had left the night before, via Army Transport Service. He reminded people that whole blood would supplement plasma, not replace it, and those one hundred thousand pints of plasma would still be needed every week in Europe.

After V-E Day, this changed. As soon as medics in Europe felt they could get along without further deliveries, whole blood was flown from eleven East Coast centers by Navy Transport Service to the Navy Distribution Center established on Guam after the island was secured in the summer of 1944. Whole blood had been going to Guam from the West Coast since Guam was ready to handle it.

Only type O donors gave blood that was used as whole blood. All other donations were used for plasma. The type O donations were marked with a traceable source so that someone whose donation went to the front as whole blood had a chance for a personal connection with the recipient. It might have been a letter from a parent or from a hospitalized patient himself. Seldom was it a person-to-person meeting, but when it did happen, it was a thrill to all.

Out for Blood is a reminder to remember. It is so easy to forget. But you can't remember what you never knew. As veterans of World War II returned home, many did not talk about where and how they spent their days in harm's way. This book will give readers a glimpse of what they were not told.

There is much to be learned from *Out for Blood*. The author hopes that she has provided a good read for the learning.

Anastasia Kirby Lundquist
June 2014
Auburndale, Massachusetts

PART I
DECEMBER 7, 1941

1. STATESIDE

It was a Sunday afternoon on December 7, 1941, in a suburban neighborhood. This was a quiet time, an at-home time. There was no dashing off to a mall for holiday shopping—there were no malls. Indeed, state law forbade the opening of retail stores on Sunday.

The father in this suburban family sat in his easy chair in the living room, reading the Sunday paper and nodding off after a hearty midday meal. He wasn't being kept awake by a crowd roaring out at him from a sports event on television. There was no television.

The mother was in the kitchen, cleaning up after her roast dinner with all the fixings. The children had washed and dried the dishes—there was no dishwasher—and the mother was doing the finish-up. The roasting pan would be soaking in the sink where the father would scrub it later.

On December 7, in this suburban home, the son—a live-at-home college student—was in his room going over his notes for an upcoming exam. There was no computer. His older sister was at her desk in her room writing a letter. There was no e-mail.

Radios were turned on both upstairs and down, but no one was paying close attention to them. That is until an emergency signal cut in indicating that the network was about to interrupt the program in progress with a news flash: "The Japanese have attacked Pearl Harbor."

"My God!" said the father, coming to with a jolt, the newspaper spilling onto the floor as he called out, "Mother, come quick!" The mother wrapped her wet hands in her apron and hurried into the living room, calling out on her way, "What, what, what is it?"

"The Japanese have attacked Pearl Harbor!" her husband blurted out.

"Oh, my Lord in heaven," she gasped.

Upstairs, their son had heard the announcement on his radio. He shouted out, "Hey, Sis. Come quick! Listen to this: the Japanese have attacked Pearl Harbor!"

His sister moved quickly into the hall and stood in the doorway to her brother's room. Neither spoke. They just listened. They were stunned by what they were hearing. They wondered how bad it was, and what would happen now. They waited for more details.

On that Sunday afternoon, a radio producer was parking his car outside a building in the city where he kept a small studio as a retreat for writing. He had his car radio on as he drove through town, listening to a regular Sunday concert by Walter Damrosch. The maestro was not only an outstanding conductor; he was a great teacher, too. Each week he would feature a certain instrument of the orchestra, explaining its importance in the piece being played. That Sunday, it was percussion instruments, and at the moment, it was the gong.

The network also used a gong to alert its listeners that a news flash was imminent. Our producer thought the gong he heard was part of the music lesson, so he was totally unprepared for any news flash, much less what came. He was shocked. He sat in his car to listen for more details. Then he gathered his papers and hurried upstairs to his studio where he turned on his radio and went about his work. He, too, wondered "What now?" as did millions throughout the country, indeed throughout the world.

Some Americans were frozen in shock; others were enraged. How could this have happened? How could we have let it happen? Didn't anyone see them coming? Wasn't anyone watching? Who was supposed to be watching? Who was responsible?

The world is full of chronic blamers who are not so much interested in picking up the pieces as they are in finding someone to blame. Names! They want names. But they were not alone on December 7. As the news sunk in, there were many questions. For example, it was known that a Japanese envoy was in direct consultation with our State Department even as his country's aircraft were on their way for the surprise attack. When a large flight of planes had been detected by radar approaching Oahu, they were presumed to be a flight of our own B-17s that were expected to be coming in from the States, so they received no attention.

Even before people stateside had learned of these details, a psychological thaw was creeping in. The emotions of the blamers and the irate turned to compassion. There were so many victims, military and civilian; so much devastation, ships and planes, buildings and facilities. These people, these places were ours, and people stateside grieved for them.

In spite of their concern for others, the compassionate turned their thoughts inward. How would each individual be affected personally? They did not have to wait long for an answer. All newspapers and radio stations carried the announcement that the president would address the nation on Monday evening, December 8. Everyone who could do so was by a radio, waiting for the president.

As the clock hands reached the appointed moment, a cold, flat voice came on: "Ladies and gentlemen, the president of the United States."

Then the emotion-packed but contained voice of Franklin Delano Roosevelt:

1. STATESIDE

My fellow Americans...

Yesterday, December 7, 1941—a date which will live in infamy—the United States of America was suddenly and deliberately attacked by naval and air forces of the Empire of Japan.

The United States was at peace with that nation, and at the solicitation of Japan, was still in conversation with the government and its emperor looking toward the maintenance of peace in the Pacific.

Indeed, one hour after Japanese air squadrons had commenced bombing in Oahu, the Japanese ambassador to the United States and his colleagues delivered to the secretary of state a formal reply to a recent American message. While this reply stated that it seemed useless to continue the existing diplomatic negotiations, it contained no hint of war or armed attack.

It will be recorded that the distance of Hawaii from Japan makes it obvious that the attack was deliberately planned many days or even weeks ago. During the intervening time, the Japanese government has deliberately sought to deceive the United States by false statements and expressions of hope for continued peace.

The attack yesterday on the Hawaiian Islands has caused severe damage to American naval and military forces. Very many American lives have been lost. In addition, American ships have been reported torpedoed on the high seas between San Francisco and Honolulu.

Yesterday, the Japanese government also launched an attack against Malaya.

Last night, Japanese forces attacked Hong Kong.

Last night, the Japanese attacked Guam.

Last night, Japanese forces attacked the Philippine Islands.

Last night, the Japanese attacked Wake Island.

This morning, the Japanese attacked Midway Island.

Japan has therefore undertaken a surprise offensive extending throughout the Pacific area. The facts of yesterday speak for themselves. The people of the United States have already formed their opinions and well understand the implication to the very life and safety of our nation.

As commander-in-chief of the Army and Navy, I have directed that all measures be taken for our defense.

Always will we remember the character of the onslaught against us.

No matter how long it will take us to overcome this premeditated invasion, the American people in their righteous might will win through to absolute victory.

I believe that I interpret the will of the congress and of the people when I assert that we will not only defend ourselves to the utmost but will make very certain that this form of treachery will never endanger us again.

Hostilities exist. There is no blinking at the fact that our people, our territories, and our interests are in grave danger.

With confidence in our armed forces—with the unbounding determination of our people—we will gain the inevitable triumph— so help us God.

I ask that the congress declare that, since the unprovoked and dastardly attack by Japan on Sunday, December 7, a state of war has existed between the United States and the Japanese Empire.

The small groups that had gathered around radios to hear the president's speech dispersed at its conclusion. Some walked away slowly, silently, alone. Some couples hurried off, grasping each other's arms and talking nervously, scared by what they had heard and what it might mean to them personally. Everyone was horrified by what had happened at Pearl Harbor, even though they did not have the whole picture. Nobody did...yet. Washington did not want the enemy to know the full extent of its success—or lack of success. The Japanese knew that they did not get the aircraft carriers they were after. *Lexington, Enterprise,* and *Saratoga* were not "in" when the enemy came calling.

Saratoga was in San Diego for overhaul; *Lexington* had left to deliver planes to Midway; *Enterprise* was returning from delivering planes to Wake and was due in Pearl on December 6. Fortunately, bad weather changed that and a delay was ordered in its Pearl Harbor arrival.

Although the enemy had missed the carriers, their planes had found sitting targets on Battleship Row and in the harbor where some of the Navy's best lay quietly at anchor on that peaceful Sunday morning. The raiders thought that they had knocked out more ships than they actually had, and they were amazed to see some of these survivors turn up to engage them in battles later on in the war.

The bombs spared some ships, but so many were damaged or destroyed. We all knew the details eventually. The whole world knew that the *Arizona* exploded and sank with over a thousand men trapped within her hull. Today that ship serves as a symbol of that "Day of Infamy." The *Arizona* Memorial at Pearl Harbor is visited by throngs of people, many taking the boat from the visitors center at the National Historical Park on shore out to the memorial in the harbor next to Ford Island, above the remains of the sunken ship and her 1,177 crewmembers who are still onboard.

Anyone watching ships of the United States Navy entering or departing Pearl Harbor is impressed by the crews of those ships who, even today, man the rails at attention, rendering honors to their fallen comrades of yesterday who are entombed below. It is a deeply moving sight to behold.

On December 8, 1941, the cries of the blamers were once more gaining momentum. "Who was to blame for Pearl Harbor?" they demanded. Again they wanted names. But they withdrew their demands when it was announced that the president had called for the creation of a board of inquiry. He asked Secretary of the

Navy Frank Knox and Secretary of War Henry Stimson to recommend two Navy officers, two Army officers, and one civilian for the board.

President Roosevelt accepted the recommendations of the two secretaries. They were Adm. William H. Standley, USN (Ret.); Rear Adm. Joseph M. Reeves, USN (Ret.); Maj. Gen. Frank B. McCoy, USA; Brig. Gen. Joseph T. McNarney, USA; and the civilian, Supreme Court Associate Justice Owen J. Roberts. The five met informally with the secretaries in Washington on December 17. Justice Roberts was named chairman, and, forever after, the five were known as the Roberts Commission.

The five flew to Oahu to conduct interviews with everyone involved with the December 7 attack, including the commanders: Adm. Husband E. Kimmel, USN, and Gen. Walter C. Short, USA. This was a painful experience for all in the Pearl Harbor community because they were still in a state of personal and professional trauma. Kimmel asked Rear. Adm. Robert Theobald—then commander of Destroyer Flotilla One in the Pacific Fleet—to serve as his counsel. As the questioning continued, Theobald urged Kimmel to replace him with legal counsel, but Kimmel declined. "I don't need a lawyer," Kimmel said. "I want you."

The commission worked hard and fast, returning to Washington to present its report to the president on January 23. They had found General Short and Admiral Kimmel guilty of "dereliction of duty" and "errors of judgment."

It answered the cries of the blamers.

It was reported that neither man had considered retirement, but on February 7 the Navy and War Departments announced that both Kimmel and Short had applied for retirement. Their requests were accepted by the president.

After the war was over, Congress requested that the case against the two Pearl Harbor commanders be reopened. The new hearings resulted in a finding of "errors of judgment" only. The blistering charge of "dereliction of duty" was dropped. This was truly an easing of a terrible scourge for these two officers, but it came too late. Two seasoned commanders had been required to sit out World War II in retirement, under a cloud.

On December 7, 1941, our country's concern was with Japan's attack on Pearl Harbor. On December 8 came the president's declaration of war against the attackers. On December 10, our country's attention was turned to Europe where Germany and Italy declared war on the United States.

Up until that time, most wars were fought against one country at a time, facing off against each other in one place. The U.S. and its allies fought World War II all over the world—on different continents, in different countries, on different oceans and seas, in different climates, with different geography, different cultures, and different languages—a veritable mélange of differences, all at the same time.

2. WHAT NOW?

After the declaration of war, it was clear to the people stateside that things would be different henceforth. The mainland may not have been hit, but we were all together now—at war. In some lives, changes would be minor; in others they would be drastic. Life would never be the same again for many, but they did not know it yet.

As we return to our suburban family, change was not immediate, but it wasn't too long before the father was giving up his weekly date with the hilarious Jack Benny and his radio show. The father, Charles Kirby, was out on the street, equipped with hard hat and flashlight, patrolling the neighborhood as an air raid warden. Amid concern that Germany might send planes across the Atlantic to bomb the East Coast, a blackout was in effect.

Streetlights remained dark; storefronts were blackened; window shades in homes were required to be drawn on lighted rooms. If a shade was up, the warden had to make his way to the front door, ring the doorbell, and tell the resident to get that shade down. An even more realistic threat came from German submarines. Lights on shore created a backdrop to silhouette ships approaching coastal ports, providing ready targets for prowling U-boats. The blackout was essential.

The mother's concern in this suburban household was like that of all the other mothers in the country. Would her son have to go to war? What might happen to him? Would he be all right? Beyond this constant worry—that never did let up—hers was a matter of inconvenience. Would she be able to get a roast for her Sunday dinner every week? Would her butcher have one to give her? Would she have the stamps needed to procure it?

Rationing began, and there were major shortages of nonrationed items. Gasoline was for necessary travel only. People stood in line to get sugar and butter—and stockings. Some people simply went without as many items grew scarcer. Many suffered serious deprivation during the war, but they offered little complaint since no bullets ever crossed their paths. This was when margarine came into the picture in a white oblong block with a little yellow capsule attached, which was blended into the white block to make it look like a pound of butter.

In addition to her culinary trials, Lillian Kirby, our suburban mother, had an unexpected change in her life. She had to go to work in her daughter's book shop when her daughter, Anastasia Kirby, was tapped by the American Red Cross to take the position of assistant director of their newly opened Boston Blood Donor Center, operating under contract with the Army and Navy.

The student son in this suburban family returned to school on December 9. Boston College was a Jesuit school, so December 8 was a holiday because it was a holy day, the Feast of the Immaculate Conception, ironically the officially designated feast day of the United States of America.

There was much distraction in all of his classes. It was a combination of patriotism—young men wanting to get into the fray immediately, to go after the enemy—and of fear of being drafted. Administrators and professors urged the students to stay in school as long as possible, at least through semester finals; otherwise they would lose credit for the whole term. When school resumed after Christmas vacation, there were changes. Classes were combined with seniors and juniors grouped together in one classroom for certain subjects. In one room, the son noted that there were empty seats. Where were the former occupants? They had been drafted.

Since 1940, all able-bodied males between the ages of 18 and 45 had been required to register under the Selective Service Act. Each person had a number. On December 13, 1941, the draft was activated in a special event held in Washington on Capitol Hill. A huge glass fishbowl was filled with the numbers of draftees. Secretary of War Henry Stimson was there to do the drawing. President Roosevelt sat across the fishbowl from him, ready to read the number pulled out of the bowl.

The media was present *en masse.* Of course there was no television, but there was radio with all the networks represented, along with wire services and newspapers from all over the country. According to plan, Secretary Stimson was blindfolded. Somebody called out "Go fish!" and he dug deep into the bowl and pulled out a number. He passed it to the president. Everyone was quiet.

Each radio announcer held his microphone close to his face, ready to repeat the number read off by the president. The Mutual Broadcasting System was a major network at that time, and its Washington representative was at the ready by his mike. He did not gasp, gulp, or stammer as he repeated the number just read by the president. After all, he was a professional. But afterward, Steve McCormick did all of the above because it was his own number that had just been announced. (Steve was a graduate of Boston University and of Cambridge High and Latin School, where he had been a classmate and member of the senior drama cast with the author of this book.)

There was more activity on Capitol Hill regarding the draft. As written, the law stated that draftees were not to leave the Western Hemisphere. That had to be changed.

The prospects of being drafted worried our suburban student. He did not want to be drafted. He did not want to be a GI. He wanted to be a Marine. When a Navy doctor arrived on campus to examine students for officer training, our student got in line. He was turned down because of his eyes, as he had worn glasses since he was a little boy. The Navy doctor, knowing that this student wanted to be a Marine, told him to go downtown to the Marine Corps Recruiting Office and enlist. If he passed the initial test, he would be sent to officer training...so said the doctor.

Without consulting with anyone, parents or teachers, he did just that. He went to the Marine Recruiting Office where he was examined and turned down again. This time it was because of weight, so he went home and fattened himself up and returned to pass the physical successfully. His name on a special piece of paper, with all the blanks filled in, declared him to be ready to become a Marine.

He was told to go home and wait to be called, ready to leave the day following the call. It did not come until April. Candidates were not sworn in individually but by platoons of seventy, so each had to wait until there were sixty-nine others. After the long wait, it was a hassle to get ready overnight. But after much rushing around on everyone's part, he was set to go.

His parents drove him to the courthouse where the Marines-to-be were to meet for their swearing in. As of April 6, 1942, he and sixty-nine others were officially members of the United States Marine Corps. They said their painful good-byes, and the Marines were bused to a hotel to await an early morning entrainment to Parris Island.

There was pride mixed with the pain of departure, a mixture that remained within the hearts and minds of his parents throughout the war years—along with constant prayers for his safety. Mr. and Mrs. Charles F. Kirby drove home in a sort of tearful silence. Pvt. Charles F. Kirby Jr., USMC, boarded the train the next morning in a state of exhilaration—and wonder. He was what he wanted to be. He was a Marine, but where would it take him?

When the announcement of the attack on Pearl Harbor was gonged into the life of our radio producer, change came almost immediately. He acquired a new title: director of war programs for WEEI, the Columbia Broadcasting System's key New England network station. From then on, he spent his time writing and producing a series of programs called *This Is Your Fight* and other special events to let the ordinary citizen know what he or she could do for the war effort.

Early in April, after giving a pint of blood to the Red Cross and knowing of the great need for donors, he decided that he would produce a program about the Blood Donor Service. He thought it would be effective to have a group of popular radio personalities giving their blood in a live broadcast direct from the center, explaining the procedure as they went along.

When he went to the center to see if his idea was acceptable, he was told, "You'd better see Miss Kirby." This he did and found that Miss Kirby was as enthusiastic about his idea as he was. She would make the necessary arrangements at the center when a mutually convenient date was set for the broadcast. He would contact the station's promotion and publicity departments to arrange for coverage. Because the producer had already donated a pint of blood, he knew exactly what he was writing about.

When the appointed day came, the producer, Henry Lundquist, arrived with both his scripts and his narrator, Fred Garrigus. The engineers were there with their gear, and the personalities with their "personalities"—and a little apprehension. Popular sportscaster Jack Maloy and talk show hostess Priscilla Fortescue arrived, along with many announcers whose names and voices were familiar to the vast New England radio audience. It was hoped that listeners would feel that if these people they had come to know so well could give their blood, the listeners could, too.

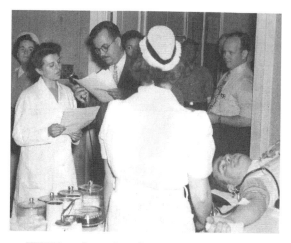

WEEI broadcasts from the center with Dr. Delilah Remer on duty. Fred Garrigus is conducting the interview while sportscaster Jack Maloy is donating.

The program met the producer's expectations. The radio audience came forward with pints and pints of blood, as did the staff of the radio station, including station manager Harold Fellows and other top executives. And they kept coming throughout the war. There were many Gallon Club members. Florence Mitchell, the general manager's secretary, gave fifteen pints. The producer was a "two galloner."

Time went by until one day in July "Uncle Sam" came calling. Our producer, Henry Lundquist, was drafted. Harold Fellows went to the Draft Board at once. He said that he needed this man who was doing more for the war effort than he ever could do if they gave him a gun and marched him off with a lot of boys half his age. The Draft Board concurred, and the producer was deferred.

Meanwhile, there were many government agencies in need of professional assistance in their expanding work. They came knocking on Lundquist's door. CBS had already wanted him in New York. The Office of War Information also made a bid. The Army and Navy extended invitations. Finally, the station manager said that he would not stand in the way if his producer wanted to accept one of these offers.

Our producer decided to join the Navy. On July 8, 1942, he was sworn in, becoming Lieutenant Junior Grade (Lt. j.g.) Henry W. Lundquist, U.S. Naval Reserve (USNR), with orders to Harvard University for indoctrination and then to First Naval District Headquarters in the radio division of the Office of Public Relations, known as PRO. But before he could even be fitted to his new uniform, his orders were rescinded. No indoctrination. He was to report directly for active duty.

On August 6, 1942, two members of the Boston media reported for duty in the First Naval District PRO: Lt. j.g. William G. Schofield of the *Boston Traveler* (an evening daily) and Lt. j.g. Henry W. Lundquist of radio station WEEI. This began a close Navy affiliation between these officers and a lifelong friendship.

Within months, Bill Schofield left PRO to go to sea where he remained as officer in charge of Armed Guard aboard merchant marine ships in the Mediterranean and on the Murmansk Run for most of the war.

After reporting for duty at PRO, Lieutenant Junior Grade Lundquist

Newsmen from Boston's newspapers give blood.

served as radio officer for the district with collateral duty as blood donor officer for headquarters, duty assigned to him by the commandant, Rear Adm. Robert A. Theobald, who had been commander of Destroyer Flotilla One in the Pacific Fleet on December 7, 1941, and who was counsel during the Roberts Commission hearings for Admiral Kimmel.

3. A "GREAT ROMANCE"

About the time that my brother was going off to war with the Marines, I went to a local hospital to visit a sick friend. He was a Jesuit priest who had been a bright, active, productive, wonderfully creative person, full of ideas that he never left idle in his head. He put them into action. He had been a college professor and prefect of studies at Holy Cross College in Worcester, Massachusetts, for several years, but his greatest success was in the promotion of children's books and reading for young people. He had founded a Book of the Month Club for boys and girls with headquarters in the Empire State Building in New York City, and had operated bookstores there and in Boston. He had written children's books, lectured about them, mounted enticing exhibits, and produced elaborate book fairs.

Now he was hospitalized and I went to visit him. At the nurses' station, I was told that he was too sick for visitors and I should not go in to see him. I said that I would just stand in the doorway to his room and wave, to let him know I was thinking of him, and then be on my way. When I did so, he beckoned me in. I entered and stood by his bed. He was pale and seemed very weak, but he had questions for me.

We had worked together in books. I had been radio editor for his book fairs, interviewing the many authors he brought to town for his programs. Now I was into blood, and he wanted to know all about my new work. When I told him that the Red Cross was working under contract to the Army and Navy, which had such a tremendous need for blood plasma for their wounded on the battlefronts all over the world, his eyes widened and he seemed to brighten. When I described some of the people who were giving blood, there came a slight glow to his pallor. When I told him about the interviews I was having with casualties back from the front, those who survived because of plasma, his eyes seemed to sparkle.

"What a romance!" he said. "What a great romance! To think that someone can give blood here in the States and it can go clear across the world to save a stranger's life on a battlefront. What a romance! One of the greatest!"

The nurse had come quietly into the room. She did not speak. She just stood there glowering at me as if to say, "So this is standing in the doorway and waving, huh?"

I looked at her contritely and said, "I was just leaving." Then I smiled at the patient and said, "I have to go now." I smiled again and he smiled back.

The nurse did not smile. I said, "I'll see you again," and left.

I did not see him again. The Reverend Francis X. Downey, SJ, died on April 14, 1942, at age 55. What a loss! But what a legacy he left. How many hundreds of boys and girls were introduced to the romance of books that took them through time and space to know people and places that their lives could never touch in reality? This man knew what romance was, that our donors were part of a great romance. A rich association came to an end for me when I lost this dear and treasured friend.

As the days and weeks and months of 1942 moved toward 1943 and beyond, the number of donors responding to appeals for blood increased. At the same time, casualties were coming home to recuperate before returning to service.

They were survivors, some because they had received plasma on a shrapnel-infested beach or in a foxhole in the jungle before being carried off to an advance aid station for treatment. Some had been close to death on an operating table. All were glad to be alive and grateful to the folks at home who helped keep them alive. The medics interviewed were lavish in their praise of plasma and in gratitude to the donors who helped them through their crises at the front.

This combination of donor and survivor is what our dying Jesuit called the great romance of the war. Now we could see what he meant in these real-life examples. It was indeed a romance. There were thousands and thousands in the cast of characters of this romance—donors, recipients, witnesses. The recipients hailed from every corner of the United States and became casualties in remote corners of the world.

The witnesses, also from all over this country, were the comrades who stood by their wounded buddies; the chaplains who ministered to the wounded; and the doctors, nurses, corpsmen, and other medics who met these casualties in these far-off places and worked tirelessly and heroically to make sure these casualties remained survivors.

The testimony of these witnesses was graphic and dramatic… and convincing. It assured donors that their blood made the difference between life and death for so many, that contributions from the home front made it possible for the medical corps to save hundreds of thousands of their patients.

The donors also came from everywhere. They were everybody. And everyone was a "somebody." Indeed, each individual who walked through the front door of the center to give blood was a VIP—all equal. Blood wasn't like money, where those who had a lot could give a lot to make up for those who didn't have much and could only give a little. With blood it was a pint apiece. That meant six thousand VIPs at a pint apiece each week for each month until the war was over. This was the quota set for Boston by the Army and Navy, which held the contract under which the American Red Cross operated. This was an enormous challenge, but the American people were equal to it. They did it.

These donors came from all walks of life: blue collar, white collar, no collar, Roman collar, lace collar. Gracious ladies in fancy hats and white gloves arrived in chauffeur-driven limousines; executives were dropped off by taxicabs; still others walked because they did not have fare for the subway. One man came by wheelchair, not being pushed by somebody else, but propelling himself through more than five miles of unfriendly city streets. This was long before curbstones were required to be wheelchair accessible. And one trip was not enough for this generous man. He was back again, same route, for a repeat donation.

Our donors came from all neighborhoods. They came from tall tenements painted dark colors to cope with the smoke from city factories. There were service flags in most windows here: more than one blue star in many windows, a gold star in some. They came from sprawling white mansions on the outskirts of the city. The shades were all drawn in one house here. Nobody was home. The owner was operating in a tent hospital in Europe. His two Navy sons were at sea in the Pacific somewhere. His wife was a Red Cross volunteer working all day at the Blood Donor Center. At night she stayed with her daughter who was expecting her first child while her husband was "over there."

Some donors came in groups. Some came alone.

A woman with a gold star pinned to the lapel of her coat—signifying that she had lost a son in the war—was still hurting so very, very deeply but came to give her blood so that some other mother's son might have it if he needed it. Hers didn't, because he was one of those about whom Ernie Pyle wrote in his book *Here Is Your War* (1943): "I heard of a high British officer who went over the battlefield just after the action was over. American boys were still lying dead in their foxholes, their rifles still grasped in firing position in their dead hands. And the veteran English soldier remarked time and again, in a sort of hushed eulogy spoken only to himself, 'Brave men. Brave men.'" Ernie Pyle's next book was entitled *Brave Men* (1944).

Another gold star mother was not wearing her pin. She had not had time to change her clothes. She had worked all night in a defense plant, hurried home to get her five grandchildren off to school, then rushed to the center to keep her appointment. She had five children of her own—three boys and two girls. One of the boys was in the service; she didn't know where. One was missing in action. She knew where that was, but not where he was. Her third son had made her a gold star mother.

Were these donors an inspiration? Every day—so much inspiration from so many people! Like the day when there was a tap, tap, tap on the big window wall at the former center at Exeter and Boylston Streets. A man was tapping his way to the front door. When he found it, he and his companion entered and went through the donor routine. Upstairs in the donor room, he lay on the table and his companion curled up on the floor underneath. The nurse was a little uneasy but equally inspired to have a Seeing Eye dog and its master at her table.

Two months later they were back, but this time there were three other blind men with them. Three months after that second visit, they were back again, this time thirteen strong…all blind. Inspiration? Every day!

But the workers at the center were not the only ones who were inspired. The donors inspired themselves and each other. One day thirteen blind men—another day Marines. As a woman sat in the waiting area one morning—she had been so afraid that she might be late for her appointment that she arrived much too early—the front door opened and a group of Marines came in. Her heart skipped a beat. She knew the uniform well. She had two Marines of her own: a young son at Parris Island waiting for orders to move out and a husband in the Pacific giving orders for his men to move on. She watched the sergeant in charge of the little group and listened to him call out, "When you hear your name, take your registration and sit down and wait to be called."

A Marine with an *A* name came and sat beside her.

"Good morning, Corporal," she said.

He smiled. "Good morning, ma'am."

"You Marines shouldn't be doing this," she said, "We civilians should be doing it for you."

"But we're the ones who may need it. It's sort of insurance. Besides, there's nothing to giving. I've done it before."

"I have, too," she said, "and it is easy."

She heard her name and stood up. She looked down at the Marine. "Good luck to you, Corporal," and she held out her hand.

Military and civilian donors gather over coffee in the refreshment room.

The Marine was on his feet immediately, shaking her hand warmly.

"Thanks, ma'am, and thanks for the blood."

"You're very, very welcome," and she turned to start the donor route, her eyes a little blurred. All along her way she heard the same comments: "What a great looking bunch of Marines! What an inspiration!"

It was that, all right. And there was other inspiration that nobody noticed. It was within the donors themselves. How could they not be inspired by what they were doing? They knew that the blood they were giving would soon be on its lifesaving journey. They knew that this was exactly what was going to happen because they heard it from witnesses who had been there when it went to work.

None other than a Navy chaplain had told them, "There is no doubt in my mind whatsoever but that plasma saved my life."

The prognosis declared in sick bay aboard the chaplain's heavily damaged ship after the Battle of Tassafaronga, where he had been badly burned, was "He can't make it." But he did, and this is how we happened to learn about it. He told us himself.

4. THE PADRE

The Reverend Arthur McQuaid was a Roman Catholic chaplain, who, like many Navy priests, was known as "the Padre." When he came home on medical leave following his ordeal at sea, he was asked to speak to parishioners at Saint Margaret's Church in Lowell, Massachusetts, where he had been a curate for nine years before entering the Navy. He knew that he would be limited in what he could discuss about operations in his remarks, so he went to First Naval District Headquarters for guidance. He was directed to the Office of Public Relations where he was received by the commanding officer, Cmdr. Neil Rex Collier, USNR.

Chaplain Lt. Cmdr. Arthur F. Mc Quaid

The chaplain explained that he was home on medical leave after being badly burned when his ship was hit by enemy fire. He added that he credited blood plasma with saving his life. Commander Collier interrupted him and asked him to wait until he could have one of his officers join them. He asked his yeoman to get Lt. j.g. Henry Lundquist. After Lieutenant Junior Grade Lundquist's arrival and subsequent intrdoductions, the chaplain went into the details of his story.

He described the hours leading up to the battle in which his ship was hit and how he was caught in the fire that resulted. Even though those in sick bay did not expect him to pull through; he said that plasma did it for him.

The listeners were intent and silent until the chaplain paused and said, "That's about it." Only then did they speak. They agreed that it was a remarkable story, complimented the chaplain on his stamina in getting through what he had endured, and said how good it was to have him back. They talked of the ship and Tassafaronga and Tulagi and went over certain information that would have to be excluded and what he could discuss. Security was tight in those days.

Finally, Collier said, "I think the chaplain should meet Miss Kirby." The lieutenant concurred and the commander asked Yeoman Sands to get her at the Red Cross. When the call came through there followed a four-way conversation.

I was deeply moved by the chaplain's story and asked him if he would be willing to speak on an upcoming program. He declined, explaining that he was still recuperating and very tired. But after talking for a while, he decided that since he owed his life to plasma, he had a debt to the Red Cross and he would do one thing for Miss Kirby. I was elated, needless to say, and suggested a radio interview since it would reach more people.

Commander Collier asked Lieutenant Lundquist, his radio officer, to try to get time on the radio station where he had been in charge of war programs before coming into the Navy. Then he could help the chaplain and with the facts that could be incorporated into my script for the broadcast.

4. THE PADRE

On the night of April 14, 1943, the chaplain, the lieutenant, and Miss Kirby reported to producer Fred Garrigus at WEEI. At precisely 10:30 p.m., Mr. Garrigus threw the cue to the announcer.

ANNOUNCER: At this time, WEEI presents one of the truly remarkable stories to come out of the war in the Solomons, the story of Lt. Arthur F. McQuaid, Chaplain Corps of the United States Navy. This program has been arranged by WEEI's War Program Department with the cooperation of the American Red Cross Blood Donor Service. Chaplain McQuaid will be interviewed by Anastasia Kirby, Assistant Director of the Boston Blood Donor Center.

KIRBY: This is the story of a man who was put ashore on the lonely island of Tulagi on the night of November 30... to die. That same man is sitting across the microphone from me now, very much alive, and ready to tell you the story of his escape from death in the Solomons. Chaplain McQuaid, it's a very great privilege to present to our radio audience a man who has experienced the real miracle of plasma.

MCQUAID: I assure you, Miss Kirby, that it's a far greater privilege to be that man.

KIRBY: Where on your ship were you, Father, when this disaster occurred?

MCQUAID: I was at my Battle Station which means, for a chaplain, where I was ready to aid with any wounded.

KIRBY: But it certainly wasn't a place of safety.

MCQUAID: No, it wasn't. I found myself completely enveloped in flames from an enemy hit and that was the end of active duty for me for a while.

KIRBY: Did they hold out no hope at all for you?

MCQUAID: None whatsoever. They wrapped me in hundreds of yards of gauze bandage and lowered me over the side into a Higgins landing boat to put me ashore on Tulagi to die.

KIRBY: It's a grim picture, Father, but a thrilling one in view of what followed.

MCQUAID: The Navy underestimated its own power – its power over death through plasma.

KIRBY: Do you remember being given the plasma?

MCQUAID: Strangely enough, I remember the first injection vaguely, but I was unconscious when they gave me the other two pints.

4. THE PADRE

KIRBY: You received three in all?

MCQUAID: Three pints and I often wonder who the people are to whom I am indebted, who are responsible for my being in Boston this minute. My thanks go out to everyone it might have been.

KIRBY: Chaplain McQuaid, how did you progress after Tulagi?

MCQUAID: I was evacuated from the island fairly soon after landing there. I was pretty badly burned: face, shoulders, legs, hands. I went through two weeks of blindness and two months being unable to walk. It's only very recently that I have started to regain limited use of my hands. As you can see, they are still pretty bad.

KIRBY: I can see. Ladies and gentlemen of our radio audience, what you can't see are two hands so completely burned that not one fragment of flesh was untouched.

MCQUAID: I'm only one person. There are hundreds and hundreds of others, some out there still, some back here in the States on sick leave. They're boys, like myself, given up to die but staged a remarkable comeback following plasma administration. You people at home here don't know the remarkable power of your blood donations. You can't thoroughly appreciate it until you've seen a boy brought in gray and deathlike. Frequently the doctors themselves say it can't be done only to see color and life come slowly back into that boy's face and then a flicker of pulse, sometimes even immediate consciousness.

KIRBY: Have you seen many people receive it?

MCQUAID: I have seen hundreds get it—at base hospitals, on ship, and with emergency medical units. Plasma is truly a remarkable and powerful weapon over death.

The interview continued with the chaplain, telling us what had been happening to him during the four and a half months since he was put ashore to die on Tulagi. His was quite an experience, and he gave plasma the credit for his being alive. He thanked the people who had been giving blood for his life.

After the broadcast, we went to the Hotel Lincolnshire for a nightcap and some lighthearted conversation to offset the grimness of the story just told. The program was deemed a success. The radio station had been very much pleased and we three were, too. We felt sure that listeners would have been inspired to give their blood. Later we found out how true that was when donors told their nurses that's why they came.

At the end of the evening, Chaplain McQuaid decided that he would do one more "thing" for the Blood Donor Service. That one "thing" grew into many "things" that took him into factories to speak to workers and into various communities where local committees had arranged a meeting in a school or church hall or the Town Hall—often with a school band, local dignitaries, and much publicity and promotion. The Blood Donor Center provided the program. There were war movies such as *The Battle of Midway*, courtesy of the Navy, and military personnel home from the front where they had seen and experienced plasma at work. The chaplain called these events our "medicine shows," and he continued to participate in them because he saw their value. They not only were successful in signing up new donors, but, perhaps more importantly, they were able to show people who had already given how important their donations were...how important *they* were.

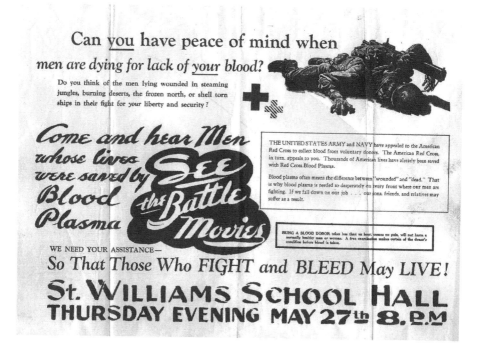

One night when we were on our way to John Hancock Hall on Berkeley Street in Boston for one of these events, we ran into in traffic. Nothing was moving, and we were conscious of the time. We couldn't keep an audience waiting. The passenger in the car next to us got out and went up ahead to see what the holdup was. When he returned, he explained, "It's some kind of a parade. There's a bunch of uniforms marching up the street. They're still coming. They look like policemen, but I don't know what it can be."

We knew. It was our audience, the Auxiliary Police of Boston marching to our "Medicine Show." The chaplain was impressed. "Looks like we hit the jackpot tonight, Kirby!"

And so we did. The committee in charge had organized their auxiliary members, who filled John Hancock Hall. When we arrived backstage, we found a lineup of dignitaries waiting for us, including Boston Mayor Maurice J. Tobin, as well as the police commissioner and a variety of superintendents and committee members.

In making arrangements for the meeting, I had explained to my police contact that the Padre could not shake hands with anyone. The burned flesh had not yet healed, and he wore gray suede gloves most of the time. I asked that word be passed to the other men.

What a useless suggestion that was! When a man meets another man, his arm is on automatic. It goes out to shake hands immediately. That's the way it was with the police that night. Every man, from the mayor on down the line, put out his hand to the chaplain and the chaplain put both his hands up in the air. "Sorry, can't do it," he said. "My hands are still bad." It was quite a sight: the Padre with his hands up in the air in front of the uniformed police as if to say, "Don't shoot. I surrender."

The presence of the mayor and ranking police officials made the evening very special, with many of the force responding to this kind of leadership. The evening helped raise awareness and provided new donors for the Blood Donor Service, which pleased the police and our guest speakers.

In mid-May 1943 and now promoted to lieutenant, Lundquist felt that there was enough outstanding material coming through from the various fronts to support a weekly broadcast for the Blood Donor Center. Would Miss Kirby be interested? Of course I would! But I was not unmindful of the work entailed in producing a weekly show and the commitment involved on top of all the other demands. On the other hand, the benefits would surely be great and, therefore, worth the effort.

Harold Fellows, general manager of the radio station that would air the show, was very much interested and promised to have his people handle publicity and promotion. Commander Collier approved and pledged whatever help PRO could provide. Wesley Fuller, director of the Blood Donor Center, agreed to the plan, so it went forward.

We had to create a title and format for the show. Since Lieutenant Lundquist had planned, written, and produced a series similar to that being considered, he was a tremendous help in getting things underway. The series would open in July with a special show planned for that date. It would feature Chaplain McQuaid's story but with a new and extraordinary addition. There was one problem, however. We had no assurance that the two principals in the program would be here in July. That was too much of a risk for our opening. We decided to transcribe...just in case. It was a fortunate decision because the Padre was called back to active duty in June.

Just before he left, he made a farewell speech at Converse Rubber Company in the Boston suburb of Malden, which they valued so highly they ran it in their company publication, *Conversations*, produced by and for their employees.

Because of the blood plasma in which you folks here at Converse have such a great interest, because of that plasma I am not only here this morning, but I am first and foremost, very much alive. The story I might tell is nothing personal; it is simply the story of every man who has been out there in the battle areas all over the world, and the story of those men, who, unfortunate as I was, or am, were tagged by the enemy.

The Night of November 29th, —which was November 28th here, in the Greater

Chaplain McQuaid and Anastasia Kirby with workers at the Converse Rubber defense plant.

Boston area—was a Saturday. It accounted for two major casualties: first, Boston College, my Alma Mater, was defeated by Holy Cross, and secondly and more seriously, was the case of the Coconut Grove fire. That was the night we were ordered into battle to destroy a Jap fleet......At the present time, you are doing everything you can do for the war effort. If you want to do the real thing for the war effort, if you want your boys to come back to you, then for God's sake put your name on the blood donor list. I certainly will be proud if any names are added to this list because I came here this morning – I will be delighted to hear that it will have been worthwhile. I am back in the States because of somebody, but those other boys out there are looking to me to plead for them for the blood that is going to be so essential that they may live...Thanks a million!

When it came time to say good-bye to the Padre, I had a final meeting to tell him how deeply grateful I was to him for all that he had done for the Blood Donor Service. Before I could remind him of how many pints of blood he was responsible for sending out to those that he had left behind, he took both my hands firmly in his and said earnestly, "Don't you thank me! I thank you. You gave me something worthwhile to do while I was recuperating. You probably kept me from cutting out paper dolls. You worked me hard, but it was worth it and I thank you."

We knew that we would miss him, and we certainly did.

The Padre was back on active duty when his special story aired in Boston on the debut of *Life to the Front*, the title chosen for the new series broadcast weekly until the end of the war. The format that introduced the opening program, and every one after that, explained its intent:

> *"To all the men of the armed forces of the United States...who—on every fighting front in the world—daily risk their lives in the service of their country...the American Red Cross Blood Donor Service dedicates this program...that they might live."*

The opening broadcast was called "What a Small World."

5. WHAT A SMALL WORLD

Today, when people say "it's a small world," they usually are talking about telecommunications or air travel or some electronic link between people and places. It's different when the Navy says it, as they have been saying it for years. With their experience, they, more than anyone else, know that the world isn't small at all—it is very, very big! But as they sail its many seas and touch on all its continents, they keep bumping into old shipmates from some place, some time ago, and they remark over and over, "What a small world!"

On December 1, 1942, two men in the U.S. Navy met for the first time in a Higgins boat on the sea off Lunga Point in the Solomon Islands. One was a lieutenant in the Chaplain Corps; the other was a boatswain's mate second class. They had just left their respective ships, the heavy cruisers *Minneapolis* and *Northampton*. The two men and their ships had taken part in an important event, the Battle of Tassafaronga, named for a point on the coast of Guadalcanal.

The two were among others on their way to the island of Tulagi. The boatswain's mate went there to get first aid and dry clothes, having just been picked up out of the water after the sinking of the *Northampton*. The chaplain was being put ashore to die.

The *Minneapolis*, like the *Northampton*, had been hit by a Japanese Long Lance torpedo. Although not sunk, the ship was severely damaged, its bow blown off back to its forward gun turret, the ship engulfed in flames and smoke. The chaplain had been caught in the fire and critically burned.

The hours leading up to the night of November 30 had been busy and tense. Sunday morning the chaplain had said mass on the *Minneapolis* and later held general services. In the afternoon, he had gone over to the *Northampton* to conduct divine services on her deck. It was a beautiful sunny afternoon.

At midnight the American task force, under the command of Rear Adm. Carleton H. Wright, stood out of the harbor of its operating base. They were underway for a full day, traveling several hundred miles. They formed into a column. *Northampton* was the last in the line of heavy cruisers, which included *New Orleans* and *Pensacola*. Behind them was the light cruiser *Honolulu*. The *Minneapolis,* Admiral Wright's flagship, was first in the column. During the day, Capt. Charles. E. Rosendahl, the skipper of *Minneapolis,* apprised the ship's company of the purpose and the nature of the upcoming operations. The chaplain toured the ship to touch bases with the men. When he went below decks into the engine room, he found a good-natured group in the "black gang," the engineers who work in the hot machinery spaces below decks. They joked with him, "What's the matter, Father, coming down to get your morale boosted?" The chaplain said that the men were lighthearted but serious, and none seemed afraid.

When darkness came they went to general quarters. The chaplain had selected a battle station nearest to all the guns where he might be needed to help with possible casualties.

The task force reduced speed as it moved into the narrow, treacherous waters of Lengo Channel along the northeastern coast of Guadalcanal. Navigation was difficult as they headed into what became known as "Iron Bottom Sound."

Several hours later, the shapes of several unidentified surface ships were sighted in the pitch-blackness. Within a few minutes, six enemy vessels were discernible. The *Minneapolis* opened fire with her main battery of eight-inch guns. Her first salvo was a near hit. By now the Japanese had reached their disembarking point. They had to be stopped. The U.S. Marines, once again holding the initiative after the fierce Japanese counterattack of a few weeks before, had to be protected. Salvos from the *Minneapolis* and other ships hit the Japanese destroyer *Takanami*, immediately disabling her; she sank several hours later.

Attention soon shifted to another target. A second group of Japanese warships rounded Cape Esperance after the first group of vessels. They hugged the shoreline, waiting for the auxiliaries to disembark their troops. Although this second group was also stopped from landing, the Japanese destroyers managed to fire a spread of torpedoes at the *Minneapolis* and other U.S. cruisers.

The flagship was hit. Badly!

The *Northampton* was worse. She was going down.

At this point, the chaplain's service to the Navy took a drastic turn. Instead of being ready to assist with the wounded, he needed assistance himself. And he received it. He was helped into sick bay and immediately given a unit of blood plasma...but little hope of survival.

The medics decided to get him off the ship to the nearby island of Tulagi where a medical evacuation center had been set up. They wrapped him in yards and yards of gauze bandage and lowered him over the side of the *Minneapolis* into a Higgins boat for the trip ashore. The Padre went alone, because no corpsman could be spared to accompany him. There were too many casualties aboard in need of critical care.

On the way, the boat crew came upon the boatswain's mate clinging to a casing. They picked him up and took him along with them. When they landed, they hurried the chaplain into the emergency unit where he was immediately given another unit of plasma, but the same prognosis: "He'll never make it!"

The boatswain's mate watched and listened. The man he saw on the Higgins boat lying on a cot was wrapped in his bandages like a mummy with still another plasma tube running down into his arm and the doctors shaking their heads. The sailor knew he would never forget the chaplain, but he was also sure he would never see him again.

Eight months later and eight thousand miles from the Solomons, Chaplain Arthur F. McQuaid and Boatswain's Mate Second Class Julius R. Mays sat around the microphone in the studio of the Columbia Broadcasting System's New England outlet, WEEI in Boston. They were recording the opening program of the new radio series, *Life to the Front*, that would begin on July 15, 1943, and run the length of the war. It was necessary to record the program in order to bring both men together. The Padre was returned to active duty in June. The story that these two men brought back from the front was extraordinary, and we felt privileged to debut our series with it.

As I introduced my two guests to the radio audience and described their trip to Tulagi, Julius Mays was shaking his head: "I can't believe you're here, Padre. I can't believe it's you. It seems like a miracle."

"I'm here all right," said the chaplain, "and it is a miracle. The miracle is plasma. There is no doubt whatsoever in my mind but that plasma saved my life, especially that first pint they gave me in sick bay on the ship."

The boatswain's mate continued to shake his head. "The medics said you'd never make it, and from the looks of you I didn't see how you could."

"The Navy underestimated its own power, its power over death, with plasma. I'm here to say a big 'thank you' to the American people."

"Where did you go from Tulagi?" Mays asked the chaplain.

"They evacuated me to a hospital in Auckland, New Zealand, and I was there for quite a while. I was blind for two weeks; I couldn't walk for two months."

"You sure were bad, Padre."

"I guess I was. The flames just wrapped themselves around me. My face was bad, and my hands and my arms up to the shoulders, my legs up beyond my knees. Except for the hands, I'm as good as new. And these are coming along nicely, too."

Chaplain McQuaid paused. "But I see that our boatswain's mate here is wearing a Silver Star ribbon. You don't get that for perfect attendance."

A copy of the citation for his medal had been given to me for the interview, and I proceeded to read it.

"After his ship had been badly damaged by a torpedo hit and set on fire, Mays, although menaced by terrific heat and bursting ammunition from the boat deck, twice climbed the flame-enveloped structure of the main mast and assisted in evacuating wounded personnel who had been injured by an explosion and blinded by oil and smoke. His heroic conduct was in keeping with the highest traditions of the United States Navy. Signed, Frank Knox, Secretary of the Navy."

"Can you fill in the details, Mays?" asked the chaplain.

"Well, my battle station was below decks as battle telephone talker in the damage control party. After we got hit, we were so badly off, there wasn't much a damage control party could do. So when a call came to get some morphine up to some wounded men on the main mast, I ran and got it and went up and gave it to the fellows who needed it most. One had both legs broken by the concussion, and he was hurting so much that he would rather stay where he was than be moved after I brought him down."

"And then what?" asked the Padre.

"Well, I tied a couple of lifebelts around him and pulled him to where the water would float him off when the ship rolled over."

"Did it work?" I asked.

"Yes, ma'am, it worked. When the *Northampton* rolled over, the wounded man floated clear."

"And that's not all, according to my information," I added.

"Well, we brought two other wounded down from the mast…at least they say I did. I don't remember coming down from the second trip, but I must have, because I had gotten a powder can from somewhere and was floating around on it. Then I was picked up by the same boat that had taken the chaplain here off his ship, and it took us both to Tulagi."

"By the way, Mays," asked the chaplain, "did you ever hear what eventually happened to your shipmate in the lifebelts?"

"Yes," he said. "I heard that he got picked up by a raft and later was taken to the hospital where he recovered. He had a rough time but he made it."

"What a wonderful sense of satisfaction that must be for you, Mays," said the chaplain.

"It is, sir. But what a wonderful satisfaction it must be for blood donors in Boston to see you back home alive because of plasma."

"What a small world," I noted, "when you think of blood going out from the United States all the way to the Pacific and coming back to Boston in the chaplain's veins."

Life to the Front was off to a great start, and the chaplain returned to active duty soon after. But he did not remain at his new post very long. As he walked across the base one day, he was stopped by a couple of sailors coming toward him. After exchanging salutes, they asked, "What's the matter with your face, Padre?"

The priest put his hand up to his cheek and it came away all bloody. He was literally sweating blood. The tropical climate of the new base was too much for his damaged skin. He was immediately removed from that post and assigned to another that, fortunately, had just become available. He was sent to New Jersey to serve with an old shipmate from the *Minneapolis*, his former skipper, now Rear Adm. Charles E. Rosendahl and chief of U.S. Naval Airship Training and Experimentation at the lighter-than-air base at Lakehurst.

The admiral had long been an expert and enthusiast in the field. In addition to his promotion, Secretary Knox had presented him a Navy Cross for "heroic and inspiring leadership as commanding officer of the *Minneapolis*."

When the Navy released its official report on the *Minneapolis* months later on January 31, 1944, it contained not only extensive details of the battle but also a grim and graphic account of the extremely difficult days of salvage afterward.

When Rosendahl assessed the damage to his ship, he determined that the engines were operative and ordered a course for Lunga Point, where, if it became necessary to abandon ship, the cruiser might be beached on friendly territory on Guadalcanal. But the ship's speed gradually increased, so he changed course for the secluded harbor of Tulagi, eighteen miles away.

The salvage operation received help from the Seabees and a variety of Navy ships that passed through Tulagi Harbor. The men worked under extremely difficult circumstances make their ship seaworthy enough to attempt the long journey home for final restoration to active service.

Rosendahl was profuse in the praise of his men and their extraordinary dedication to their ship. These statements were genuine. He also praised the ship and the people who built her. "No story of the *Minneapolis* would be complete which did not contain praise of the superb construction and tough materials that enabled the ship to take the punishment it took that night of the 30th and still survive."

McQuaid had another "small world" experience. He wrote to us from Lakehurst early in 1944. It was New Year's Day when he was about to say mass in a little chapel on the base there. He needed an altar boy, so he asked for a volunteer from his congregation. A young Marine came forward and served.

After mass, as the priest was removing his vestments, his altar boy said, "You weren't here last New Year's Day, were you, Father?"

"No," said the Padre, "I wasn't."

"I bet you a dollar I know where you were."

"All right," replied the priest, pulling out a dollar bill and laying it on the table. "Where?"

"You were in the hospital in Auckland, New Zealand."

"You're right on it!" The chaplain pushed the dollar bill toward the Marine. "How did you know?"

"You were in the bed next to mine."

The Marine explained his hospitalization. "I wasn't sure it was you because you were in such bad shape out there; your face was so disfigured that no one could recognize you today," the Marine added. "But when I saw your hands as you were saying mass, I knew it must be you. There couldn't be two Padres in the Navy with hands like that."

As the Marine pocketed the dollar bill, the two shook hands, agreeing that it sure was a small world.

PART II
THE SOLOMONS

6. GUADALCANAL

This broadcast of *Life to the Front* is the graphic description of the first days after the Marines landed on Guadalcanal, from one who arrived on the "Canal"—the name the troops gave to the place—on August 8 and was in action up to the important crossing of the Tenaru River. His name was Cpl. Roy Pearson of Lynn, Massachusetts. He was interviewed by Lt. Francis L. Sweeney, USNR, of the First Naval District's Public Relations Office.

SWEENEY: This young man, a corporal in the Marine Corps, is typical of the American fighting man. He's young...rather good-looking... well educated...a tough fighter...daring, without being stupidly reckless...a man who can think for himself when the need arises. Heroes? Sure, they're all heroes when you think of what they've done, and are doing, and have yet to do. But they're not heroes to themselves...and you don't think of them as heroes when you're talking to them either. They're just American kids, come home again for a breather. This corporal happens to be a local boy. He's Corporal Roy Pearson of the United States Marine Corps. You went right into the Marine Corps from school, Corporal?

PEARSON: Almost right away. I finished school in June…and I joined the corps in August… August 7, 1940.

SWEENEY: Were you in any action before you hit the beach at Guadalcanal?

PEARSON: No—that was my first action—and as it turned out—it may be my last for quite a while.

SWEENEY: Well, let's hope it won't be too long before you're fit, Corporal…but let's hope the war doesn't last too long, either. Tell us about the landing out there on Guadalcanal.

PEARSON: Well—the whole convoy came in late on the 6th of August—and that night the Navy did a grand job of shelling Jap positions. I'm not fooling. We would have been lost out there without the Navy. The Navy just poured shells into the Japs all night. Then—the next morning—we went over the side, and ashore in landing boats.

[The term "Japs" is today considered derogatory and offensive, but during the war it was commonly used when referring to the enemy in the Pacific. It is repeated here and elsewhere in this book when quoting directly from the script.]

SWEENEY: That was the morning of the 7th?

PEARSON: Yes, sir…the 7th – —exactly two years to the day since I enlisted with the Marines.

SWEENEY: What kind of a reception did the Japs give you when you hit the beach?

PEARSON: Not bad at all. There was surprisingly little opposition—just a few snipers, and it didn't take us long to clear them out. But we found out why soon enough—the Japs were waiting for us at the airfield, and the reception there was plenty warm. But even so, it didn't take us very long to clean the Japs off the field…and into the jungle where they set up new defensive positions.

SWEENEY: Were the Japs using the airfield at the time?

PEARSON: No, sir—they had about a week's work still to do. I guess that's one reason why we moved in so fast out there—to take the island before the Japs could get the field ready for use.

SWEENEY: So instead, we took the field and finished it for ourselves.

PEARSON: That's right. The Seabees came right in with us, and the minute we took the field they went to work on it. They had it finished in just four days. Planes were landing even sooner than that.

SWEENEY: And all the while the Japs were in the jungle just beyond the field?

PEARSON: Yes, sir. For a short time there wasn't very much action…we were getting organized. We'd send out patrols to locate the Jap forces—to feel out their strength. That way we learned a lot about the Japs and jungle fighting…and we learned fast.

SWEENEY: You usually do learn fast when you have to learn the hard way. It's either that or you don't learn at all. When did you get your first hard fighting?

PEARSON: About a week after we landed on the island. There's a little hill just about a thousand yards from the airfield that we call "Bloody Knoll." We had it…and the Japs tried to take it back. The battle lasted three days—the 13th, 14th and 15th. It was pretty hot going. But

SWEENEY: Hand grenades? You mean you were so close to the Japs you just lobbed hand grenades at them?

PEARSON: We were even closer than that, Lieutenant Sweeney. You see the knoll was pretty steep, and the Japs kept trying to climb it. So all we had to do was pick up a grenade, pull out the pin with our teeth, reach out over our foxholes...and roll the grenade down the side of the knoll. That's all there was to it. Everybody was loaded with grenades. Even General Vandergrift was there—with his uniform coat just bulging with grenades. Anyhow, we kept "Bloody Knoll."

[Marine Corps Gen. Alexander Vandergrift commanded the 1st Marine Division at Guadalcanal, and was awarded the Medal of Honor for his actions in the Solomons. Vandegrift later became the eighteenth commandant of the Marine Corps, and the first active-duty U.S. Marine to hold the rank of four-star general.]

when the "Battle of Bloody Knoll" was over, we still had the hill. We won that battle with hand grenades.

SWEENEY: That was the middle of August. Then what?

PEARSON: It was sort of quiet for a while, patrols, skirmishes, and sniping. The next big battle was the battle of the Tenaru River, the last few days of September. It started on the 27th.

SWEENEY: That's where you got hit, isn't it?

PEARSON: Yes. I was hit on the 28th.

SWEENEY: Go ahead—you're telling the story, Corporal.

PEARSON: Well, the Tenaru River was about ten miles beyond our main lines, and we had a force of about four thousand men on one side of the river, near Red Beach, at the river's mouth. It was our job to cross the river.

SWEENEY: And how many Japs were there on the other side?

PEARSON: We don't know just how many they had, but they had more than we did, and they were making life pretty miserable for us, because they had 91 mm trench mortars, which were heavier than ours. That first day we didn't do too much because we were trying to find out where they had their machine guns and how their forces were dispersed, and things like that. But the next day, plenty happened. At about noon on the 28th, we were still waiting to get across the river, and then the air support we had been waiting for came up. The planes—Marine and Navy—bombed and strafed the Jap positions. And then one of our destroyers moved in close to the beach and began to shell the Japs… so our commander decided it was time to move along.

SWEENEY: Corporal, you told me once just what sort of troops you had with you. I think your audience would like to hear that.

PEARSON: Well, on one side of us we had "Bailey's Marine Raiders"—I guess they made quite a name for themselves. We had a good machine gun company on the other flank… and a mortar company behind us, lobbing mortar shells over our heads. Old Lou Diamond, the most decorated Marine in the corps, was in that mortar company.

[Master Gunnery Sgt. Leland "Lou" Sanford Diamond was 52 years old at Guadalcanal.]

SWEENEY: I imagine it helps a lot to know you've got good men on all sides of you?

PEARSON: It sure does, sir. All we had to worry about was the Japs on the other side of the river, and that was plenty to worry about. You see, according to maps we had, there were just two shallow places in the Tenaru where we could cross, but on the other side we knew the Japs had two machine guns set up, but we hadn't been able to locate them. We had to clean out those two machine guns before we tried to cross, so there was just one thing to do.

SWEENEY: What was that?

PEARSON: Do something that would draw the fire from the Jap guns, so we could spot their locations, and clean them out. So the CO asked for a squad to volunteer to go out and draw the Jap fire. Well, the fellows in my squad looked at each other...and then we said we'd go.

SWEENEY: Wait a minute—you said you'd volunteer to go out—just to draw the Jap machine gun fire—knowing what your chances would be?

PEARSON: Well, somebody had to do it. We figured it might as well be us. So we went. We had hardly got started, hadn't even reached the ford in the river, when the Jap machine guns opened up and caught the whole squad in a cross fire. We all dropped, and I went down with bullets in both legs and my hip. I dragged myself into some underbrush and just stayed there.

SWEENEY: How long did you have to stay there?

PEARSON: Just about half an hour, I guess. The minute the Japs opened fire, our boys bracketed them and went to work on them. It took that half hour to clean them up—and the minute they did, the Marines crossed the Tenaru.

SWEENEY: What your squad did wasn't in vain then. You did what you set out to do. How many men were in the squad?

PEARSON: Well, at that time, my squad numbered nine men. Of the nine, three are in Australia now—okay. I'm here at the Chelsea Naval Hospital. The other fellows—they're still on Guadalcanal— they won't ever come home.

SWEENEY: They won't be forgotten, Corporal. Now, you say you laid there in the under- brush a half hour. Who picked you up?

PEARSON: Hospital corpsmen came in right after the first wave of Marines crossed the Tenaru. And with the corpsmen, acting as stretcher-bearers, came the musicians who played in the band. Make no mistake, those guys work hard—and was I glad to see them! The corpsman gave me a shot of morphine to ease the pain and used my first aid kit as well as his own to stop the bleeding. Then they made a stretcher out of a poncho and carried me back to the first aid station.

SWEENEY: A poncho? Didn't they have stretchers there?

PEARSON: They had run out of stretchers—it was a pretty busy day. From the station I was put in a truck and taken to the field hospital where they were working like mad to take care of all the cases coming in. It was just a shed with a tin roof, shaded by palm trees, with about 15 or 20 cots in it. And about the first thing that hit my eye was poles stuck in the ground beside each cot, with a bottle of plasma hanging from it. Just as soon as one bottle of the plasma was used, a corpsman would come around and hang up another for the next man.

SWEENEY: You had some of the plasma, didn't you? How long did it take?

PEARSON: Yes, sir, I did. I was given plasma just as soon as I arrived. I don't know just how long it took—maybe ten minutes or so. I wasn't observing too much, what with the wounds and the morphine...but I was conscious all the time, and I know that almost every man they brought in there got plasma. That night I spent in an air-raid shelter, because we never knew when Jap planes would come over and bomb the hospital, or Jap warships throw a few shells our way. The next morning I was flown out of Guadalcanal to a mobile hospital unit in the New Hebrides. I was operated on there, and they removed the one bullet that hadn't gone clean through. When I woke up I was in a plaster cast from my chest down to my feet.

SWEENEY: You had more plasma there, didn't you?

PEARSON: Yes, my medical record shows that I had some more plasma after the operation.

SWEENEY: How long were you there, Corporal?

PEARSON: About three weeks. Then the hospital ship *Solace* brought me to Auckland, New Zealand, for a while. Then another trip, this time on a freighter, that landed me in California on November 13. I had another operation there, had my casts changed again…and then home here last April.

SWEENEY: And I know you had still another operation there, and that you're still wearing a brace. How about that brace, Corporal? How much longer will you have to wear that?

PEARSON: I don't know. Not too long, I hope. But at least I'm home—that's more than some of the other fellows are. I'm home.

7. THE ARMY RELIEVES THE MARINES

As Marine Cpl. Roy Pearson's transport was landing him in San Francisco for still another operation, Lt. John J. Kelly Jr. of the U.S. Army arrived on Guadalcanal as part of the reinforcement of the First Marine Division.

An interview with the lieutenant on *Life to the Front* on October 11, 1943, told us more about the campaign that Roy Pearson had described. This is how it went:

ANNOUNCER: Today, *Life to the Front* brings to you listeners the story of life at the front... told by a man who recently returned from the front...a lieutenant in the United States Army. Miss Anastasia Kirby, assistant director of the American Red Cross Blood Donor Center of Boston, is here with the lieutenant, and we'll let her tell the story about Lieutenant Kelly.

KIRBY: And it's quite a story! I expect that some of you listeners recall the words that Robert Louis Stevenson wrote from the South Seas..."I can think of no worse fate that can befall a man than to spend the remainder of his life in the Solomon Islands, condemned to die on Guadalcanal." Well...it's from that very place, from Guadalcanal, that our latest story of plasma comes. It's brought to us by a young man who spent thirteen long months in the Pacific Theater and came out wearing the ribbon of the Medal of the Purple Heart...along with a presidential citation and more than one star in his Pacific campaign bar. Lieutenant John J. Kelly, Jr., of the Signal Corps of the United States Army. Lieutenant...how about it? Was Stevenson right?

KELLY: He was quite right. There's nothing good to be said for Guadalcanal. There's heat and fever and rain and mud and insects...that not only defy classification but defy every protective effort, too. Definitely, Stevenson was right.

KIRBY: How long were you out there, Lieutenant?

KELLY: I was in the Pacific area for 13 months. I was on the Canal for two months.

KIRBY: How much of those two months did you spend in the front lines?

KELLY: Twenty-three days on the first stretch.

KIRBY: You reinforced the First Marine Division, didn't you?

KELLY: Yes. We landed on Guadalcanal on November 11...Armistice Day...and were cordially welcomed by a Jap raiding party of 33 planes.

KIRBY: Did you return the salutation?

KELLY: We did. Our ships pulled away from shore and set up an antiaircraft barrage that accounted for 32 of 33 planes.

KIRBY: Well, that was a royal acknowledgement of their welcome.

KELLY: The Navy did a top job out there... and still is, for that matter. Two days after we had landed—on November 13 to be exact—the Japs came back and started to shell the beach in order to knock out our shore installations. In the battle that ensued, our Navy sank approximately 20,000 Jap troops.

KIRBY: These were your first days on Guadalcanal.

KELLY: And what followed when we went up to the front was infinitely worse.

KIRBY:

I suppose living conditions just aren't to be mentioned.

KELLY:

Not too much in detail. We spent hours, sometimes days, in foxholes that had six inches of water in them. We lived for three weeks on C-rations before they were able to get real food up to us. It surely was a great day when we saw the jeeps coming through the jungles, over the ridges, with our supplies. The Japs were on the lookout for them, too, and managed to blow several of them up. It was something to watch those little jeeps in the distance, bravely coming through shellfire and explosions, continuing along when another had been blown to bits next to it. That was what they went through every time they brought supplies up to the front. And that included medical equipment with your Red Cross blood plasma.

KIRBY:

I never realized how much those poor little bottles of plasma go through.

KELLY:

On Guadalcanal it was plenty. But we were glad to have it there. Plenty of us were plenty glad!

KIRBY:

Lieutenant, you said that this was your first stretch...the 23 days that started when you went up to relieve the Marines on the 13th of November. Did you go back up later?

KELLY: Yes, I did. My battalion had been relieved from the front and returned to Henderson Field to rest for a while...

KIRBY: Rest! What kind of rest could you get on Guadalcanal?

KELLY: Not the same thing you call rest home here. But compared to the front lines, it really was something. All we had to do was defend the airport against small groups of Japs who were constantly infiltrating through, trying to blow up our planes. We suffered mostly from nightly bombings aimed to knock out Henderson Field.

KIRBY: So after you were all rested up with this little workout, you went back up to the front...

KELLY: And that was the beginning of the end for me on Guadalcanal.

KIRBY: Then this is where the history of your Purple Heart starts?

KELLY: That's right. Another battalion had moved onto the island and, needing battle-experienced officers who had not been hit. I was one of those men transferred. It was January 11th when I went up to the front again.

KIRBY: Were you on some special mission?

KELLY: Yes, we were to put up a barbed-wire entanglement. I had taken my platoon out into the jungle and we were working feverishly to set the barbed wire up between two hills, when the Japs spotted us and laid down a mortar barrage. They swept the whole area with exploding shells and we were caught in it. That's when I got mine.

KIRBY: Where were you hit, Lieutenant?

KELLY: One of the shells exploded so close to me that it blew off the side of my foot. When I looked down I could just see a mass of ragged flesh and blood...my shoe was cut right off. I was sure my whole foot was gone and my one fear was that I would lie out there without help,

KIRBY: So that you paid for your Purple Heart with a broken leg and a blown-off foot.

KELLY: And I was lucky. Most of the other men of my platoon didn't get out.

KIRBY: It seems a pretty high price to pay.

KELLY: War is costly, no matter how you look at it. Every minute of every day somebody is paying for it somewhere.

KIRBY: That's something that I think we frequently forget. But let's get back to Guadalcanal. Did they find you in a foxhole or did you make your way out into the jungle for your own help?

KELLY: After the Japs stopped firing, I crawled out to where I could just barely see two figures, but they were dead, so I called for help and then waited until two men ventured out into the jungle looking for wounded. They improvised a stretcher with my combat suit and started out on the long and treacherous journey with me.

KIRBY: Were you conscious during all this?

KELLY: No, I passed out after we had been subjected to Jap fire again and I had been dumped onto the ground. I didn't regain consciousness until I woke up in a field hospital after my first operation.

KIRBY: Your first...how many did you have?

KELLY: Several...but I'm almost through, I think. They'll take out my last shrapnel soon and that should be the end. I certainly never thought then that I'd ever get off the island, much less be able to walk and get back to a job in a matter of months—but that's exactly what happened.

KIRBY: The Medical Corps scores again. You're a good example, Lieutenant, I should say, of the result of all those lifesaving factors that Major General Kirk has listed as responsible for keeping our death rate so low at the front.

KELLY: Oh yes, I remember...the surgeon general listed number one lifesaver as blood plasma; number two, the excellent surgery; third, sulfa drugs. It's doubtful if I'd be here today if it weren't for all three of these. First—plasma—to keep me alive while they did the job. The second—the job itself—the surgery. Third—sulfa drugs—to reduce the chances of infection.

KIRBY: Well, I should think you'd had enough of hospitals for one year.

KELLY: Too much. During the time I was in the Pacific, after I had been hit, I was in five different hospitals...Army, Navy, and Marine Corps medical units... evacuation centers...base hospitals...I had a taste of all of them.

KIRBY: The doctors work under pretty trying circumstances over there, don't they?

KELLY: Terrific! I can remember one battalion hospital that had been set up in the middle of the jungle on Guadalcanal. I had just carried some wounded men down from the front lines and brought them in under the canvas that was the roof of the hospital. They had to have it for protection because they did everything in this little battalion unit—from administering first aid to performing major operations—right under the trees that were under the canvas.

KIRBY: You mean that the canvas was just thrown over the trees...not set up as a tent?

KELLY: You must remember that on Guadalcanal the growth is so heavy that you couldn't cut it away. If you chopped a path through the jungle you couldn't find it in a few days...the vegetation grows so fast it would be all covered over. That's the way it was in the hospital, so they threw the canvas over the trees...they had to have it to keep the rain out.

KIRBY: Did it rain much?

KELLY: Every day.

KIRBY:

Every day?

KELLY:

That's right. But to get back to the trees...the doctors and corpsmen used the boughs of the trees to hang their bottles of your Red Cross blood plasma onto. And as you'd come into the unit, you'd see these familiar flasks of yellowish liquid hanging up here and there all around the woods that was the hospital. This day of which I speak, there was a very large number of wounded men brought in and the litters were all lined up while the doctors were working as fast as they could, taking care of the men, one right after the other.

KIRBY:

Was this well away from the Jap encampment?

KELLY:

There wasn't much of any place in the jungles of Guadalcanal that you wouldn't find Jap snipers in the trees. That's why we spread our men about so as not to serve as any more of a target than possible. This battalion hospital unit was the one and only place where you'd find men grouped together. It was necessary here because it took three or four people to perform an operation or care for a casualty. The Japs continually fired at these groups and made things pretty tough for the doctors.

KIRBY: You mean that the Jap snipers fired from their trees into the hospital?

KELLY: Right into the midst of the wounded and the doctors as they worked. One day I saw them shoot a bottle of plasma right out of the hand of the corpsman who was holding it for a plasma transfusion. Pieces of glass and plasma just sprayed all over the place...all over the boy who was getting it.

KIRBY: What did the corpsman do?

KELLY: Reached for another bottle of plasma. That boy was dying. There was not time to lose. They fixed up another one and went on with their work as though nothing had happened.

KIRBY: That's what hurts...you boys out there being blown up, the doctors and medical corps working under the trees, having bottles of plasma shot out of their very hands...and they calmly pick up another bottle and go on with the job, because there is NO TIME TO LOSE...a man is dying...a man's life is at stake... never mind their own safety...while we at home here have to work furiously every day of the week to get anywhere near the minimum number of pints that the Army and Navy expect of us. It's always a struggle because people are always putting off giving their pint. They figure there's PLENTY OF TIME.

KELLY: People who can't appreciate the need for their blood...NOW...ought to see a few instances of field surgery and field amputations. Going through the jungle, it's not at all uncommon to come upon a small medical unit working on a man...operating, amputating...always with a bottle of plasma suspended from the butt of a gun that's been slung in the ground beside the patient, or hanging from a tree, or just being held quietly by the hospital corpsman who is assisting. You couldn't see one such sight and not realize that if you've got something our soldiers need... something you'll never even miss...then the quickest means of getting it to them would be all too long.

KIRBY: Then may we appeal today to our listeners to remember those men...those boys...whose fate it may be to spend the remainder of their lives...their young lives...condemned to die in the Solomon Islands.

During convalescent leave, Kelly spoke to other groups, as well. Here are his remarks on one occasion:

We took very few prisoners and the Japs took none. I recall one day a patrol went in search of water. They had two officers and about 25 men. While at the waterhole they were ambushed by Japs and a number of men were killed. One officer got back, but the time he had spent in Jap territory was too much for his mind, and he was unbalanced when we found him. My platoon pushed through this area a few days later and we found the other officer tied to a tree with his hands and feet hacked off and his body mutilated by bayonets. There were other cases so revolting I would be embarrassed just standing here telling you about it. There wasn't enough food to talk about, although at the end we were getting two meals a day. The Japs knew all the tricks of jungle fighting, but we had to learn from experience, which was often very costly. It was total blackout all the time. We had one boy who after a tough day was on guard shift in his foxhole. He decided to have a smoke. He lit up and a Jap grenade caught him in the face. His whole face was blown completely off, but he lived. What a price to pay for a smoke! If a man showed a glowing cigarette in the dead of the night, the platoon leader, rather than stand and expose himself, would crawl to a man's side to tell him to put it out. Many a platoon leader found a couple of Japs waiting for him when he got there. To tell about all this, one cannot feel the intense heat and the fear of death that was always present. Perhaps that is why so many men who returned with me were mental cases.

The next morning I was taken to Henderson Field and there they decided that I might pass on in the plane and so back to the hospital I went for more operations. Next morning I felt better, so they flew me to the island of Efate in the New Hebrides group. After an eye operation and a siege of malaria, I went to Suva in the Fiji group. From there, I returned to the United States where I was hospitalized until the 31st of July.

8. THE SEABEES

The men of the Naval Construction Battalions are known as the Seabees, and are a "can do" outfit that proudly proclaims: "We build. We fight." Their motto tells it all: "With willing hearts and skillful hands, the difficult we do at once, the impossible takes a bit longer."

Their record proves it. Before becoming the Seabees, they were known by the rather generic "United States Navy Construction Force." They become the Seabees after December 7, 1941, when there was a desperate need to repair the catastrophic damage done by the enemy at Pearl Harbor. They are and continue to be a vital force in the U.S. Navy.

Official records show that there were more than 325,000 Seabees serving in World War II on four continents and three hundred islands. They were not combat units per se, but were trained to fight to protect themselves and what they were building, including hospitals for more than seventy thousand patients, roads, airfields, and so much more. They did heroic work, some of which was recognized with thirty-five Silver Stars and five Navy Crosses. Seabees had more than one thousand Purple Hearts awarded, some posthumously. There were more than 250 combat deaths and more than 500 accidental deaths as a result of the hazardous construction work.

The focus of U.S. forces on Guadalcanal in August 1942 was to get control of the airfield. The Japanese had been working feverishly to ready it for their planes and the resulting dominance this would give them in the Solomons and beyond. When our Marines captured it, it was a crushing blow to the enemy troops who were still left to watch what happened next.

According to our personal report from Marine Cpl. Roy Pearson, who had landed on August 7 and helped secure the airfield, the Seabees came ashore right behind them. "When the Seabees took over, they completed the task in four days. Our planes were landing even before the Seabees were done."

The Seabees had their own doctor who followed them through the Solomons. Lt. Cmdr. Louis Burton Benjamen, Medical Corps (MC), USNR, told me of the extraordinary success giving plasma to the wounded. When asked about his own experience with plasma, he described one special case:

"There was a young man whose appendix had been ruptured for five days. Everyone was worried about him," Benjamen said. "Even the doctor was concerned when he finally arrived on the scene. Men in combat become such a family: the patient's buddies were hanging around the operating tent during the surgery and during the recovery time. They knew it was risky and they feared the worst. The operation was a success and the patient came through the post-op without a problem. Everyone was elated and kept complimenting the doctor on the remarkable piece of surgery which had saved their pal."

But the doctor said, "No, that's not the reason this man was able to make it."

Doctor Benjamen gave the credit to plasma. "Yes, it was good surgery. The Navy expects that of its doctors. But you must remember that the best of surgery is no good if it's performed on a dead man. Plasma kept this man alive until I could get to him and during and after surgery. It's the people at home who saved his life."

The Navy doctor, hardened by what he had seen and been through in the Solomons, said, "I felt particularly good about this case because the young man had a new baby that he had never seen and a wife waiting for him to come home and parents worrying and praying that he would be all right. Three generations benefited from this operation and from the gift of plasma from folks at home."

We could call this another success story for the Seabees—because the doctor was one of them, after all—and another success story for our donors at home whose plasma also traveled with the Seabees in the Solomons.

And there were other islands where both doctors and donors were at work with similar success.

9. FROM THE SHORES OF THE CANAL TO THE SKIES ABOVE

The ground forces on Guadalcanal had to slog it out. From the landings, securing the airfield, taking the island, and then holding, it was costly. Every success, every setback carried a heavy price tag. The death toll was high: 7,100 Allied killed while the Japanese lost 31,000 killed and 1,000 more captured.

But there were survivors, and they outnumbered the losses by far. Some came through unscathed. Others, though wounded, managed to improve sufficiently to be sent home to complete their recuperation in a hospital nearby. Interviews with these survivors told similar stories. The men shared grim descriptions with graphic details that left no doubt that these were hard-won battles.

The casualties, and those who cared for them, had a very positive message for us. They extolled the power of plasma. It was invaluable, and they were profoundly grateful for it.

The Marines who went ashore on the Canal on August 8 learned about the Navy's action on August 8 and 9 in the Battle of Savo Island, when three heavy cruisers were lost: *Astoria, Quincy,* and *Vincennes.* Australia lost *Canberra.*

Those ground forces knew that Rear Adm. Norman Scott had a great success at Cape Esperance (the Second Battle of Savo Island) on October 15 but lost his life, along with Rear Adm. Daniel J.

Callaghan a month later in early action of the Naval Battle of Guadalcanal (also known as the Third Battle of Savo Island), November 13–15.

While there may be rivalry among the services, in war they are part of an extended family that grieves over the loss of their admirals, generals, sailors, and soldiers alike. That's how they felt about the sinking of the cruiser *Juneau* in the Solomons with the five Sullivan brothers aboard. They had sailed with her to the end. Joseph, Francis, Albert, and Madison went down with her; George died on a raft awaiting rescue.

Marines on Guadalcanal never forgot this battle, when our Navy stopped the Japanese fleet as it steamed resolutely toward the Canal with supplies and troops to reinforce their beleaguered and diminished forces holding out on the island. Our donors and listeners couldn't forget that battle either, as Chaplain McQuaid had shared how his life was saved by plasma.

As the Seabees put the finishing touches on the airfield, the Marines and Seabees watched the skies, anxiously awaiting the first American planes and hoping not to see the enemy's. It was a thrill to finally see their planes land on the airstrip they had fought so hard to capture and complete.

We had a chance to trace one Marine flier from his suburban home stateside on December 7, 1941, to the deck of the USS *Puget Sound* in Tokyo Bay after the signing of the instrument of surrender on September 12, 1945.

Remember that college student who wanted to be a Marine? The last we heard of my brother, Charles Francis "Bud" Kirby Jr., he was on his way to Parris Island. He arrived there all right; the Marines saw to that. He did not, however, get officer training as he had hoped. Someone did not see to that. He did get to Quantico because his name started with a *K*. After six weeks of boot camp, the "boots" were divided alphabetically. *A* to *J* went to

Camp LeJeune to be moved out for line duty "wherever needed." *K* to *Z* went to Quantico.

Our *K* Marine tried to find out about officer training at Quantico, but the only answer to his queries was "We don't know anything about that. Just move along." That he did, into aviation, and on to Texas A and M University for radio training and then to San Diego for Gunnery School. He was going to be a radio-gunner.

That's what brought him to the West Coast, to Miramar, where his squadron, Marine Scout Bombing Squadron (VMSB) 144, had orders for debarkation on January 5, 1943, aboard SS *Lurline*, a luxury liner turned troop transport. She and her sister ship, SS *Mariposa*, ferried troops throughout the war.

VMSB 144 was not alone. The 8th Marines were also among the five thousand military passengers sailing on *Lurline*. They had a plane escort for two hours out of San Diego Harbor. Then they were on their own on the Pacific. But they did not know where they were going.

They packed gear and uniforms for all seasons. With a fur-lined hat and jacket, could it be the Aleutians? There was much speculation, guessing, and wagering.

That finally changed when one of their regular morning training lectures was posted as "Flora and Fauna of the Tropics featuring poisonous plants, berries and insects, and venomous snakes."

All bets were off now. Attu it was not. The transport must be headed south.

After fifteen days at sea, they came to Nouméa, New Caledonia, where the harbor was crowded with everything but an aircraft carrier.

One of ships there was an old troopship, USS *Hunter Liggett*, and that's where Bud and his five thousand shipmates were ordered. Climbing over the side of the transport and down the nets should be no problem for most Marines, but when one is toting a full seabag, backpack, AND a rifle, it wasn't easy for anyone. Most made it. Then it was into the Higgins boats that would take them to the *Hunter Liggett*. Next it was off to the New Hebrides and the port of Vila on the island of Efaté.

They were the first to arrive, with only natives to greet them. They had to rough it for a month, working day in, day out to prepare a place for those who would follow them in. Seabees they were not, but they labored—pilots and gunners and ground crew alike—until the job was done and they had established a working port.

They did find an active Navy port elsewhere on Efaté. The USS *Chicago* was there with ships on either side of her, seemingly holding her up. Bud had a twinge of nostalgia. As a boy, he had gone aboard the *Chicago* with his father for lunch in the wardroom as guests of a family friend who was the ship's supply officer, who later became Chief of the Supply Corps Adm. Murray Royar.

When it was time to leave Vila, VMSB 144 knew where they were going—Guadalcanal was their destination. They would go to the New Hebrides for briefings and training about the Canal. At Espiritu Santo, they found an enormous staging area with temporary quarters for their preparation period.

Before they had a chance to untie the knots on their seabags, their orders were changed. VMSB 144 was needed to relieve a squadron that had taken hits, suffered losses, and needed immediate relief. VMSB 144 was to be flown up at once.

This was a squadron that flew Douglas SBD Dauntless dive bombers with a two-man crew—a pilot and a radio-gunner who rode backward in the rear seat. About thirty-six of the VMSB 114 Marines, with their gear, boarded a DC-3 for a four-and-one-half-hour flight to Guadalcanal. Toward the end of the trip, the pilot came on the PA system: "We'll be landing soon, and you'll have to be ready to get off immediately. You can't waste any time. Get your gear and yourselves off the plane and off the runway and into the jungle where you'll wait to be picked up to be taken wherever you're going. Remember, move fast. I have a cargo of wounded to get aboard and back to the hospital in Espiritu Santo as soon as I can get them there, so move fast."

VMSB 144 moved fast. They didn't even look back until they were all huddled around their gear among the trees. Then they turned to watch. The plane's propellers had never stopped turning. They saw wounded men lying on stretchers on the ground beside the plane. Litter bearers were running with other patients. When the plane was loaded to capacity and the last litter shoved aboard and the cargo hatch slammed shut and secured, the corpsmen who were left behind disappeared into the jungle across the airstrip. The newly arrived Marines watched the plane taxi down the runway, lift, climb, and circle around, finally disappearing into the clouds. Only then did any of the men of 144 speak. Someone noticed a couple of potholes still smoking from an enemy passover the night before, so they were told later. These Marines had no doubt about where they were and what they were about. It was not exactly a gentle welcome: a cargo of wounded and knowledge that they were relieving a shot-up squadron. They no longer wondered what lay ahead for them. They were there. They were in the war.

When their truck finally came jouncing through the jungle, they gathered themselves and their gear together and climbed aboard. They hoped that they would not be asked "where to?" because they did not know. The driver knew. They were headed for temporary quarters.

Eventually they settled into their permanent abode, a place known as "Skunk Hollow." These were no four-star accommodations. The men of VMSB 144 were assigned to four-man tents with earthen floors and a four-by-six-foot foxhole out front. The "ambiance" in Skunk Hollow left much to be desired, especially in the foxholes where they were often required to spend hours on end.

An enemy plane flew over the American base regularly, setting off the sirens and sending the men into their foxholes. This enemy came not to bomb but to harass with his noisy circling of the camp. He became known as "Washing Machine Charlie." The American guns could not reach him, and he knew just how low he could fly safely.

When a Washington VIP visited the Canal to learn firsthand what was going on there, he was irate to have to spend so much time in a foxhole. "Why can't we get that guy? What's the matter with our antiaircraft?" He was furious to learn that our guns weren't good enough. They needed 88 mm guns to get him, but they did not have them.

As soon as the Washington visitor could get out of his foxhole, he wasted no time in getting off the island and back to Washington (where there were no foxholes). Perhaps it was a coincidence, perhaps the VIP was responsible, but not too long after his departure, 88 mm guns arrived and were put to use immediately. Next time confident Charlie came buzzing over, he was nicked in the tail and turned abruptly and flew away, never to return.

Our Marine residents of Skunk Hollow were regularly flying missions over Munda, Bougainville, and other islands in the area. One day, as they were returning from Munda and the ground crew was watching the sky and counting, as they always did, VMSB 144 put down and taxied off to the side to make room for the next plane in.

Things were abuzz on the ground. Joe E. Brown was in town; big show tomorrow! This news raised the spirits of everyone. The troops could use a little laughter on Guadalcanal. That's what this famous comedian and movie star could give them. Everyone was excited, but it was special for one Marine who had just landed. Joe E. Brown (known as Joe E.) was a close friend. The Kirbys and the Browns had been friends for years. He couldn't wait to see the star.

As the fliers piled aboard the bus that would take them back to their camp, Pvt. Bud Kirby decided to look for Joe E. He walked a mile and a half to find him. It was a great meeting for both of them but too hectic for a real visit, what with the production crew trying to make Broadway out of the jungle.

However, Bud did meet the general who "suggested" that the private come for dinner that night and have some time with Joe.

"Where do you live?" asked the general.

"In Skunk Hollow, sir," replied Bud, as though it was Main Street.

"I know where that is," said the general as though it was Main Street or Broadway. "My jeep will pick you up."

Back in camp, Bud cleaned up, put on a fresh uniform, and waited for the appointed hour. It came. A booming announcement echoed through Skunk Hollow. "Attention Private Kirby. Attention Private Kirby. The general's jeep is here for Private Kirby. Repeat, the general's jeep is here for Private Kirby."

As the private came out of his tent, his campmates came out of theirs, mimicking the PA announcement. Bud hurried up to the command shack where the general's jeep was waiting. The general's lieutenant driver took off over the rough roads that had been hacked through the jungle growth. When they arrived at the general's tent, the table was laid...with a tablecloth! And napkins! And dishes! Bud could scarcely remember when he'd last seen such luxury!

The "brass" at table was very much interested in what was happening on Munda. They pumped the radio-gunner steadily. Of course, he was given some quiet time with the guest of honor before the dutiful driver took him back through the jungle to Skunk Hollow. Before departure, a date was set for another meeting the next day. The private said he had a mission to fly but would be back in time. And he was. A photographer recorded the meeting,

81

and a copy of the picture was given to Joe who sent it back home to California to his wife, Katherine, who sent it to Boston to Kirby's parents. This was the first time they knew where their son was.

The show on Guadalcanal was a colossal success. The laughter that roared up out of the jungle was as powerful as any guns

Joe E. Browne meets Marine Charles. F. Kirby, Jr. (right) returning from a misson.

that had roared in battle on the island. Joe E. Brown was an outstanding performer who made his mark in Hollywood and on Broadway. He was one of the great comedians of all time, and author of *Your Kids and Mine* (1944) and *Laughter Is a Wonderful Thing* (1956). If laughter is considered therapy, then Joe E. Brown was a first-class therapist.

Joe E.'s shows for the troops were therapy for him, too. He had lost his son, Don, early in the war, and he worked with an unmendable heart. He told how he had heard of the tragedy in *Your Kids and Mine.* He was playing in *The Showoff* at the Shubert Theatre in Detroit.

"Sometimes when I'm playing, I like to go out in the box office—just for fun—just to see the amazed look of people who come up to the window. Their mouths fall open, and then they recover and try to look dignified, as if they didn't recognize me.

"'Hiya folks,' I say, 'just picking up a little pin money on the side.' The crowd always gets a kick out of it, and I do, too. So this night there I was, and the telephone rang. 'This is the Army Ferry

Command in Long Beach, California,' the voice said, and I said, 'Sure, let's have the call, I'm expecting it.'

"'We want to reach Joe E. Brown to tell him that his son has just been killed in a routine flight…will you get the message to him?'

"'Yes,' I said, 'I'll get it to him. Thank you very much.'"

That was the night of October 8, 1942, when Joe E. was hoping for a call from his son, Captain Don Brown, USA, of the Army Transport Command, due to leave soon for duty in Australia.

Joe had already done shows in Alaska before this night, and he was hoping to meet up "down under" with Don when he went on a planned trip to Australia. That was not to be. Joe still went to Australia, Fiji, Midway, the Solomon and Hawaiian Islands, and throughout the Pacific Theater. He crisscrossed the world, oceans and continents alike. He rode over "the hump" with Gen. Claire Chennault, who had led the famous 1st American Volunteer Group (AVG) of the Chinese Air Force in 1941 and 1942, nicknamed the Flying Tigers, in the general's private plane…but still with that unmendable heart.

Joe E. Brown had friends among the highest-ranking military and among the lowest-rated GIs. When he returned from one of his tours, he found that he had another special group of friends: the parents of all those fighting at the front whom he had entertained.

His wife, Katherine, was waiting for him in their New York hotel along with a mailbag of letters. Joe became emotional as he read message after message of gratitude from these parents for what he had been doing for their children. Some hoped that he might come for supper on their farm so that they might repay him. Joe told Katherine that he would like to take a year off and travel around the country, visiting all these good people. Even, maybe, two years. The ever practical Katherine eyed him sternly and said, "Don't you even think of that!" Then she handed him one of the letters she had been reading. "However, you could do this one."

"I could," said Joe, as he read the letter she had handed to him. "I'm going to be in their town next week. I could do it then."

When that next week came and Joe E. was standing in front of his hotel in "their town," traffic was heavy and cabs were scarce. The doorman asked if he would be willing to share a cab. "Sure," said Joe. He hopped in with a young couple already in the cab indicated by the doorman.

"Where to, boss?" asked the driver. Joe passed him his letter with the address.

The cabbie looked at it and swung around. "Why, you're going to the White House!" He looked at Joe. "For dinner with the president! Yes, sir!" And he took off, smiling broadly. Joe had not wanted to seem to be bragging in front of the young couple: that was why he gave the cabbie the letter. The couple was awed.

Joe knew he was going to see the father of four boys in uniform and that their dad would want to know if he had run into them. The commander-in-chief was just another caring and grateful father who wanted to thank the touring therapist for what he had done for his own four sons and for all his other children in uniform on the various fronts where Joe had been.

Sometime after Joe E. Brown's departure from Guadalcanal, Squadron VMSB 144 received orders off the Canal to New Georgia. They had no regrets about leaving Skunk Hollow, but they were utterly unprepared for the upgrade in their new quarters. The tents were a cut above those in Skunk Hollow. They had wooden floors. And there were bunk beds. The bunk beds had mattresses! The mattresses had sheets. Sheets!

There was a mess hall with a cook who prepared meals around the clock. The men of VMSB 144 could sit on chairs, at a table, in the mess hall, to eat the chow that was prepared for them.

There were palm trees on New Georgia, making it seem more like a tropical resort instead of a takeoff spot for bombers. But this was war. VMSB 144 was flying regular missions over the Russells and still keeping their sights on Munda and Bouganville. They flew farther and more often but they always came back...all of them.

Eventually, the Douglas dive bombers were relieved of duty in the Solomons and sent back to the States for a new assignment. They were no longer VMSB 144. They were about to move into a new kind of flying—in Helldivers off a carrier. But before they were introduced to their new planes, they were given leave.

Bud called home as soon as he could get to a phone. It was the middle of the night on the East Coast. There was only one telephone in a suburban house in those days, and it was in a little telephone alcove in the front hall. Father stumbled down the stairs, half awake. He was trembling as he picked up the receiver. Mother and I were sitting upright in our beds—waiting—scarcely breathing. What could such a call mean?

In a choked-up voice, Father called up to them, "It's Bud. He back. He's all right. He's coming home."

"Tell him not to fly," said the ever-protective mother. "It's too dangerous. Tell him to take the train."

He flew.

10. THE NEW *QUINCY*

When his tour of duty with the Marines on Guadalcanal ended, Lt. Mathew Keough (ChC), USNR, received orders to Boston. He was to report to the heavy cruiser USS *Quincy*. This was the new *Quincy*, which had just been built in the extremely busy Fore River Shipyard in Massachusetts and was now being outfitted in the Charlestown Navy Yard.

It was a strange bit of coincidence that the old *Quincy* had sunk in the First Battle of the Solomons at the same time the First Marine Division, including Chaplain Keough, went ashore on Guadalcanal on August 8, 1942. When a group of sailors came in to the Blood Donor Center from the new *Quincy* in 1944, they were not thinking about the past. They were thinking about the present and—probably—their future.

Since their ship is home for long deployments, sailors appreciate good living quarters. What better than a brand-new ship, all shining, with the latest in equipment, nothing needing to be fixed because nothing was broken...yet. The sailors of the new *Quincy* were an upbeat lot when they came to the center to give their blood—a busload of them!

The chaplain also was delighted with his new quarters. After Guadalcanal, this was the Ritz. But he wanted something more. He wished that he had a piano aboard. It would be nice to have live music for divine services.

Now it just so happened that there was a naval officer in Boston who had something to do with "welfare." His job was to get whatever a serviceman needed or wanted and was a genuine "go-to guy." If you asked for something not too big, he probably had it in his pocket or in the backseat of his car. If the item requested was a little larger, it might be in the trunk of his car. Wherever, whatever—it was yours. If he didn't have it, he likely knew where to get it, and he would do just that—go get it for you. He was indeed a "go-to guy."

When this benefactor heard of the chaplain's wish, he obviously did not have a piano in his pocket or his car, but he must have known where there was one. A few days later, people were stopped in their tracks as they walked through the navy yard. There, high above their heads, swinging from a crane, was a piano. They gasped as it came in for a landing over the *Quincy* and dropped down upon her deck.

This benefactor was Lt. Ralph Colson, USNR, who had worked for the Massachusetts State Department of Education before entering the Navy. He was in physical education, especially schoolboy sports. He planned and supervised statewide track meets. As a schoolboy himself, he held the record for the one-hundred-yard dash, a record that was not touched through all the years until his own son came along and capped it.

As the men of the *Quincy* went through the Blood Donor Center that day, other donors and workers asked them where they had been. There was a variety of answers. Some were fresh from training; some from another ship; some from a battlefront. Those of us who could identify ribbons on a sailor's blouse knew that a man had been wounded in action when we saw his Purple Heart. And now, here he was recuperated and ready for new action on a new ship. When asked where they were going, they all had the same answer. They did not know. Even the captain did not know...then. When he received his orders, he was to head into the Atlantic.

He did not know at first but learned later that his ship was to join the fleet in the English Channel for D-Day on June 6, 1944. We at home were gratified to learn later that the *Quincy* came through without damage.

USS Quincy fires her guns off Normandy.

11. SURVIVING THE *VINCENNES* AT SAVO

When a ship is hit by enemy fire in a raging battle at sea, many of her crew cannot see what is happening. They are the "black gang" in the engine rooms, a name that dates back to coal-fired boilers, working doggedly below decks to keep all the ship's systems going. Such was the case on the USS *Vincennes* on that awful August day when she sank and many of her men met their deaths.

One year later, on August 9, 1943, to mark the first anniversary of that ill-fated day, our radio series, *Life to the Front*, presented a story of the *Vincennes*, featuring an interview with one of the survivors, the engineer officer in charge of one of those "black gangs" below decks.

When Lt. Edmond P. DiGiannantonio, USNR, was asked what it was like down there in the engine room, he said the temperature was between 120 and 125 degrees and that they had been at general quarters for sixty-eight hours. Our conversation with him on our broadcast was dramatic, but there's more to this story after the show was aired.

ORGAN:　　　FANFARE

ANNOUNCER:　　LIFE...to the FRONT!

ORGAN:

THEME MEDLEY (MONTEZUMA, CAISSONS, SEMPER PARATUS, ANCHORS AWEIGH)...FADE ON CUE AND HOLD UNDER FOLLOWING...

ANNOUNCER:

To all the men of the armed forces of the United States who, on every fighting front in the world, daily risk their lives in the service of their country...the American Red Cross Blood Donor Service dedicates this program... that they might live!

ORGAN:

UP AND TO END

ANNOUNCER:

LIFE...to the FRONT! Presented weekly by the American Red Cross Service of Boston in cooperation with station WEEI.

One year ago today, August 9, 1942, the Battle of Savo Island opened the campaign of the Solomons. Today, August 9, 1943, *Life to the Front* presents the story of Savo as witnessed by Lt. Edmond DiGiannantonio of the United States Naval Reserve, a survivor of Savo. But first, Miss Anastasia Kirby, assistant director of the American Red Cross Blood Donor Center. Miss Kirby.

KIRBY:

Like all broadcasts of *Life to the Front*, today's is dedicated to those fighting for us, everywhere. But especially is today's program dedicated to those men of the Navy who were a part of the battle of Savo just one year ago today. Perhaps many of you don't know much about the Battle of Savo because you don't know where or what Savo is. If I told you that we dedicated today's program to the survivors of the cruisers *Quincy*, *Astoria*, and *Vincennes* you'd know in a minute because those are names that the American people can never forget. Well...it's all the same. Savo is the island off which that eventful battle occurred one year ago today. It was the first of the six important Battles of the Solomons, the one in which we landed the Marines on Guadalcanal and really started things out there in the South Pacific. To pay fitting tribute to this important occasion, we have a very special guest with us today...a naval officer from the old *Vincennes* who was part of that action—a part of the Battle of Savo—out there on August 9, 1942, Lt. Edmond DiGiannantonio of the United States Naval Reserve.

KIRBY: Lieutenant, it was good of you to come here this afternoon to tell us all about this day last year because I know it's something you'd just as soon forget.

DIGI: There are times when it's good to remember it. This is one of them.

KIRBY: Well let's start out by having you tell us just where you and the *Vincennes* were at this very moment on August 9, 1942.

DIGI: At 1634, or should I say 4:34, I was aboard a transport—and the *Vincennes* was lying on the bottom of the sea. In other words—it was all over.

KIRBY: Then perhaps we should start out on Friday or Saturday and lead up to that fateful Sunday.

DIGI: Well, actually it was 10:30 on Thursday, August 6, when general quarters sounded. Our first attack was an aerial attack from high-altitude bombing planes and a few dive bombers. Next morning the dive bombers came in again with torpedo planes and we shot down most of them.

KIRBY: Where were you during all this...where was your battle station?

DIGI: I was below decks as engineering officer in charge of one of the black gangs.

KIRBY: What's it like to be down there where you're such a part of everything but you can't see what's going on?

DIGI: It's a strange feeling. Of course there's a loudspeaker system, you know, throughout the whole ship, and reports on all movements are called down to us. We're kept posted in that way on everything that's happening. When the voice comes through the speaker...bombs falling...getting larger and larger... coming toward us...there's no power on earth that can stop you from looking up at the overhead...waiting for that bomb to come through.

KIRBY: It must be—a very strange feeling! And— it must get pretty hot down there, too, doesn't it?

DIGI: Yes. All the vents and ventilators are closed and the fans are turned off while we're at battle stations. The temperature down there was between 120 and 125.

KIRBY: How long were you at battle stations?

DIGI: Sixty-eight hours.

KIRBY: Sixty-eight hours. Why that's nearly three full days!

DIGI: That's right.

KIRBY: Digi, how did the men react being under such a strain for such a long time?

DIGI:

They were tops—4.0 as we say in the Navy. And they proved their mettle when the final crash came. At 0146 the Japs came in with a surface force and we were hit by torpedoes, bombs, and numerous shells. There was no panic below...no uneasiness. After losing all power—steam, electricity, etc.—the engine room filled with smoke...I gave the order to abandon the engine room. The men left in orderly fashion. There still was no panic.

KIRBY:

About how many were there in your gang?

DIGI:

There were about twenty of us all told. We had to go through a narrow passageway to get out. We climbed up through a small opening like a conning tower hatch...if any man tripped or got panicky he'd have trapped us all because that's the black gang's only means of escape you know. But the men were orderly and there was no trouble.

KIRBY:

When you came topside what was it like, and what did you do?

DIGI:

It was pretty grim. We saw all the men who had been killed lying around on the well deck. The ship was burning furiously. Men were running through flames...as a matter of fact, we had to run through the burning hangar to get over to a life raft. I ordered the men to cut it loose from the bulkhead, put it into the water, and leave the ship. While they were working on that, I went back aft to see about getting another life raft cut loose, and as I did we were hit by another torpedo.

KIRBY: Were there any more engine room crews that got up?

DIGI: Out of about ninety I think eight or nine survived because that torpedo got all of us that were on deck. My ten men were blown completely off the ship by the explosion, and I never saw them again.

KIRBY: What happened to you, Digi?

DIGI: I never really knew what happened to me until I read the record. The explosion picked me up and blew me forty feet up against a bulkhead, and I got a concussional shock. When I picked myself up and came back to where we had all been together, I couldn't find a man.

KIRBY: I don't suppose you wasted too much time in getting over the side, did you?

DIGI: Not too much, but when I got into the water, I swam away from the ship and then a funny thing happened...I lost my hat, and right away quick I thought... that was my new cap and it had cost me plenty just weeks before. So darned if I didn't turn around and swim back and get it. You know, always in uniform, that's me! Some of the men recognized me from a raft they were hanging to off to the left, so they called to me, "Hey, Digi, over here!" When I got over there, there were some wounded men hanging onto the sides, so we got the men who were well enough out of the raft and put the wounded in and then we drifted for seven hours.

KIRBY: Seven hours that seemed like seven days, I suppose.

DIGI: At least that. The only break we had came about 0450 when it started to rain and one of the fellows had enough spirit left in him to give us our first laugh. He said, "Gee, now we're going to get all wet."

KIRBY: Were there any other outstanding events while you were in the water those seven hours?

DIGI: Yes, I got clipped myself. I turned around to watch the ship sink...when you have lived on a ship for two years, been through as much with her as we all went through with the good old *Vincennes*, you sort of want to be with her at the end. However, it was a wrong move for me because I got hit in the face either by some debris or by the raft itself, and I got a broken nose, a cracked jaw, and lost four choppers as a result.

KIRBY: That's how you got the Purple Heart, I take it.

DIGI: That's right. I got my first medical attention aboard the rescue ship, which happened to be a transport. We were picked up around nine o'clock.

KIRBY: How much medical attention did they give you aboard the transport?

DIGI: They took care of all the emergency cases...these were men who were severely burned, or were suffering from terrific shock, shrapnel wounds, etc. As a matter of fact, that was my first experience witnessing a plasma administration. As I came through the passageway, I saw the doctors giving a pint of blood plasma to a boy who was lying there unconscious. Right beside him was another boy who was in a similar condition. The minute they finished the first transfusion, and it took less than five minutes as I remember it, they moved on to the next man without any loss of time.

KIRBY: Digi, did you see any other plasma used down there?

DIGI: Yes. During the two months that I remained in an area where there was an advance base hospital, I had the opportunity to watch doctors administer plasma to the Marine casualties that had just been flown down from the Canal, and there were plenty of them.

KIRBY: Describe what a casualty looks like when he is getting his plasma.

DIGI: You and I would say that he is all through because usually he looks absolutely lifeless. Then as plasma is injected into his veins, you can actually see the life coming back... his pulse quickens, color comes back into his face...it's almost uncanny. It certainly is great stuff, and I am sure that if they had had more down there in the beginning, we would have had more survivors from the Solomons besides speeding up the recovery of those not so seriously wounded. You see plasma was used chiefly on extreme cases and not any like mine, for example—

KIRBY: I have to interrupt you. How could a broken nose and a cracked jaw and a bashed-in face, to say nothing of concussional shock, not rate prompt attention?

DIGI: Well, really, mine wasn't so bad. However, had I had plasma and other cases like mine, I suspect that our recuperation would have been cut in half.

KIRBY: Could have used more plasma if they had had it?

DIGI: You're damn right they could have used more! They can use every pint of blood plasma they can get out there...and plenty that they didn't get.

The lieutenant's message didn't help his shipmates who did not survive the Solomons, but he did a lot for those left behind fighting on. His story on this broadcast brought in many donors, as did his appearances on our "Medicine Shows"—so termed by survivor Chaplain McQuaid. These men and others visited communities where a large audience was gathered to hear firsthand reports from survivors back from the front, especially recipients of the Purple Heart like Digi and the Padre.

This naval officer brought unexpected comfort and some closure to a person who came in touch with him through the broadcast. Shortly after the program aired, a letter was received at the radio station from a woman who had missed the broadcast but heard about it from a friend. How could she find out about the *Vincennes*?

"My brother was on the *Vincennes*," she wrote, "and since receiving the official notification from the Navy Department last September that he was missing in action, I have had no further word. I understand that the officer interviewed was in some way connected with the black gang in the engine room, and, since my brother was a fireman, you can see how much it would mean to me to be able to communicate with this man because he might know something about my brother."

Her letter was forwarded to the Blood Donor Center, and a reply was sent promising a script of the broadcast and a call to Lieutenant DiGiannantonio to find out if he knew her brother.

Her next letter told us about her brother. "He is my only brother and as we lost our parents and a sister some years ago, you can understand how very dear he is to me and how eager I am for some news of him. It is not knowing what happened to him that is so hard."

Not long after this letter was received, Lieutenant DiGiannantonio happened to be sitting at my desk (waiting for me to return from trying to get a shipment of blood through an air raid) when a call came in from this sister. When he heard my secretary mention the name, he asked to take the call and talk with her. He told me of their conversation, and both of us were deeply moved. Her following letter explained:

"You can well imagine what an effect the lieutenant's information had on me and it is so hard for me to believe it is true. 'Missing in action' gives you so much to hope for and with no news for a year and hoping for a year for further word from the Navy Department, I was unprepared for such a difficult statement. I didn't half grasp the details that the lieutenant gave me. Please tell him that I am grateful to him for the kindly manner in which he broke the sorrowful news to me. I know that it was no easy task. I understand that what the lieutenant tells me is strictly off the record and I shall keep it in confidence. Please believe me what you have done for me is so deeply appreciated. It has meant so much to me to talk with you through our letters. I look forward to meeting you personally."

This caring and saddened young woman, living out of town for the summer with a young baby, was one of so many "next of kin" who had to live with the crushing news of loss. Our anniversary broadcast about the end of the *Vincennes* at Savo Island gave us something to give to her.

Although this experience undoubtedly opened wounds for the lieutenant, it must have given him a sense of satisfaction also. The "good old *Vincennes*" obviously meant a lot to Lieutenant DiGiannantonio. This very personal contact with the sister of one of his missing men must have been bittersweet as it took him back to the tragedy of the year before.

Lieutenant DiGiannantonio considered himself lucky. He was a survivor. *Vincennes* lost 332 men at Savo.

PART III
ATLANTIC CONVOYS

12. THE PREWAR ATTACK ON THE *KEARNEY*

Even before Germany had declared war on the United States, her U-boats were on the prowl, menacing shipping in the Atlantic but especially the convoys. On October 17, 1941, in the waters off Iceland, U-568 got a hit. The victim was a U.S.destroyer. The USS *Kearny* (DD 432) was not sunk, but she was heavily damaged, and eleven members of her crew killed. In addition, twenty-two of her men—including her captain—were injured. The No.1 fireroom sustained most of the injuries, caused by the far-reaching effect of the torpedo's explosion. The ship experienced fires, flooding, and major structural damage throughout.

This was not an easy situation for a crew to handle. Their captain was down; their ship had been attacked when their country was not at war. Damage control needed to work fast before damage worsened. Eleven shipmates lay dead. The twenty-two injured, some critically, were a priority, preferably to be taken to sick bay for assessment of injuries and prompt treatment. That was the ideal—but the ideal is not always attainable in crisis. Their injuries included shock, burns, deafness, broken and crushed bones, lacerations, contusions, and loss of blood. All were candidates for plasma, but there was none on board. In World War II, there was a store of plasma on every ship ready for just such cases. But this was October 17, 1941, before war had been declared.

Fortunately, plasma was available on the mainland, and the Army and Navy had been instrumental in putting it there. The full value of plasma had been realized in 1940 through the pioneer research of diligent professionals. Among the leading researchers was Doctor Charles Drew, a highly regarded teacher and surgeon who was anxious to see a program established that would provide an ongoing supply of plasma. Probably through his enthusiasm and persistence—and, of course, his outstanding credentials—the Army and Navy and the American Red Cross started a pilot program in New York City in early 1941, with Doctor Drew as assistant director.

Dr. Charles Drew

Washington was well aware of the U-boat attack. The unprovoked assault deeply disturbed President Roosevelt. Care for the ship's injured men became a top priority. If plasma was needed, it was to be made available. A plane was ordered to load up with plasma and fly to the stricken ship. With no place on the destroyer for the plane to land, the cargo was rigged with parachutes and dropped into the heaving sea around it. *Kearney*'s boat was launched and sailors rowed out to gather in the little parachutes bobbing on the water.

Kearney's damage was repaired fast enough to get her back in action where she served throughout World War II. Within six months of her own attack, she was ordered to assist in rescue efforts to remove the crew of the SS *Fairport*, which was sinking following a

German submarine torpedo attack. The rescue ship had a glimpse of what October 17 might have been for them, but at the same time, they were grateful that there was no loss of life for this ship as there had been on theirs. They rescued 123 men, including members of the Naval Armed Guard.

Kearney saw duty at Africa, Sicily, Italy, and France before reporting to CINCPAC for service in the Pacific. She left Iwo Jima, headed for the Straits of Magellan into the Atlantic. She ended her days stationed in Charleston, South Carolina, in 1945, decommissioning in March 1946. It was a full life for a ship that was almost lost on October 17, 1941. *Kearney*'s surviving shipmates always remembered the eleven crewmen killed in that prewar attack.

13. THE *TURNER* COMES HOME

The story of the USS *Turner*, sunk outside New York Harbor on January 3, 1944, isn't a story of a victorious naval victory, but rather a disaster in local waters with no enemy involved. But when researching this book, the *Turner* became a special story of heroism and the value of plasma.

The USS *Turner* (DD 648) was a destroyer of the *Gleaves* class, built at Federal Shipbuilding & Drydock in Kearney, New Jersey, and commissioned at the New York Navy Yard on April 15, 1943.

Not all the Navy's losses came from enemy fire on a foreign sea. Some came from friendly fire, some from human error, and some from an accident. That's what happened to *Turner* when she went down at the entrance to New York Harbor on that cold January day in 1944.

She was a relatively new ship, but she had proven herself in the months since joining the fleet. She served in the screen of transatlantic convoys. She was seen at Casablanca, Gibraltar, and Guantanamo Bay. As she moved in harm's way as an advance anti-submarine (ASW) scout for convoy GUS-18, she picked up a contact on her SG surface search radar. Within eleven minutes, her lookouts made visual contact with a German submarine on the surface. *Turner* opened fire, scoring a hit on the U-boat's conning tower, followed by other hits before the sub began to dive. *Turner* dropped a depth charge and then another and still another before explosions were heard telling the men of the *Turner* that they had taken out the menacing U-boat. They looked for proof, but time and circumstances made it impossible to acquire evidence. However, *Turner* witnesses were convinced that there was one less submarine to threaten the convoys.

Toward the end of December, *Turner* was homeward bound, her escort duties with transatlantic convoys completed for the time. The deployment had been demanding and the crewmen weary when they dropped anchor at Ambrose Lightship at the entrance to New York Harbor. Those on watch went to work; others hit the sack, content that it was just a matter of time before the ship received clearance to enter Ambrose Channel and be on her way to New York.

The crew felt good that night and the next morning when they reported for breakfast. The two mess compartments were filled; some Sailors had finished eating, while others were filling their trays and looking around for a place to sit down. At 0616, a violent explosion rocked the destroyer. Trays and food and chairs went flying. Men were tossed around like rag dolls.

What had hit the ship? A torpedo? An underwater mine? Nothing had been expected. Then the crew realized that the explosions were coming from within the ship. Fault in her own ammunition? Explosion followed explosion. Fires broke out everywhere. They were not only eating through the framework of the ship, they were eating the clothes off the bodies of the crewmen. One of the men who survived this horrible ordeal told his son in later years that when the day started he was wearing wool pants, a denim shirt, a wool sweater, and hat. After the first explosion, his pants became shorts, and the sweater was patches. Burns covered his arms and legs, and all the hair on his head was gone. This man was Seaman Second Class Albert L. Cover. When the end came for the *Turner,* he was one of the survivors taken aboard the rescue ship. All he had left were his shoes and a leather belt. The rest had been burned or blown off his body.

His son, David Cover, who gave this account to the USS *Turner* Association, said that he had seen his father's medical records listing second- and third-degree burns over 65 percent of his body. "I knew his case was critical because a priest performed the last rites on him three times during his recovery."

Another description of the plight of the men of the USS *Turner* that fateful day was told by John MacDonald, a second-class petty officer and the ship's baker, who was coming up the ladder to the mess decks when the initial explosion occurred. He could neither see nor hear after the blast, and all his clothes and his hair were burned off in the fire that followed.

"I tried to find my way out. The steel inside the ship and the hatch I tried to get out of were buckled from the explosion. Not able to see, I kept feeling around for ways to get out and finally felt cold air from the snow outside. Next thing I knew, a snipe put a life jacket on me and threw me over the side. A boat from the destroyer escort USS *Inch* (DE 146) had picked me and a few others up and brought us to their ship. I was seriously injured and in the hospital for a great amount of time."

This information was provided to the USS *Turner* Association in the year 2000. It wasn't a case of some people remembering. There are some things one can never forget.

Still another member of that crew was around in 2000 to recall that awful day for the men of the *Turner*. This man was Machinist's Mate Second Class Robert Freear, remembering sixty years later how he had just filled his tray in the main mess and moved into the forward mess compartment to sit down to eat. This was a fortunate move for this man because everyone in the main mess compartment died.

After the explosion, Freear was out for five to ten minutes and when he came to, he saw nothing but flames and heavy smoke and heard nothing but the screams of those who were trapped in the wreckage and were burning to death. "Breathing was next to impossible, so I crawled with my face close to the deck for better air. In time I found five men who were trying to find their way. Eventually, we arrived topside on the foredeck and found ourselves in a howling blizzard. I will never forget the exquisite sensation caused by snow coming into contact with red hot skin.

"Looking aft with one eye open, I saw the sight of a destroyer completely out of operation. Both sides had huge holes blown out. The number two 5-inch gun turret had disappeared, and flames were rushing out of the holes in the sides and on top of the superstructure. To the great credit of the men on the foredeck, there was no panic.

"A Coast Guardsman brought his boat, approximately sixty feet in length, up to the port side of the foredeck and threw lines up to us, and eventually we all boarded and got safely away. Those Coastguardsmen spent 20 to 30 minutes alongside the ship rescuing us, knowing of the imminence of explosion and realizing that they had hundreds of gallons of gasoline on board. However, they stayed alongside until the last man was taken off. The Coast Guard deserves a great deal of credit for this rescue.

"We were about thirty yards from the *Turner* when the second major explosion occurred. We watched her sink, and when some of the depth charges were under water, there was a tremendous blast. It seemed as if acres of water rose thirty to forty feet," Freear said.

"We were six miles out, the most agonizing miles of my life, as we were being taken to an Army hospital at Red Bank, New Jersey. The searing pain of the burned areas of my body were incredible. When I passed over my threshold of pain and mercifully went into shock, I felt nothing and saw nothing because my eyes were blistered shut," said Freear.

"The treatment at the Army hospital was outstanding. The personnel met the emergency of many difficult cases (one man had 90 percent second- and third-degree burns and survived) with expertise and cheerfulness," Freear said. "We had a medical corpsman at our bedside twenty-four hours a day, checking our blood count and body fluids...we required hundreds of quarts of blood plasma."

There was not enough to meet this extensive—and ongoing—need, but the Coast Guard came to the rescue in a first mission of its kind.

A Navy HNS-1 helicopter, flown by instructor pilot Lt. Cmdr. F. A. Erickson, USCG, of the Coast Guard Aviation Unit at Floyd Bennett Field, came through the blizzard with cases of plasma lashed to the helicopter's pontoons. This mission of mercy and heroics was a lifesaving experiment and as such a piece of history. It was the first-ever use of a helicopter in a lifesaving role.

Lt. Cmdr. F. A. Erickson, USCG

"Later we were transferred to Brooklyn Naval Hospital where we, again, received excellent treatment and nursing. In spite of complications which most of us developed from the blast, we came through," Freear said. "No one was lost!"

The recollections of the *Turner* disaster were put forward by these survivors as a testimonial to their shipmates: those who came through and those who did not. Said Freear, "These thoughts were offered as a memorial to those who were blown to bits, slowly burned to death, drowned, or suffered severe injuries."

When the *Turner* went down in the waters off Ambrose Light, her captain went down with her. Cmdr. Henry S. Wygant Jr. and fifteen of his officers and 123 of his men were lost.

This was a terrible tragedy, a great loss to the Navy, especially Task Force 68. The Navy can always build another ship and find a crew to man it, but those killed can never be replaced.

The *Turner*'s death toll was tragically high, but the survival rate among the victims rescued was outstanding. A detailed report regarding victims who were brought to the hospital at Fort Hancock, New Jersey, was issued by Capt. Saul Hochheiser of the Army Medical Corps. It was so thorough that the surgeon general of the aAmy referred to it in his statement about the *Turner* disaster.

The blood from more than 320 donors was used in saving the lives of the thirty-five most severely burned survivors.

Although this is not a report of plasma's use in the front lines, the Fort Hancock medical report concerning the use of the lifesaving plasma processed from blood collected by the Red Cross is one of the most detailed released at the time.

According to the report, most of the victims "needed plasma transfusions because severe burns and accompanying abrasions, 'blast' lungs, lacerations, and fractures had accelerated the production of traumatic shock, deadly after-effect of loss of liquid from the bloodstream."

The doctor's lengthy and detailed report explained the extent of each man's burns and the degree of those burns and the amount of plasma given to each man each day. He seemed to be aware of where his plasma was coming from and grateful to the folks at home for giving him what he needed. "During the first twenty-four hours after the explosion, the thirteen worst cases averaged 2,211 cc. of plasma each, representing the blood donations of approximately 117 persons."

The most satisfying part of his report was the last paragraph: "Within less than a month after being admitted to the Fort Hancock hospital, they were all well enough to be transferred to the Brooklyn Naval Hospital for convalescence or return to active service."

Doctor Hochheiser's report was most valuable to me, as was the *Turner* research sparked by that worn two-page report, which had been previously ignored. Although these pages are concerned essentially with the great connection between the people on the home front during World War II and their men in uniform wherever in the war world they might have been, there was another important intent. There is a hope that some of the millions walking the world today will learn of their heritage that they are here because the life of a father or grandfather was saved by the gift of one of our blood donors. It is a special piece of heritage that people should know if it applies to them.

When David Cover told of his father's experience on the *Turner*, he concluded his remarks with a very touching observation: "It is a strange feeling knowing that I am alive as are my sisters as well as a brother who died at age 37 because some person or persons that I will never know saved my father's life. I am just happy to have been able to get some information out about the people behind the event. I guess I am just trying to say 'thank you' somehow to those unknown people."

Much has been said about the *Turner* disaster not being the result of enemy engagement. Officially, the cause was listed as defective ammunition, but some witnesses claim to have seen German U-boats. Regardless, *Turner* was the victim of one of the Navy's greatest—and always dreaded—enemies: fire aboard her ships.

14. THE DALBEY STORY

When a young graduate of the University of Oklahoma came east to attend the U. S. Maritime Service Radio Training School at Gallops Island in Boston Harbor, it was a natural move. He had been a radio announcer in Oklahoma City and a ham operator with an amateur radio license since he was twelve years old. He took his interest in radio to a new level: maritime communications.

At Gallops Island (sometimes called Gallups Island), he joined hundreds of prospective Merchant Marine radio operators studying radio theory, typing, electricity, and the maintenance and repair of receivers, transmitters, and direction-finding apparatus. These students would be able to handle whatever problem might occur on a ship in merchant service. In addition, the student earned his second-class radio telegraph license. There was also a history lesson for anyone interested. Carl Dalbey would have been one of those.

The island had been a fortification for Boston during the Revolutionary War and a training ground for troops during the Civil War. In the late 1800s, Gallops Island served, as the much bigger Ellis Island had done, in receiving and processing immigrants and quarantining them when necessary. In the 1940s, men were being prepared for critical service at sea in World War II. This is the place where this Oklahoma boy joined that service.

I first met Carl Shepard Dalbey Jr. when he came to the Blood Donor Center to give blood. He was one of the first 368 trainees to sign up in the school's blood donor drive. They represented the forty-eight states of the union as these volunteer donors formed a huge cross, dwarfing a twelve-by-eighteen-foot American Red Cross flag. Commanding Officer Cmdr. Sherman W. Read, USMS, announced, "Our goal is one thousand pints of blood for our comrades-in-arms overseas."

368 donors form a Red Cross.

Carl Dalbey not only gave his own blood, he also helped to get others to give theirs by speaking at blood donor programs. He had some extraordinary stories to tell. Following his graduation from Radio Training School, he signed on as radioman on a merchant marine ship sailing in an Atlantic convoy. The name of the ship was the SS *Potlatch.*

Potlach was underway about 650 miles east of the Virgin Islands on June 27, 1942, when she was torpedoed by an enemy submarine, U-153. *Potlach* was traveling unescorted at seven knots due to heavy smoke coming from the stack. She had stopped several times during the day to check the water content in the fuel oil. At 2152 the enemy struck on the port quarter near the engine room about ten feet below the waterline. The explosion blew a hole through the deck, threw the trucks and tanks on deck into the air, buckled the deck plates, and damaged the steering gear.

As Carl Dalbey rushed to the radio room to send his messages, all he could hear was "the terrific concussion of metal hitting on metal." He stayed at his controls until the last minute, as did the gunners. The ship was armed with one 4-inch gun, along with four 20 mm guns and a pair of .30-caliber guns. The gunners manned their stations until the aft gun was awash and then they jumped overboard. The ship immediately began settling on an even keel and sank by the bow in five minutes.

Forty-eight survivors crowded into a lifeboat with a capacity of thirty-nine. U-153 came close to their boat and gave them cigarettes. They asked if there was something else they could do for them. Their commander spoke perfect English, Dalbey said. "Before diving, they circled the wreckage and picked up some of the tires from our cargo, leaving the forty-eight of us to set out on what was to be a thirty-eight-day journey in the scorching Caribbean sun."

As my interview with Dalbey continued, he explained, "You just sit and think about the folks at home, maybe pray a little. We had some pemmican, some malted milk tablets, and a little water.

Squalls came along, and we caught water in some sail. It kept us going for days. One of the boys—he was pretty young and inexperienced—kept drinking seawater. We couldn't stop him. Finally, he'd had just too much and he died. We gave him a sea burial with the Lord's Prayer and then...we prayed some more."

After fifteen days adrift, an island was sighted. "It was uninhabited," said Dalbey, "but there was water there, even if it was poor quality, and we tried to catch some wild animals. We didn't have our land legs yet and the results were funny. We found a few berries and ate some raw snails. Some of the men had tried eating seaweed because they thought it would do them some good."

They set out again, and six hours later came upon another island, but alas, it too was uninhabited—not even any berries left. They stayed a day and then set sail once more, ever mindful that every time they went ashore they risked serious damage to their boat going in over the coral reefs.

"Now the going was really rough," recalled Dalbey. "We tried to see who could tell the tallest yarns, but pretty soon we just sat there and said nothing. Most of the men were tough seamen and could take it, but it was rough on some of us who were green and new to the game."

Dalbey said the ship's old cook died the night before they sighted the third island. "We kept him in the bottom of the boat because we were all too weak to lift him overboard. We finally buried him on the island after we landed."

This island had a small fishing village where an old woman gave the some gruel—the first real food they'd had for days. "Later, we got a man to take us around the island to a larger village where we hoped we could get word to the mainland, but it was inland and we had to walk barefoot over the hot coral rocks and sand. I just about made it to the schoolhouse they turned over to us before I fell. I didn't think I could make it but I finally got to my feet and made it inside."

This was Aklins Island. From there, the forty-six survivors were put onto a small sailboat and then taken aboard a yacht, the *Vergenmere*, owned by a prominent British yachtswoman named Betty Carstairs. She was a Standard Oil heiress who had sailed and raced extensively in the Bahamas and had bought up many of the islands there in a desire to preserve their native integrity. Her yacht brought the survivors to Nassau. From there, they were flown to Miami. Dalbey was hospitalized and later sent to New York for further treatment. His body weight had dropped from 124 to 97 pounds. Finally, he returned to his parents' home in Oklahoma City to recuperate.

The master of the SS *Potlach*, Capt. John Joseph Lapoint, was awarded the Merchant Marine Distinguished Service Medal for especially meritorious service "under stress and hazards. He had sailed the crowded boat to the nearest land only navigating by the sun and the stars."

Following his convalescence at home, Carl Dalbey was ready to return to sea. Once more, he returned to Boston to sign on as radioman on another Merchant Marine vessel on convoy duty in the Atlantic.

Once more his ship was hit. It happened somewhere off the coast of Nova Scotia. The ship was not sunk, but damage was extensive. One of the local residents who came down to see what had happened in the night said, "She had a hole in her side you could drive a schooner through."

Six of her men had been able to bring her to shore, beach her, and save the cargo. Carl Dalbey was asked by another local, "You and those five bring her in?"

"Yes, sir, we did...the captain, the first mate, two engineers, a seaman, and I'm the radioman."

"That was a mighty job for six men."

"It wasn't easy," said Dalbey.

"You look pretty young for that work," offered the native.

"I'm young, sir," said Dalbey, "but not for the work."
"You six all that's left of the crew?"
"Just us, but we saved the cargo."
"What were you carrying?"
"Landing barges. They're waiting for them across."

This beaching of their ship was no minor matter for the six survivors. For Carl Dalbey, it might well have been too much. But it wasn't. He was ready to resume his service, signing on once more as radioman on another Merchant Marine cargo ship.

Ten days before his departure, he spoke for the Blood Donor Service in the Boston suburb of Belmont. Mrs. William B. Burbank, the local blood donor chairman, never forgot what he told his audience in the Belmont High School auditorium that night. People listened intently to his description of that ordeal in the Caribbean. His conclusion hit home. They were all deeply touched:

"I did not receive any blood plasma out there because they had none on the island or the yacht that rescued us...but all of us could have used it because the shock we had suffered was terrific. When you sail with the Merchant Marine you see plenty of explosions and torpedoing, flaming oil, men burned horribly. You know what it is to need things. What the men on the high seas need from you is your blood for plasma, because that's the only place it can come from—you! Those boys out there depend on you. They believe in you. Don't let them down. Make sure there's plenty of plasma out there for them."

Dalbey felt confident in his next voyage. They were traveling with a large convoy—always a good feeling for every man on every ship because there was safety in their numbers that kept the U-boats away. "Unless," as one man said, "you have to drop back!" The optimist in Dalbey believed that no one would get torpedoed three times in a row. How wrong he was! His ship was the SS *William*

B. Frye—one of the new Liberty vessels—on her first voyage across the Atlantic.

They were well on their way when the new Liberty ship developed engine trouble and had to slow down and drop back out of its assigned position in the convoy. When repairs were completed and the ship moved on at full speed to catch up, a pack of German subs was ready to move in. One hit the ship with a splintering effect. The *William B. Frye*'s guns hit back, and the sub submerged, giving the merchant ship hope because a surface ship's speed is greater than a submarine's under water. However, another U-boat was ready, and *William B. Frye* was hit again, this time fatally.

Dalbey had run for his radio controls and sent out his messages. For six of the seven minutes that the ship remained afloat, he stayed at his transmitter, wiring ahead to the convoy. In the seventh moment, he grabbed some portable equipment and went into the water.

It was early spring, North Atlantic, icy waters, high seas. He swam to a raft that was already dangerously overcrowded. One more person would have capsized it and sent them all into the water. Dalbey tried to lash his equipment to the side of the raft, but because of the high seas, he was unable to do so. He threw his radio to a shipmate and said, "Take this. Use it!" He was immediately swept away by the violent waves.

Carl Dalbey was never seen again.

His shipmates called him a hero. They probably owed their lives to the messages he worked so diligently to send. A British destroyer rescued them after picking up the *William B. Frye*'s SOS.

In June of that year, the U.S. Maritime Service honored him by posthumously presenting an officer's commission. His parents from Oklahoma attended the special ceremony held in Boston. His mother accepted for her son.

WEEI transcribed the event, and it was used in the August 13, 1943, broadcast of *Life to the Front*. There were one thousand trainees listening on their radios at the Gallops Island School that day to hear the story of one of their own. Included in that broadcast was Dalbey's last will and testament, which had been read at the memorial service at the Seamen's Institute in Boston.

"I, Carl S. Dalbey Jr., being of sound mind and body, do hereby designate the following to be my last will and testament. In the event of my death, I bequeath to my dear mother Mrs. Henrietta Boyd Dalbey, all monies, stocks, bonds in my name. To my friend, William Huffman, I leave all of my personal effects that he may find useful—the rest of which may be disposed of as seen fit by my mother.

The above constitutes my worldly goods. My greatest possession of all, however—my faith in Him and the Everafter—I bequeath unto all the poor in spirit who may, as I have, find comfort in His blessings."

There were many long personal letters between me and Mrs. Dalbey after the Dalbeys returned to Oklahoma. Although still grieving the loss of her son, Henrietta Dalbey turned her tragedy into productive pursuits. Aware of the need for more attention to the men of the Merchant Marine Service, she wanted to establish a Merchant Marine Auxiliary in Oklahoma City and in Boston, working with Mrs. Leslie G. Neal, widow of the first engineer on the ill-fated *William B Frye.*

In one of the newspaper clippings sent to me, I found a notation that Leslie Neal had been in a successful business for fourteen years when war was declared. He felt the need to go back to sea in the service of his country. In that same paper I read that, in their work, these ladies had used Carl Dalbey's words, spoken in his speech for the Boston Blood Donor Service: "Your men need you. Don't let them down." The paper printed the whole speech.

A front-page story in another Oklahoma City newspaper gave details of the disasters at sea and announced the memorial service to be held in the First Presbyterian Church that Carl had attended.

I learned also of the memorial service at the Seamen's Church Institute in New York City attended by many prominent people. Mr. and Mrs. Dalbey had given a room in their son's memory with his name on the door. This was a place where many a weary seaman could seek respite in the future during wartime and after.

Carl Dalbey was gone and with him hundreds of other men of the Merchant Marine. Lost also were members of the U.S. Navy Armed Guard serving aboard these convoy vessels.

I always remembered the blond boy and his words in behalf of his fellow seamen: "Make sure there's plenty of plasma out there for them."

A monument was erected at Gallops Island to remember the men who had died. It read, "By their deeds measure yours."

As a postscript, the five-acre Gallops Island known to the Radio Training School is now part of the fifty-acre Boston Harbor Islands National Recreation Area. Gone are the barracks, dining hall, auditorium, classrooms, and labs that provided every type of equipment to be found on a Merchant Marine ship. Nothing should be unfamiliar to the seaman, except, of course, the weather and its devastating storms and the enemy lurking under the waves.

PART IV
THE QUEST

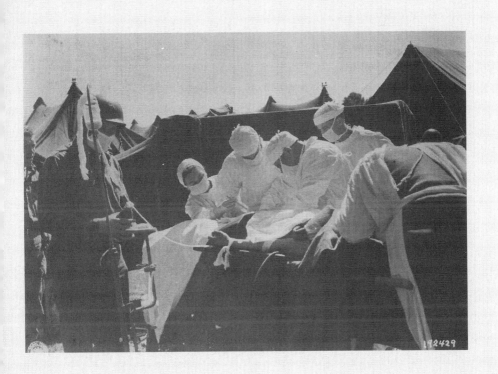

15. RULES AND REGULATIONS

The world is full of rules and regulations, and the Blood Donor Service was no exception. In the center we worked within medical limits such as temperature, weight, blood pressure, pulse, and hemoglobin, along with a series of questions in a medical history. And then there was the matter of age. A donor had to be between twenty-one and sixty.

Those between eighteen and twenty who wished to donate were accepted if they had permission from a parent or legal guardian and a signed and witnessed official release form. It was distressing to have to turn away someone with permission that was not witnessed. It was equally difficult to tell a big, strapping nineteen-year-old who wanted to give his blood for the troops that he had to go home to his mother for permission.

When a group of giggling girls came in from a local college dormitory, waving their permission slips that they had just received from home, they might have been a little nervous about the upcoming procedure, but they were thrilled to be a part of the great romance. A few of them envisioned handsome Marines lying wounded on a battlefront somewhere just waiting for the girls from the dorm to save their lives. There were others who were very quiet, very serious. These girls had someone close to them on a battlefront and hoped he was not wounded. But if so… at least they were doing something about it … for him… or for someone else in need.

There were no romantic notions among the over-60 group or those approaching that special age; only frustration. Many were repeat donors, waiting to make the Gallon Club but the nearest date for their next donation would take them over their 60th birthday. No red ribbon in their blood donor pin for them. Not even if the family doctor wrote a letter stating that his patient was medically qualified to give. Most of those so disqualified expressed their annoyance, even anger, in person or over the phone. Few wrote letters. One man, however, did write and his message came in on a postcard.

78 Hastings St., West Roxbury. 9/16/43

78 years. Am operating a commercial plant nursery in Canton. Work every day from daylight till dark. No tobacco, no liquor – no glasses – own teeth. Eat everything – anytime. The sap in an old tree is just as good as that in young one. How about tapping me? If mine is not 100%, tell me why please. Thanks.
  Yours and the Master's,
  G. H. Taylor

Our answer to this able gentleman was – what else? Of course, "Washington says we may not take you." Their decree was based on directives from the National Institute of Health, the Army and Navy, and the National American Red Cross. Locally, we did not have a say.

Rules and regulations are a problem for many who are told what to do – or worse – what not to do. Sometimes they are defiant, breaking the law. Other times, they just sneak up the down staircase or in the exit only. Enforcers of certain rules are inclined to look the other way. It's easier.

Take, for instance, item (e) under the section on Age of the Blood Donor Center's regulations. "Married donors, between 18 and 21, who are economically independent and living apart from their parents, may be accepted without permission of parent or legal guardian, but, if possible, written permission of the mate should be obtained." How hard should one try?

One directive did allow us to accept military personnel between the ages of 18 and 21 without parental permission. It seemed to be presumed that they no longer belonged to their parents. They now belonged to Uncle Sam and he was presumed to be willing. However, we were forbidden to solicit the military. If they came in, we were to accept them. But if they came in a group, it had to be with permission of their commanding officer.

There was never a need to solicit the military; they came on their own. They knew what they were doing. It was a wonderful sight to see them arrive in the rickety old gray Navy Yard bus. It would grind to a sudden stop outside the center, and the creaky door would open to reveal bell-bottom trousers on the high step in the doorway. Then the sailors in those bell-bottoms would bounce down the high step and line up on our broad sidewalk, squaring their caps for a picture. It was indeed a picture! They had a good time coming to the center, and they gave everyone there a good time.

We never knew where they were going when their ship left the Navy Yard, nor did they know their destination much of the time. And we never knew how many of them came home after the war was finally over.

Besides abiding by Washington's rules, we had a few of our own. Photographers and reporters were not allowed to roam through the center looking for a subject. It isn't that we did not like publicity; we did! With our demanding quota, we needed it. But we were protective of our donors' privacy. When a big business group came in with their own photographer to get a picture for an article to be published in their house organ—often a slick magazine—I was delighted to help.

Sometimes a company that was a heavy advertiser in metropolitan newspapers would request coverage of their group donation. The city editor called this a BO (business office) must, and he usually sent a photographer. Again, I worked with the cameraman. Also, if a city editor sent out a man for a "filler" when he had space, I worked with him to find a good shot, set it up, and help with a caption. We were certainly not against publicity.

One day I was called by the front desk to come in a hurry because there was a man there with a group of girls and a photographer, and they were in a bit of a rush and wanted to go right up to the donor room to get a picture. I went quickly. There was, as described, a group of girls—very good-looking girls—and a photographer and a man who seemed to be in charge. Our volunteer on the front desk stepped over and introduced me. I said "good morning" and extended my hand to the gentleman. He accepted my hand but went right to his business, explaining why they were in a hurry. His photographer had another job to get to, so they needed to go right up to the donor room for a picture.

"It'll be a great picture with these good-looking girls," he said. "Great for the Blood Donor Center."

I gulped, and then explained how the donor room was the last stop on the donor routine. The girls would need to go through the medical desks first. Then I asked, "What time is your appointment?"

"Oh, they don't have an appointment," he said. "They're not going to give blood. They're just here for the picture. They're dancers, you know; they have to dance every night at the club. They can't give blood."

I wanted to explain that many of our donors performed physical labor, but I decided not to do so. Instead, I said the only photographs allowed in the donor room were of donors. He argued the benefits of a picture with his good-looking girls. The girls did not appear enthusiastic. They probably had resented getting dressed up early in the morning for a picture...and now! Their boss man, of course, was exasperated with me and our impossible rules and regulations. I decided to make a gesture of conciliation.

Since they were all here with their photographer, we could set up a picture of the girls around the registration desk, making an appointment. "Of course," I added, "we would expect them to keep the appointment."

He turned to the girls. Most of them shook their heads and turned away. Two of them agreed, and I took them to the desk and let the photographer do his job. I helped with the caption and then walked with them to the door, offering some pleasantries and our thanks for their interest in the Blood Donor Service. I don't know whether they kept their appointments.

There is little doubt that this noted publicist rated me as an incompetent ingrate to have turned down such a great picture. He just didn't understand our ways.

16. NONDONORS

The thousands of people who came through the center every week were a source of great admiration, even inspiration. The thousands who did not come were a source of great distress. We needed them and we did not seem able to reach them.

There was the "mañana" crowd, good people who wanted to come and meant to call for an appointment. "I'll do it tomorrow." But tomorrow never came. The elitists felt that going to the Blood Donor Center was for the common folk. How could they tell who might be sitting beside them? If they had faced us with their objection, we could have told them that on any given day, there might be prominent names in big business and industry, leaders in government, mayors of cities, stage and screen stars, distinguished educators, or prominent socialites. Our elitists would have felt themselves quite comfortable. Of course, most of our donors thought they were sitting beside the most important VIP of all: a wounded man at the front, on land or at sea, waiting for a chance at tomorrow.

Fortunately, the elitists were few. Unfortunately, however, the "scaredy-cats" were many. They had always been afraid of needles, probably due to a bad experience in childhood. We could not tell them that the deft insertion of a blood donor needle by a skilled nurse was nothing compared to a bayonet or shrapnel or a bullet cutting through the flesh of a battle-worn man at the front. They knew that, but the thought of a needle was too powerful. We just had to leave them alone.

But the skeptics were different. The world is full of them. Unfortunately, they were undermining our program, and we had to do something about them. Some skeptics merely wonder, some seriously doubt, and some are chronic disbelievers. Plasma was an unknown to most people before the war, so naturally some felt so skeptical about its claims or would ask, "Is this stuff really as important as the people who are out for blood say it is?" Our answer—"Yes indeed!"—was not enough. They needed more convincing, and since they were discouraging prospective donors, we had to find more.

We needed to give them some proof, something tangible, something that they could see and understand. We feared that it would not work if we gave them a picture from a remote island in the Pacific that they had never heard of before, whose name they could neither pronounce nor spell. We needed a familiar place like Sicily. Early in our geography lessons in grade school, we learned that Italy was a boot with Sicily at its toe like a football ready for the punt. Only Sicily was not oval; it was triangular. Of course, true Sicilians did not require a geography lesson to know where Sicily was.

Radio and newspaper reports on the progress of the war as it moved from Africa to Sicily made it obvious that our skeptics would know what was happening at the front. They would be aware of the many casualties, so we reminded them of the medical care required for the wounded. We told them about plasma at Sicily. We told them how a medical unit went in by parachute, with every doctor descending with his chute billowing over his head. He dropped to the ground like an angel of mercy, plasma strapped to his back, ready to go to work.

Was that plasma stuff really important?

Was this picture of Sicily enough to make a donor out of a skeptic? We think it was. But you just never know.

We also had to deal with the "no show" who failed to appear as expected; it was a problem. But when a group failed to show up it could be disastrous to the quota. We had to keep reminding ourselves, and everyone else, that the quota in our case was not a matter of numbers. It was lives.

One morning a letter was received at the center from a group who had failed to keep an appointment the week before. They didn't call to cancel, which would have left an opening for walk-ins. They wanted us to know that they would have come if they had been permitted to come on company time like some other companies allowed. Since it was on their own time, they just did not come.

It seemed appropriate to answer the letter in a specially written episode of *Life to the Front*. Most of our dramatizations were true stories with the principal character coming on in person for an interview at the conclusion of the program. This story was fiction, but fiction based on fact. The reason that there was no one to interview at the end of the program was that they were all in prison or dead.

It was a story of Bataan, called "On My Own Time."

ORGAN:	"AMERICA" DOWN UNDER THE FOLLOWING
ANNOUNCER:	On April 9, 1942, Bataan, stronghold of the Philippines, went down under the white flag of defeat. Today, you will find the heroes of Bataan in Japanese prison camps…buried in unmarked graves in the ruins of Bataan, or beneath the calm blue seas of the Philippines. That included the nurses along with the troops.

Those were the Americans, sacrificed, so that years later we in America might still be untouched—free. This is the story of one of those heroes, one of the women of Bataan. It is a first-person story.

ORGAN: UP FULL...AND THEN OUT

NURSE: I was a nurse on Bataan. I fought beside dozens of other girls who, like myself, had been brought up to the touch of cool, crisp linen...the whiteness of hospital walls...the clean smell of things being sterilized...and copious stores of things needed—things helpful. All that we took for granted—until we hit Bataan—until we started to fight—and fight we did...daily, madly, for life, for mere existence.

We were fighting to bring a little peace to mangled bodies. We were trying to make whole men out of pieces of men... and we did...sometimes we did. I saw them, just little boys, really, hurt and dirty, saw them dragged in, heard them groaning in pain...

VOICE: (GROANS OFF MIKE)

NURSE: But still fighting to get back.

SOLDIER: But I gotta get back.

NURSE: Take it easy, soldier, you're out of the fight a while.

SOLDIER: But I tell you, I gotta get back. They're waiting for me. (GROANS)

NURSE: There you see; it's killing you and you want to go back.

SOLDIER: But you don't understand, sister, you don't know what it's all about. There's a war going on up there and they've got a miserable half of what they need—

NURSE: (CUTTING IN) I don't know what it's about? I don't understand? What do you think we do here all day—and all night...brother!

SOLDIER: Well—

NURSE: How do you think I can stand here and look at you and not know there's a war going on?

SOLDIER: I know...but—

NURSE: You don't know anything. Now lie back and don't give me any more trouble. Lord knows I've got enough to do without arguing the war back here with you.

SOLDIER: I won't lie back. I can't. I tell you I gotta get back there, and leave my leg alone.

NURSE: Sergeant, lie back.

SOLDIER: Why you… (GROAN)

NURSE: Lie back, Sergeant.

SOLDIER: Yes, ma'am.

DOCTOR: Any cases for surgery here, lieutenant?

NURSE: Yes, doctor, three of them over there in my group.

DOCTOR: What about this man?

NURSE: Well, sir, he's got a bone sticking out of his leg like a coat hanger but insists that he's going to get back to the front.

DOCTOR: How'd you plan to make it, son? Fly?

SOLDIER: Aw, gee, Doc, I can't be that far gone. I gotta get back. I promised. They sent me down here to get supplies. They need them. Honest, Doc, it's pitiful up there. They haven't got anything. You haven't got any idea.

16. NONDONORS

NURSE: It seems, doctor, the men in the front lines think we're running a rest home back here with full and plenty and we don't know there's a war going on.

DOCTOR: This bone will need setting.

SOLDIER: Can I get going then? You see, sir, they're depending on me to bring supplies back.

DOCTOR: There are no supplies for you to take back. I can't touch this until this man's had plasma. Shock would be too great. So prepare the plasma, Lieutenant.

NURSE: Sir, there is no more plasma.

ORGAN: (CHORD...FADE OUT UNDER)

NURSE: No more plasma...no supplies...fewer men for relief...that was Bataan as the days wore on.

           That night, our Captain Lanis talked with the doctor in charge, Colonel Steele.

COLONEL: You ask me what we're going to do, Captain Lanis.

CAPTAIN: I know, Colonel. I know but there must be reinforcements somewhere. There must be some relief in sight.

COLONEL: I tell you, Captain Lanis, there is no hope in sight. There are supplies, yes, some feeble store of supplies over at our sister base, but they've got no way of getting them to us. As a matter of fact, they've lost some of the few people they had over there, and I've been thinking seriously of sending a few of our nurses to them. What do you think of that?

CAPTAIN: But Colonel, how could we take any of our people? We're hopelessly understaffed as it is. We need at least a dozen more nurses right here. Now the girls are working a twelve-hour duty. If we take four or five away...well, I just don't see how you can do it.

COLONEL: If I told you that they have less than one-half the number of nurses over there that we have here, what would you say to that?

CAPTAIN: I can't believe it, Colonel. I can't believe it. Doctor, where is our relief?

COLONEL: I don't know. I have never in my life had such a feeling of futility.

CAPTAIN: And every day we get more wounded.

COLONEL: Yes, and every day what little we have in the line of supplies gets lower...

Well, think it over and let me know which nurses will go.

ORGAN: CHORDS

NURSE: There were three others and myself and Captain Lanis who went. The trip was a nightmare. When we arrived, we found that our new home was a good deal worse than the one we had left. There they had a few supplies that we had lacked, a little more food and we carefully did that justice, and some plasma.

I saw one of the nurses pick a bottle up, hold it in her hand, rubbing her fingers over it as though it was a precious gem, or, maybe, alive. We laughed at her, although, in our hearts, we felt the same way, but she didn't mind, she just laid the bottle down and looked at us with a sort of faraway expression.

VOICE: (OFF MIKE) I saw a boy die yesterday because there was none of this to give him.

NURSE: We stopped laughing because we had seen things like that too. We knew what she meant. Then we dragged our stiff old bodies over to the shack that was to serve as nurses' quarters. We flopped down on the cots that we found there and Captain Lanis looked from face to face.

CAPTAIN: Girls, I know just how tired you are because I have been every inch of the way with you, and I feel as though my bones belonged to somebody else. You were in no shape for the trip before we left. By now, I know you are all completely exhausted.

But...some of us must go to work immediately. We have just received word that another load of wounded is coming down and should be here immediately. The girls who are working now have been on since yesterday.

I'd like one of you to rest now, to serve as relief. We'll work it in relays so that there'll be no chance of everyone passing out at the same time. At this point, I think we all realize...it is will that will keep us going, not our bodies. That's all.

ORGAN: BRIDGE

NURSE: Captain Lanis was growing older. It killed her to work her girls as she had had to do since we came to Bataan. She was tired too. She had gone every inch of the way with us as she had said she had. Nobody spoke.

We just sat, staring. Then we pulled ourselves to our feet to get ready. I laughed a little and everyone looked at me so I stopped. I was thinking of how we got into a fresh uniform from a nice fragrant shower—with our hair just so, and our caps just so—and how we rustled down the corridor and reported for duty back then.

Now, dirty clothes were shabby jumpers like the outfits mechanics wear when they roll on the floor under a car, greasing it. That was a nurse's uniform on Bataan. And our hair! Mine looked like a snarled old wig that should have been thrown away a long time ago. But it was on my head. That's what we looked like...the nurses of Bataan.

ORGAN: (KIPLING'S RECESSIONALS)

NURSE: As I walked into Captain Lanis's office, or should I say, her little tent, I found her talking on the telephone. From the conversation, I knew that she had made contact with Colonel Steele back at our old base.

CAPTAIN: We arrived in good order, sir. It was a miserable trip but the girls stood up under it beautifully.

COLONEL: (ON FILTER MIKE) I would expect that.

CAPTAIN: We're all so numb now, we feel nothing, so, really, we're a little better off than we were before.

COLONEL: How did you find things there?

CAPTAIN: It's far worse than I expected, sir. The place is hopelessly inadequate and as far as I can make out, the doctors and nurses just haven't been sleeping. What few things they have, those will be gone by morning. I am sure.

COLONEL: How many wounded?

CAPTAIN: They don't even know...there are that many.

COLONEL: Still coming in?

CAPTAIN: A truckload just arrived. Our girls are going on duty immediately.

COLONEL: Good. I'm glad you got there on time.

CAPTAIN:

Yes, but I wish there had been a little time for the girls to sleep. God knows they need it.

NURSE:

When I heard the wounded arrive, I hurried across the clearing to the surgery shack. The doctor was working on a new arrival. A hollow-eyed nurse was fumbling with a plasma flask. Their last one, I wondered. I pushed the nurse aside, out of the way. I touched her arm and said, "I'm here. Go!"

The doctor called "Scalpel!" and he had it…from my hands…which somehow, miraculously, had been scrubbed. The operation progressed. The doctor's face became wet and shiny in the lamplight. He bent lower, worked somehow faster. He called "sponge…"

But he never got it…

Just then, Japanese dive bombers came over and dropped their payload on the target, which was our Red Cross, international symbol of mercy which nations are bound to respect. The surgery shack was a heap of burning ruins, bones, matted flesh, and warm blood. Nobody survived. I died on my own time.

This broadcast delivered a harsh message for anyone who complained about being overworked during the war, but it was reality. Fortunately, the story enabled donors to understand the importance of their blood at the front when the doctor called for plasma. Most donors came on their own time, and were glad to do so.

What about the rumormongers—were they a factor? Absolutely! Were there true saboteurs among them? How could we tell? We did know that many sabotaged the efforts of dedicated workers trying to establish a blood donor program in a workplace or a community setting. Sabotage is not uncommon in wartime. We think of it as big and dramatic and deadly, like a bomb detonating on a bridge over a deep chasm as a troop train, loaded with men and supplies, approaches at high speed.

Rumormongers only hinted at sabotage. They were elusive. If we did not know who or where they were or what exactly they were saying, we could not refute their claims. However, that changed one day in July 1944 when the following letter was received at the Red Cross Boston Metropolitan Headquarters and sent over to Wesley Fuller, the director of the Blood Donor Center.

"It has been called to my attention that soldiers who have been given blood transfusions from Red Cross Blood Banks overseas have had to pay for this blood plasma. I am writing to you for authentic information on this subject.

"At first hearing of this report, which was over a year ago, I dismissed the rumor as ugly propaganda. But within the last week, I have had reason to believe this is not just a rumor.

"I work at Zenith Associates which is a war plant and among the recently hired is an ex-'WAC' (Women's Army Corps). She was in the North African campaign with our Army, was wounded, and given blood plasma. She says she had to pay for it. The subject came up when the management asked for a group of volunteers to sign up for the Blood Bank. (We have gone in as a group three times I believe.) When the ex-WAC heard of this

project, she blew (to put it mildly). She has created a disturbing undercurrent of resentment among those who are easily influenced by any loud voice. It disturbs me to see this happen.

"Whether or not the soldiers have to pay, I shall continue to give my blood. I know how necessary and vital blood plasma has become. It is the very least any of us who are in good health can do.

"But I should certainly appreciate some concrete facts from the Red Cross to put before the others at Zenith. If it is customary to charge the soldiers and sailors for plasma, let us know it. If it is not the custom but has been done in some isolated cases, please let me have the information from you."

The letter was signed with the writer's name and home address.

Mr. Fuller treated the letter very seriously and immediately called Zenith and talked with one of their executives, Mr. Douglas Sloane, who also treated the matter seriously. He said that he was not aware of any ex-WAC in their employ. Both men agreed that they needed more information. Since Mr. Fuller was in the process of leaving the civilian world for the Marine Corps, he turned the letter over to me to follow up.

After trying unsuccessfully to reach the letter writer, Mrs. A., I wrote to her on August 3, explaining the concerns of both Mr. Fuller and Mr. Sloane and their need for more information from her so that we could pursue the matter. "Meanwhile," I wrote, "let me say that the rumor is definitely untrue. The Red Cross is merely a collection agency for the Army and Navy, sending blood to the laboratory for processing into plasma for shipment according to the Army and Navy requirements. (At present they estimate their needs for 1944 at over 5,000,000 pints.) The entire cost of procurement of this blood is borne by the Red Cross and it is turned over to the Army and Navy without charge to them. The Red Cross, accordingly, has nothing to do with the distribution of blood to the various medical units of the Army and Navy. This is entirely under the direction of the Surgeons General of the Army and Navy.

"We are most anxious to know the circumstances under which this person claims to have had to pay for plasma since it is definitely not the custom of the Army and Navy to charge their people for any medical treatment administered to those wounded in action. If there are any peculiar circumstances in her case, I am sure she will be very happy to explain them. I trust she will be equally glad to retract her criticism of the Blood Donor Service when the whole matter is cleared up.

"May we thank you very much indeed for your inquiry and you interest...and may we hope to hear from you soon."

A telephone reply came from Mrs. A. on August 9. She had just returned from a Rockport vacation. She said she would like to keep her name out of the situation but would write to us when she returned from the second half of her vacation, listing the name of the ex-WAC and additional information.

Two days later she called again because she "couldn't rest." She had to get the facts to us. The name of the girl was J. C. She said she claimed that she had to pay for plasma when she received it after she was wounded in North Africa and that a friend of hers, also an ex-WAC, was still paying for it. In a moment of "confession" to Mrs. A., she stated that she had had both knees broken in boot training while going over the obstacles. Accordingly, she couldn't stand up too long and had to be relieved frequently to go sit down and rest.

I immediately called Zenith and made an appointment to meet with Mr. Sloane in his office on August 11. He brought in Mr. Hoag, their production manager, and Miss Berry, personnel manager. The Zenith group seemed cooperative, congenial, efficient, fair, and interested. Mr. Hoag knew the girl as someone he saw every morning when he came to work. As he walked through the plant on his way to his office, he said good morning to the employees whom he passed. Each returned his greeting with a cordial reply, except for Miss C., who turned her back on him and did not speak.

When her personnel form was brought out, it showed no record of WAC service although there was a specific section to be filled out if the applicant had had military service. She listed the last three places of employment (all that was required) with the first being from September 1942 to January 1943. Under "Identifying marks: scars etc." she listed: "bullet scar, left knee."

I was ready to follow whatever recommendation Zenith might have in handling the case. When they decided to call Miss C. in to investigate the rumor, I suggested it be instead to get information. When she arrived, the interview fell to me. She answered questions, showed no reluctance to talk, and claimed to be an ex-WAC who went overseas in July 1942. She said that she entered the WAC when it took over the Ferry Command, but she did not know exactly when that was except that it was sometime prior to July 1942. She arrived in Africa—Oran—sometime in September. They were in France first. She was wounded over there and was sent back in January or February 1943. She spent the next year in hospitals or stations in the United States until discharged at First Service Command in February 1944 when she came to work for Zenith. As far as Red Cross was concerned, she "wouldn't give a nickel to it or for it." As for plasma, she knew many people who had to pay for it. She denied that she had had it, but another WAC whom she knew—now stationed at Fort Oglethorpe in Georgia, a WWII training center for the Women's Army Corps—received plasma in Oran when she was wounded on the airfield there. When she arrived home, this friend showed Miss C. a bill for plasma with the remark, "I didn't know we had to pay for this, did you?" She said she knew others who had to pay for it. They had been wounded at Oran and Morocco and other places where she hadn't been but about which she knew.

When asked for the name of the WAC at Fort Oglethorpe, she said she couldn't give us that because she wasn't sure about it. She couldn't swear that the girl had had to pay for it. She said she would try to get the bill from the girl by writing to her and that I would hear from her through the personnel department. Otherwise, she couldn't swear to anything.

Our attitude throughout was one of looking for information that we felt she could give us. The interview had consisted of a series of questions that brought forth answers that in themselves were untrue in some cases and, in others, were contrary to the information that she had listed on her personnel blank. From then on, I felt that it was Zenith's problem and that they, not we, should investigate.

Mr. Sloane said they would check with the Army about her service record. We would wait for the letter from Georgia. Meanwhile, I would get an official statement from the Army on the selling of blood plasma. At a later date, Zenith would call their entire personnel together for a short talk that I would present about the need for donors.

When I returned to the center, I decided to call the Army base for my own information. I talked with Col. Walter Brown (pre- and postwar owner of the Boston Garden). He referred me to a department that handled such matters. When I asked if the Army had a record of their ex-WACs, I was assured that they did and they would check the name that I had given them. They would get back to me.

When the call came, there was more information than I had anticipated. There was no evidence of this person ever having been a WAC. We were now in a criminal situation: impersonating a WAC was a federal crime. The matter would have to be turned over for investigation.

I explained that I was looking for information for my own report, and that Zenith would be pursuing the case officially. When I called Mr. Sloane about this information, he said that they had decided to terminate Miss C.'s employment. They felt that the company didn't need this kind of person.

Not long after this, I had a visit from an Army investigator. He wanted whatever details I could lend to the case including my interview with the subject and my conversation with Mrs. A., along with her name. Since this was now an official government investigation, I felt I could not withhold her name. I explained my predicament and asked that the name not be put in the report. He felt that as long as he and I had the name, and he now had the information from Mrs. A. and from the meeting at Zenith, he would not need to use the name elsewhere.

It was understood that Miss C. was out sick, but when she returned, they would be there to take her in. That never happened, however, because our girl left town, with no forwarding address... not a trace.

Was she a saboteur? She certainly had some of the earmarks: leaving town without a trace, under suspicion, under investigation, guilty of undermining a vital government program in wartime, and impersonating a WAC. But a true saboteur would be smart and careful. There were so many discrepancies in Miss C.'s statements in the plant, in our meeting, and on her employment form that it was almost laughable. I think this was a girl who liked to talk, liked to hear herself talk, and liked an audience, all of which Zenith provided. There was something wrong with this person, but a saboteur? She was heavily flawed if she was one.

In October, I went to Zenith to speak to their employees about blood donors and the heroic work that plasma was doing at the various fighting fronts. I told them that I had brought an official statement from the Army that plasma was never sold to their soldiers. Although I did not refer to their former fellow worker, I think they made the connection. When the first group signed up, I am sure Mrs. A. felt pleased. It was her caring, concern, and action that was responsible. She was a great example of what we all should do and be. She was interested in facts—the truth—and she did something about it.

It was also a pleasure to deal with the executives at Zenith. Rumors can be handled when they can be connected with facts. But it was not a pleasure to have had to deal with such an unfortunate case as this.

17. PEOPLE AND PLACES

With war raging on so many fighting fronts throughout the world, there could be no letup in the demands placed upon the American Red Cross Blood Donor Service by the Army and Navy. The quota set for each Blood Donor Center in the country was not just a suggestion, a goal toward which a center might aspire. It was a requirement. It was a requirement based on the needs of the armed forces on all of these fighting fronts. What a tremendous task, to find six thousand people (Boston's quota) to give blood within a week's time. To find six thousand more the next week—and every week thereafter—was a little overwhelming.

It required every help possible: publicity, promotion, organization, and outreach of all kinds. It probably helped to be under contract to the Army and Navy, which were waiting for those pints every week because they had wounded waiting for them all over the world. The centers could not fail. They had no choice. And they did not fail because there were so many wonderful people who stepped forward to lend their expertise and leadership, use their positions and connections, and give their time and talent—besides their pints of blood. Many of these generous people, and the places I went because of them, were memorable.

Some I can never forget.

The Commissioner

I remember one special woman who held a prestigious position in the city of Boston, as the commissioner of the Alcoholic Beverage Commission. Her name was Mary Driscoll, and I came to know her well under unusual circumstances.

She wanted to help in the pursuit of donors, so she called a meeting of the owners or managers of all the bars, taverns, and cocktail lounges in the city. She asked me to speak to her group and help them plan a blood donor drive. Attendance at her meeting was disappointing. Miss Driscoll was not only disappointed, but she was distressed and annoyed.

Where were her people? She decided not to wait until the next day to find out. She would do it that evening. She would check on those who had let her down by their absence. She and I climbed into the backseat of a long black car driven by the president of the Liquor Dealers Association, Mr. Murray, and we rode through the darkened city: down little side streets, up back alleys, wherever there was a tavern in the town not represented at Miss Driscoll's meeting. We parked outside each establishment to rate a visit, and Mr. Murray went in while Miss Driscoll and I sat chatting in the car. We talked of the war and of plasma and of Boston. She had wonderful stories of the city. It was a memorable evening that I cannot forget.

There was little variety in the explanations that Mr. Murray brought back. The boss was sick and the bartender was alone. The boss was alone because his bartender was sick. Somebody's wife was sick. Everybody's children were sick. It sounded like a citywide epidemic before our tour ended. They all knew, of course, that Mr. Murray was merely the courier, that it was Miss Driscoll who wanted to know—and that she was outside in the car waiting for the report. When she called another meeting to try again, attendance was much improved—even very good!

When they tried to work out a plan to encourage their patrons to sign up, my advice was that they suggest to the patrons that they come to the center on their way to the tavern rather than on their way home from it.

Miss Driscoll was a woman of distinction. I felt privileged and delighted to have known her. I shall never forget her.

Red Sox

One day in the spring of 1944, a call came in from the Red Sox at Fenway Park. It was from Barbara Tyler of the Boston Red Sox front office, asking me if I would keep an eye out for Mr. Tom Yawkey, the owner of the team, who was coming in to give blood. Of course I would. Knowing the time of his appointment, I happened to be near the entrance when he arrived. After an exchange of greetings, I took him to registration, presented him to the volunteer on duty, and said that I would see him after he had gone through the checkup desk.

When he was ready to give his blood, I walked with him to the donor room, introduced him to his nurse and the doctor, and said that I would see him in the refreshment room later. I was informed when he was through donating and joined him over coffee.

We lingered over coffee, talking about the Red Sox, the war, the wonder of plasma, and the importance of giving. I reminded him of the great value of what he had just done, and there was some discussion about what the Red Sox might do to stimulate an interest in giving. Finally, we chatted as we walked to the door, where we shook hands and exchanged thanks. Mr. Yawkey was off to Fenway Park. I had a call from Barbara Tyler that afternoon, thanking me for what I had done. I assured her that it had been my very great pleasure.

A few days later, I received the following letter:

BOSTON AMERICAN LEAGUE BASEBALL COMPANY

24 JERSEY STREET
BOSTON, MASS.

THOMAS A. YAWKEY, President
EDWARD T. COLLINS, Vice Pres. & Gen. Mgr.

ZONE 15

FENWAY PARK
HOME OF THE RED SOX

May 24, 1944

Miss Anastasia Kirby
48 Merrill Road,
Watertown 72,
Massachusetts

Dear Miss Kirby:

      I appreciate very much the courtesy
shown me yesterday down there at the Blood Bank.

      I would like you to have the enclosed
pass, and hope you will use it many times during
the season and enjoy the games.

      I will keep in mind the matter we
discussed.

      Sincerely,

      T. A. Yawkey

L.
Enc.

Thomas Yawkey offers a Red Sox pass.

The Rabbi in New York

On a Saturday morning in early December 1943, I was rushing
from a wedding in one town to a temple service in another. Luck
was with me when I found a parking space on the street beside
the temple but not when I looked for an entrance. A huge door
was a magnificent piece of art and beauty but not a way in. As I

155

hurried around the corner, looking for the temple meetinghouse entrance, I saw an events board in the front yard. Every day of the week was listed with the name of a "rabbi" or "doctor" next to it. Every day but Saturday. There it was only one "miss." The sign said, "Saturday morning Service—Miss Anastasia Kirby."

I gulped but there was no time to look again. When I opened the meetinghouse door, I was greeted by a waiting escort who led me down the aisle and up onto the stage. She handed me a book and told me to read from back to front. Then she departed, leaving me to look out at the congregation, listen to the cantor, and read my book.

Eventually, the cantor moved to center stage and addressed the congregation. He explained that Rabbi Abrams was very sorry that he could not be with his people that morning. He had to be in New York City for a very important meeting. "However," the cantor announced, "we are pleased to have in his place, Miss Anastasia Kirby." He nodded to the substitute and retreated as I moved forward.

I was a little awed by the situation and certainly challenged. If the rabbi had entrusted his Saturday morning service to me, I had to respond properly. There had to be something spiritual in my talk. It proved to be easy. For a donor to give blood on the home front to save the lives of the wounded on the far-off battlefronts was much more than a physical gesture. There was a very special connection between the giver of blood and the receiver who was in dire need. Such an act of brotherly love was indeed spiritual.

I hoped that I had done right by Rabbi Abrams. When I received a letter from him later that week, I knew that I had succeeded.

What an unforgettable experience, to take a rabbi's place for a Saturday morning service.

Under the Portico

A busload of dairy farmers was on its way to the center to give blood, when their driver was told to swing around by Beacon Hill.

The driver objected, "Beacon Hill is way out of the way." The head farmer told him that he had been told that they were going to stop at the State House. The driver grumbled. "Narrow streets… no parking anywhere near the State House…what were they doing up there?"

"We'll be parking under the portico of the State House," announced the farmer-in-charge. Before the driver could offer any more objections, the farmer explained to him and to all his passengers, "We're going to meet the governor."

The notation on my calendar had listed "Gov. and Dairy Farmers under portico at State House." I felt a little puzzled, but I was there when the bus pulled in and the farmers hopped off. There were greetings and handshakes and Leverett Saltonstall, the fifty-fifth governor of the Commonwealth of Massachusetts, appeared with his aides; then we had more greetings and more handshakes.

The publicity-savvy farmer-in-charge made a nice little speech. The governor responded with brief remarks, and a photographer came out from behind the bus and positioned us all for a picture. The mastermind of the event had disappeared but almost immediately reappeared, bearing a large plastic cow. He thrust the bovine into the governor's and my hands as we stood together in front of the farmers grouped behind us.

The governor and I looked at each other, speechless. He had one end of the cow and I had the other. Neither of us let go. I believe he held the front end and I held…the other.

The photographer called out "Say cheese!" and snapped the picture.

Everyone cheered. Somebody grabbed the cow. There were more handshakes and expressions of thanks. Then the farmers scrambled onto their bus—glowing. They had met the governor! Even the bus driver was smiling.

Everyone waved as the bus pulled out from under the portico. Somebody propped the cow up in the bus window. I waved back—to the cow, too, I suppose. The governor and I exchanged comments and handshakes before his aides nudged him back to his desk. This had not been an ordinary item on their day's agenda.

Governor Saltonstall was a fine man, a successful politician who came from a long line of gentlemen farmers. That's probably why our publicity-savvy dairy farmer had been able to arrange this rendezvous under the portico.

As I started back to the Blood Donor Center, I wondered if the dairy farmers would bring their cow in with them when they gave their blood—along with their photographer, of course. Would they ask me to cow-sit if they did?

Should I take the long route back? This was only a fleeting thought. After all, that cow came with a busload of pints for plasma. The farmer-in-charge and all his fellow farmers deserved all the hospitality available. I hurried back.

Gin

An invitation to a bottling plant provided quite a challenge for me. The company turned out fifths of gin—and probably other spirits also—but all I recall is gin. The management gave me a cordial reception when I arrived; I was taken into the room where I would be meeting their employees.

It was the labeling room where bottle after bottle came through from another room on a conveyor belt. Workers lined the moving belt, ready to apply a label to each bottle as it came by them. There was no letup. Bottles kept coming and the women kept labeling. The job required constant attention.

As I stood beside the manager, waiting to be introduced, I was fascinated by what I saw. He sort of shouted out my introduction and then turned to me and nodded. I smiled and nodded back, waiting for the conveyor belt to be turned off. It did not happen and the manager shouted to me to go ahead. I went ahead, but I was totally preoccupied by the bottles that were also going ahead, one after another down the labeling line.

All speakers know that they should look into the faces of their audience and hope, of course, that the members of their audience will look back. Not so today! If this audience looked up at me, they might miss a bottle or slap a label on askew. That would never do, and I worried about the possibility. It was a terrible distraction, a challenge to keep my mind on my business.

When I am speaking out for blood, I have a message to convey, an important one, an urgent one. This day the gin bottles took over, and I didn't really know what I was saying. When I finished, I stepped aside and nodded to the manager. He led me to the door. As I left, I waved to the labeling ladies and hoped that they would not wave back. It was suddenly so quiet as we walked to an executive office where we exchanged thanks. They were pleased because I had made them feel good about themselves in their contribution to a noble cause. If only they could have turned off their machinery!

As I left, they presented me with two bottles of gin. I was not accustomed to receiving gifts for my efforts but I thanked them warmly, of course. Then I walked to my car, clutching my gin tightly in my arms. It was not in delight and gratitude. It was in fear that the bag might break and the bottles slip out and crash on the pavement, drenching my feet in gin. That would be no way to return to the center.

Mr. Barry

A white-haired, white-mustached gentleman whom I met in a synagogue one rainy Sunday afternoon left me with one of my most memorable moments in the pursuit of blood.

The synagogue planned to dedicate an outdoor service plaque in their side yard to honor their members in military service. I had been invited to speak at the ceremony and had just arrived when suddenly the rains came and we were all forced inside. I was escorted up to the stage and led to a red velvet cushioned seat in an arched niche beside the central focal spot that contained the Ark. I sat quietly, impressed with what I was seeing around me, until this gracious gentleman arrived and was introduced as Mr. Barry.

As we sat talking in our arched niche, I became aware of a group of young men who seemed to be in charge of something. They were looking at me and pointing. I was puzzled until one of them pointed to his head and then back toward me. Then I realized that all of the men were wearing their hats and it wasn't because they had just come in out of the rain. We were in a synagogue where men are always covered. The young men were not pointing at me. They were concerned with Mr. Barry who sat with his hat in his lap.

I mentioned this to Mr. Barry and he quickly put his hat back on. When the program got underway with our national anthem, we stood and Mr. Barry removed his hat and placed it over his patriotic chest. No other hats had moved so I nudged Mr. Barry and whispered that he should return his hat to his head. He frowned but did as I suggested. When it came time for prayer, Mr. Barry reached for his hat as he bowed his head. He had it off before my elbow could reach his ribs, but he got the point and replaced it.

Then I began to worry. If he was to move to the lectern to present greetings from the Commonwealth, which, I believe, was why he was there, what would he do about his hat? I could not tag along behind him with some whispered chiding. I decided to prepare him with an explanation of how a man never removed his hat even when speaking. Something else happened, however, and the automatic male reaction kicked in and off came the hat. My sotto-voce, elbow-to-ribs routine followed, and the hat returned to the gentleman's head.

We got through his remarks but we still had my speech to go. I feared that when I stood to move to the front of the stage, he would stand with me and remove his hat. I managed to get in another little lecture about customs before I was introduced. Once I stepped forward, I didn't look back. I hope that I didn't speak of the need for six thousand hats.

At the conclusion of the ceremonies, I shook hands with my friend, Mr. Barry, and told him that I hoped that I would see him again, although I secretly hoped that it would not be in a synagogue. Then I hurried off to my car before Mr. Barry had a chance to reach for his hat.

I shall never forget this charming, lovely gentleman—or his hat.

The Boston and Maine Railroad

When the Boston and Maine Railroad decided to go out for blood, they went all out! The people in charge had the approval of top management or else they were part of it because there was evidence of expertise and freedom in their arrangements. They had erected a large stage in the train yard and draped it with red, white, and blue bunting. An American flag flew from a tall flagpole on one side of the stage. A podium center stage was equipped with a first-class PA system. And then they brought their train workers off their jobs to gather around the stage. These people had really gone all out for blood!

As I climbed the steps to the stage, I looked out on a mass of engineers' caps. It was quite a sight to behold and I shall never forget it. The audience was attentive and responsive, and the planners were delighted with their production that morning. Of course, I was, too. There was more to come.

The gentlemen in charge invited me to attend a meeting of their supervisors in a boardroom upstairs at North Station. It was a long narrow room with a table down the middle and chairs on either side between it and the walls. As I took the guest seat at the head of the table, I noticed a window at the far end of the room, but I could not see through it. Soot from the trains, I supposed, but that was only on the outside. As each supervisor sat down at the table, he reached for the ashtray at his place, and immediately lit up.

The meeting opened with my hosts describing what had just happened in the train yard and explaining why I was there. The supervisors were puffing away on their Lucky Strikes, their Pall Malls, their Havanas, and a variety of other labels. As the meeting progressed, I was beginning to feel the effects of all the labels. I was not one to pass out but I began to feel that I might do just that. I was about to be introduced. How could I ask to be excused? If I did, could I make it to the door without collapsing?

How would that look...the only woman at the meeting and representing the Army and Navy and their wounded at the front. Visions of a burning Navy ship filled with smoke and flames and the injured passing out went through my mind. My distress was such a nothing! My head told my body that it could not succumb. So I did not. Was this mind over matter or remembering a mother's words, "You can do it if you try"? However, when I was introduced, my head ruled, and I managed a decent speech, but it was brief and my departure without delay.

I shall always remember the Boston and Maine Railroad for all that they did for the Blood Donor Service that day. I shall never forget the mass of engineers' caps. Nor can I forget the supervisors and their contribution to the success of the tobacco industry.

Miss Kirby at the Boston & Maine railyard.

18. THE BIG O

It is said that everything and everybody needs organization for success and that successful organization requires leaders. World War II produced outstanding leaders, and not all were in uniform. History has recorded the famous names of generals and admirals and other high-ranking officers who distinguished themselves by their brilliant wartime leadership. And many a GI will never forget the lifesaving leadership of a comrade who led him out of harm's way in the thick of battle.

But back on the home front there were leaders, too.

Washington had established official programs in which the public might participate, but on the grassroots level people needed leaders. There seems to be a strong desire in human beings to give of themselves in crisis, but they need help to do so. Leadership comes naturally to many. Let there be a need and they spring into action. The Blood Donor Service had its share of outstanding leaders. It is doubtful that the quota would have been met week after week after week without the groups organized by these leaders. Of course, a group did not have to be a busload.

One day it was a group of nine: all sisters, sisters-in-law, and wives of men at the front. Each of them might have come alone on nine different days, but when one of them said, "Let's all go to the Blood Donor Center together and tell our guys we did it," they made a statement. Who knows how many pints of blood that statement was worth when witnesses told their friends about those nine girls they saw at the Blood Donor Center.

Probably the earliest busload was organized by a church in East Cambridge. The pastor rode the bus with his parishioners, the true shepherd with his flock. That first busload was followed by others throughout the war.

When the IRS called requesting an appointment, no one was worried. This time they were coming to give, not to get. Eighty members of his staff came with the chief collector himself, Dennis W. Delaney. Another group arrived with Chairman Jeremiah W. Taylor.

Union leaders were known to be great organizers. I saw evidence of this when I sat beside William Green, the head of the American Federation of Labor, at a session of its annual convention. We were on the stage of the grand ballroom of the Hotel Statler in Boston, looking out upon hundreds of members seated wall-to-wall waiting for the program to begin. I felt that my remarks would not fall on idle ears when I was presented by Mr. Green. What an opportunity for the Blood Donor Service!

Of course, not all such opportunities were in grand ballrooms. One took place in the street outside a shipyard with a local union leader. He had circulated flyers among the workers in the shipyard telling them to come to a rally for blood donors outside the gate at the end of their shift. When I received my flyer, I was skeptical, but I arrived at the appointed time. As we stood in the gutter outside the gate, eating Eskimo Pies from an ice cream tipcart that had just pulled up, I mentioned my concern. "How can we expect these men to stop on their way home after a long day's work?"

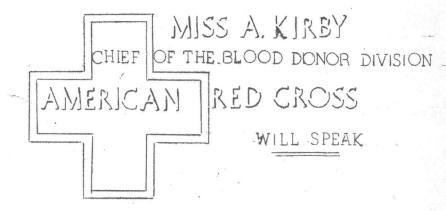

OPEN AIR RALLY

FRIDAY - JUNE 10th

12:15 NOON

OUTSIDE THE ATLANTIC WORKS GATE

MISS A. KIRBY

CHIEF OF THE BLOOD DONOR DIVISION

AMERICAN RED CROSS

WILL SPEAK

AMERICA IS FIGHTING FOR ITS LIFE!

BLOOD IS NEEDED
TO HELP WIN THE WAR

Issued by Local 25, Industrial Union of Marine and Shipbuilding Workers
of America, C. I. O.

uopwa/3

Unions helped rally support for blood donations.

He smiled and said simply, "They'll come." When the bell sounded and the gate opened, the workers came streaming out of the shipyard and gathered around the makeshift platform. I smiled at their leader and nodded just before he spoke. I understood. But when it came my turn to speak, I was conscious of time. I wanted to keep my speech brief and still give them a personal message. These were the men who built ships for the Navy to take into battle. They were important people. Now they had a chance to make sure that their blood would give the Navy the plasma needed for the sick bays on those ships. They understood and they produced. That union leader knew his men!

There was ongoing organization of groups by Red Cross chapters throughout the area covered by the Boston Blood Donor Center, and that included visits by the mobile unit to cities and towns more distant from Boston. As the war continued on and the needs of the Army and Navy did not decrease, more and more people became repeat donors. These chapters held Gallon Club parties for those who were entitled to wear a red ribbon on their blood donor pin. A simple social held at the Red Cross chapter house in Newton drew together a diverse group with a blood donor connection. The CEO of a major company came alone and stayed through the ice cream and cake! Two women arrived together with one telling the host that her friend bought a new hat for the party. An auto mechanic who worked under cars in a greasy coverall came in a new suit. Being blood donors for someone on a fighting front meant a lot to these people who continued giving until the war was over.

Winchester's celebration was at the country club. Their blood donor chairman, Ruth Hilton, had signed on after hearing Chaplain McQuaid's radio interview in April 1943. There's a letter from her signing off in September 1945. Their Winchester program featured a reenactment of *Life to the Front* with professional talent from WEEI. A culmination of a great evening was a surprise visit from Army Capt. Angelo L. Maietta, MC, who was at Normandy's beaches on D-Day, and who was home on a brief leave.

The Winchester Gallon Club party.

Waltham had a Gallon Club with officers, regular meetings, membership cards and organized groups going to the center. After they had given their blood, they divided up for dinner, half going to Howard Johnson's, the other to the Hotel Lenox.

Malden had many young men in uniform, and local manufacturing plants were producing materials for the armed forces, so the town understood the war effort. They sent groups to the center and they kept them coming. When Malden planned a Gallon Club party, it was set to be a banquet and was anonymously underwritten by a local defense plant. There must be a statute of limitations on "anonymously," so it can, and should, be told that Converse Rubber Company picked up the check that night. Many Converse employees attended as Gallon Club members, including a table of Converse executives.

A special feature on the evening's program was the presentation of an orchid corsage to the first woman Gallon Club member. The recipient was touched, explaining that she had never had an orchid corsage before although she had picked wild orchids in a swamp near her home when she was a missionary in India. The corsage had been given by a local florist who had been approached, along with other florists, by the Malden blood donor chairman, acting on an idea I had passed on from a volunteer in Scituate, Massachusetts.

The candy industry, centered in Boston and Cambridge at the time, had its own blood donor chairman. His name was Sam Sidd, an executive with the William F. Schrafft Company. He obviously worked with the blessing of his company's owners: President William V. Wallburg and Vice President and Treasurer George F. Wallburg, great-grandsons of the original William F. Schrafft, who started the business in a little storefront in the North End of Boston with his family living upstairs. Now the company was housed in a tall, multifloored building with its name in large letters on its roof. Long after the last chocolate was dipped, the building and the name remain as a landmark for directions.

Sam Sidd's attention included big and small companies. He felt that everyone should be a part of this important war effort and help it succeed. We visited the big airy New England Confectionary Company in Cambridge, home of the famous NECCO Wafers, where the candies were being produced for servicemen overseas. They had a blood donor chairman already in place who gave us a tour of the plant. It was a state-of-the-art operation. Even today, people seeking a nearby address are directed to the NECCO building, just like Schrafft's. Today, NECCO Wafers are still being turned out at the new state-of-the-art facility in Revere, Massachusetts.

In contrast, we parked in back alleys, entering rear doors into dark hallways, passing big ash barrels filled with huge blocks of chocolate, before finally stepping into the brightly lit salesroom. There were displays of boxes and boxes of chocolates adorned with colored ribbons and plump rosettes. Eye appeal seemed as important as content. Some companies employed women who did nothing but make rosettes.

There was a drugstore on nearly every corner in those days. Each had a counter displaying boxes of chocolates. This was big business, especially at holidays. How many mothers are still around who recall Mother's Day and a Whitman Sampler with Whistler's Mother on the cover?

When Sam Sidd called for a dinner meeting for his candy contacts, he had a good response. We met at the upstairs dining room of Schrafft's West Street Restaurant in downtown Boston. The candymakers enjoyed meeting each other and swapping ideas on how to promote blood donors. They were enthusiastic about the program we had planned. The guest speaker was a Marine who had seen action on Florida Island in the Solomons.

Corporal Fuller was a flamboyant personality who wore his cap at a rakish angle and his greatcoat slung over his shoulders, and he carried a swagger stick. He wore a Purple Heart among many ribbons, so many that Lieutenant Lundquist was curious. When he asked his friend, Maj. Ara Miller, commanding officer of the Marine barracks where Fuller was stationed, the major said, "Hank, I wondered about that, too. So I went into my files and pulled out his jacket, and there are papers for every one of those medals. They are all authentic."

Corporal Fuller and Miss Kirby.

Both men agreed that Fuller had quite a background.

The corporal told the candy group that the islands were tough on the Americans because the Japanese had much better training at jungle fighting. "They knew where all the caves were and could hole up in them and wait for a Marine platoon to come along. Then they would fire on them and take most of our guys out before we knew where they were." Then he described what he decided to try. "I watched a group of Japanese go into a cave and wait. I decided that if I went in after them, they couldn't identify me in the dark. It was pitch black in the cave and outside, too. When I fired, they fired back and kept firing at each other while I crawled out and left them to take out each other."

Fuller was hit, but because he had positioned himself near the entrance to the cave, he was able to drag himself out and into nearby brushes and wait until some Marines came by. "It worked," he said. "The next platoon that came by was safe, and I got picked up and taken to an aid station. I did lose blood, but they gave me plasma as soon as I got there. It turned out okay."

The diners were inspired by Fuller's talk and welcomed a chance to meet and talk with him. We had a congenial and productive evening.

A special invitation to the Schrafft plant was a great success; I brought a couple of guests with me. Whenever Lois Wilson and Eddie Nugent were in town playing in pre- or post-Broadway plays, they always offered to help. The large group of Schrafft women chocolate-dippers was thrilled to have two movie stars come to visit them. They were an inspiration because they were repeat blood donors.

The Boston Postal District offered an excellent example of leadership from the top on down through all the employees. The postmaster himself was a donor, and he appointed one of his men to be chairman of its Blood Donor Program. As soon as they had assembled a committee, the postmaster invited me to meet with them in his office.

He seated me at his desk—in his chair—while he stood off to the side among his men. With the postmaster, Chairman Fred Lofchie, and their enthusiastic committee, success seemed inevitable. And it became a reality.

On January 30, 1945, *Life to the Front* featured the Boston Postal District as an example of leadership and organization. We had a

Postal workers launch their campaign.

capacity studio audience to meet their fellow blood donors and to watch a performance by Franchot Tone, the noted stage and screen star in a drama written especially for the show. The postmaster himself was present explaining in an interview, "I was born in the wrong year. Otherwise I would be a member of the Gallon Club like so many of my men of whom I am so very proud." He gave credit for the success of the program to Chairman Lofchie, who passed the credit on to the committee. There was plenty of credit to go around. During eighteen separate blood donor drives, they had donated more than 3,600 pints of blood! They were not finished!

Two members of the committee were already veterans of the war, having received medical discharges and been returned to civilian life and the Postal Service. Each man had been given plasma and a Purple Heart. That's why they were such dedicated members of the committee and such an inspiration to the radio audience in our interviews. I started with Howard Sills.

"You were Navy, weren't you, Mr. Sills?"

"Yes ma'am, I was a boatswain's mate second class aboard the USS *Vincennes* when she sank in the Battle of Savo Island on August 7, 1942. My battle station was in number two turret. We took a direct hit on the gun, and I got hit.'

I asked him how he got off the ship if he was wounded, and he said, "I don't remember leaving the ship. I just remember hitting the water."

With so many men in the water trying to get away from the ship, so many of them wounded, I wondered how he managed. Was there a raft for him and help getting him into it? He set me straight on that.

"There was no raft, and we took care of ourselves. Five of us got together. We had three life jackets between us. We took turns swimming around and resting."

"Were there other wounded?" I asked.

He answered quickly, "Oh yes, but we still took turns even though it was almost six hours before we were rescued."

Sills explained that they received first aid immediately on the transport that picked them up, but that it wasn't until he was on the hospital ship USS *Solace* that he got his real treatment. "And I needed a lot," he said, "and I received lots of plasma." Then he smiled and added, "You know, nobody knows what it feels like until you get a little blood into you. I wasn't talking or even seeing much until I got mine. I was very down, but after plasma, I just came to and was talking and laughing with the doctors and the corpsmen."

When asked where he was wounded, he explained, "I had a bad leg."

"And how is your leg now, Mr. Sills?" I asked.

"Oh, it's okay. It will always be stiff, of course, but it's all mine. I didn't lose it. I was lucky!"

When it came time to interview the other veteran on the committee, Franchot Tone joined us at the mi-

Franchot Tone

crophone. He had received a great round of applause for his earlier performance and now he asked Arthur Mitz, "You were Army, weren't you, Mr. Mitz?"

"Yes, sir, I was communications sergeant, laying mines near the Matanikau River on Guadalcanal when I was hit by shrapnel from a mortar shell and had my leg blown off."

"And yet," said Mr. Tone, "you gave your first pint of blood at the Blood Donor Center last Wednesday, didn't you?"

"Yes I did, Mr. Tone. I got a lot of plasma out there on the Canal and at the New Hebrides Hospital and on the hospital ship *Solace* and in the Fijis. I decided it was time I gave a little."

Tone suggested that it was probably more pleasant giving it than getting it, and Arthur Mitz agreed. "The battalion aid station was right out in the jungle on the Canal. The field hospital wasn't much better. What a contrast here. They even have music in the center. But I was lucky out there."

I wondered how in the world this man should feel lucky, so I asked him and he explained, "There was an artillery observer with a walkie-talkie just ahead of me, and he was blown to pieces by the shell. Even I came close to losing more than I did. I got ten other slugs. One was fifteen inches long. It almost cost me the rest of my leg up to my hip. I came pretty close."

When I listened to these men talk about how lucky they were, I realized how lucky I was to know and work with them.

19. HOLIDAYS

Holidays are celebrative by definition, especially with families who gather every year to perpetuate time-honored traditions that seem to hold them together. During the war, holidays were the most difficult days for families with loved ones overseas. Yet holidays helped because they pushed people to carry on in spite of sorrow for men lost and worry about those still fighting.

Thanksgiving

Thanksgiving was probably the hardest of all for these families. The old song applied then as it does now: "Over the river and through the wood, to Grandfather's house we go. The horse knows the way to carry the sleigh…" The sleigh may have been replaced by a plane or a van, but families still go home for Thanksgiving, no matter how far. That November weekend is considered the most heavily traveled in the whole year. In spite of gas rationing and other travel restrictions during the war, families still found their way to "Grandfather's house."

There was pain at many a table during those war years when families gathered around the turkey to find certain faces missing. In some homes, the missing man was never coming back and everyone grieved. As Grandfather said grace, even the children were quiet. The only sound came from the grown-ups sniffling, trying to hold back their tears. A brave front was not easy, but it was essential.

At one table, a young soldier home on medical leave was basking in tribute from all around him. He was their hero. And he gave them hope for others. Even if he was going back, he was home for now, a survivor who had made it through battle wounds at the front, kept alive by plasma he had received on a rough trip to the hospital. When he thanked anyone who might have given blood for plasma, there were some glowing faces among the donors at the table. There were a lot of thanks on many a Thanksgiving Day.

Patriots Day

Other holidays were celebrated when dedicated leaders organized groups to come to the center to observe a certain date. On April 19, 1945, a group of seventy came from the Boston Ordnance District to give their blood as a good way to celebrate Patriots Day, a Massachusetts holiday. Some of the groups were interviewed on the *Time for Life* weekly broadcast from the center. One girl was not finished in the donation room in time for the broadcast. Her name was Vera B. Curlanis. On May 1, the following letter arrived from a hospital in England:

Mine was not a case of life or death at the moment but to help cure an ailment received from my confinement in a German stalag, hence my being able to write so soon after the transfusion. I only wish I was able to thank you and the donor in person at this moment.

You can rest assured that you will receive the lifelong thanks of myself and anyone else who has been the recipient of this priceless gift. Maybe you could thank the donor or pass the letter along to him or her. The number is #747434.

With this and my hope for continued success as Angels of Mercy,
I remain,
Alex Kanezes

Yes, #747434 was Miss Curlanis. When she was invited back to be interviewed two weeks later on *Time for Life*, she feared that she couldn't read the letter without crying. It was her third donation, given in honor of her only brother, PFC Albert Curlanis, who was in Germany with the First Army.

Her comment was, "After seeing pictures in newspapers, newsreels, and magazines of the prisoners who have been released from some of these German camps, I must say that I get the greatest satisfaction in the world out of knowing that my Patriots Day pint of blood helped one of these poor men back on his feet."

Flag Day

June 14, 1945, did not pass unobserved in Brockton, Massachusetts, when the Red Cross chapter brought a busload of type O donors to the center. They could never have dreamed of what would happen to one of those pints of blood when the Navy Transport Service flew it to Guam. It ended up in a hospital in the Marianas, flowing into an unconscious Marine while his buddy from Brockton watched.

Father's Day

The Father's Day broadcast in June 1945 was celebrated with a father donor reading a very special letter. This father donor had given his thirteenth pint of blood on February 13, and it was given to another father's son five days later in France. There was a lot to celebrate when the recipient's father thanked the donor father:

> *Thank you very much for the blood that you donated that helped save our dear son Charles's life when he was hit in France on February 18 in his left leg and his right foot.*
>
> *As your name and Mrs. Mary Harrison's were both donors for him, he wrote and asked us folks to get your home address through the Red Cross and we just received it today.*
>
> *We want to thank you for what you did for him and his life. He is still in a hospital somewhere in England but is getting along okay. I wish you would write letting us know if you get this letter of thanks.*
>
> *We lost another son, Fay, in France, on August 3, 1944, so we felt very glad to know that our other son could be saved by your blood.*
> *Mr. and Mrs. Charles Funk Sr.*
> *Rockford, Illinois"*

Holidays may be celebrative, but they were also commemorative in World War II.

Memorial Day

Memorial Day was established in 1868 by Gen. John A. Logan, who "wanted his men remembered officially." The date to be observed was May 30 and remained so until 1971 when it was changed to the last Monday in May as a federal holiday.

Originally it was called Decoration Day because it was a time to decorate the graves of those killed in action in the Civil War. Later it memorialized all veterans and eventually all the dead. This author remembers her childhood when she carried a basket of little blue forget-me-not flowers each year to be laid on the grave of her baby sister, a victim of the 1917 flu epidemic. There were geraniums for the adult dead.

Gatherings of extended families came with their flowers year after year. It was still a veterans' event and I remember Civil War veterans grouping around my grandmother who was the widow of a veteran. John Kirby had first been a drummer boy in Company G of the 4th Massachusetts Heavy Artillery and, after the war, a member of the U.S. Marine Corps.

May 30 was well observed by parades with bands marching to cemeteries and prominent speakers and clergymen reminding the people gathered there that they were standing on hallowed ground. Besides the flowers everywhere, there were flags throughout the cemetery on the grave of every war veteran.

In the early twentieth century, Civil War veterans used to visit schools each year before Decoration Day to speak to student assemblies. As a little boy, Henry Lundquist recalled vividly the day when he sat in the front row of his assembly hall, waiting for the soldiers to arrive. Just before one veteran started up the steps to the stage, he unbuckled his sword and handed it to Henry to hold for him. Speechless ecstasy! It was something never to be forgotten.

In the twenty-first century, when Henry and I went to the Kirby family cemetery with flowers, we seemed to be alone. As we looked around, there were few flowers on the graves. But the flags were still there, placed each year on the graves of all war veterans by local veterans and Boy Scouts. They had one more flag to place in 2004. When I went to the little old cemetery on the hill, I laid flowers in front of the old stone with a new name:

Henry W. Lundquist 1904–2003

It was Lt. Henry Lundquist, USNR, who wrote the script for the Memorial Day broadcast of *Life to the Front* in 1945. He called it "Purple Hearts or Flowers." Since most people didn't know much about the medal, he thought that it would be interesting for them to hear what a Purple Heart was and who was entitled to wear one. And so he wrote:

> *"Have you ever seen a Purple Heart? It's a medal, a very handsome gold and purple heart-shaped medal, suspended from a purple ribbon. It's a direct descendent from an award established by George Washington himself back in 1782. The service ribbon is solid purple with an eighth inch of white at the ends. You see a lot of them on our soldiers, sailors, Marines and Coast Guardsmen these days. There are two ways to earn a Purple Heart in combat. One is to get killed and then the medal is awarded posthumously and goes to the man's next of kin. The other is to get wounded seriously enough to require medical attention—and then live to wear the medal or the ribbon.*
>
> *"So much for the Purple Heart. The flowers, of course, are for the dead. No need to say much about that except that this is where you—the listener—come in to see that a fighting man, through your blood, may receive a Purple Heart instead of flowers."*

Our donors knew that their blood had been at the front to keep some man alive to wear his Purple Heart, but were not there when his Purple Heart was pinned on him at retreat ceremonies.

The story of Marine Warrant Officer William H. Woerner Jr. is for them. The Marine was wounded following an artillery bombardment on Tinian.

Navy Lt. George H. Lyons, a Boston doctor, was caring for the wounded on the Tinian beach, where he administered plasma to Bill Woerner and claimed that it saved the Marine's life.

ORGAN: BRIDGE FROM "MONTEZUMA"

WOERNER: I'd like to have you know how I felt the day the colonel pinned the Purple Heart on my blouse. It's hard to explain. It was at retreat. When my name was called, I stepped forward, faced Colonel DeHaven out there in front of the division, all at attention.

COLONEL: Warrant Officer William H. Woerner Jr., "for wounds received in action against the enemy July 25, 1944, on Tinian Island, while serving with the Fourth Marine Division, the Purple Heart is presented in recognition of wounds received while in the service of your country." Mr. Woerner, this is a badge of courage. Wear it proudly.

WOERNER: Yes, sir.

COLONEL: And, Bill, it's good to have you back.

WOERNER: Thank you, sir. It's good to be back.

WOERNER: (NARRATING AGAIN) I returned to my place
                in line. I went through the formality
                of retreat mechanically.

VOICE: OFF MIKE (STRONG) Attention.

WOERNER: (QUIETLY ON MIKE) My hand snapped to
                attention.

SOUND: BUGLE CALL "TO THE COLORS" OFF MIKE

EFFECT CONTINUED IN BACK OF FOLLOWING

WOERNER: But things were happening down around
                my heart…me, a Marine with seven years
                in the corps…me getting emotional.
                I was seeing that beach, seeing the
                casualties pouring in, hearing Doc
                Lyons's calm, quiet voice. It kept going
                through my mind as though I was still
                lying on the beach with that plasma
                bottle dangling over my head.

SOUND: UP FOR A SECOND

WOERNER: Back and forth it kept dangling, back
                and forth in front of my face, as my hand

shaded my eyes as I looked straight at the flag...and I wondered whose blood had made the plasma that filled the bottle that had been emptied into my veins.

The bottle suddenly became people, and I wondered who he or she or they were. My heart was really pounding. I owed my life to them. Doc Lyons had said so.

SOUND: TO THE FINISH AND OUT

NARRATOR: William Woerner meant you. He didn't know and neither do you...but it could be that it was you...you were one of those who did something to make sure it was Purple Hearts and not flowers for someone.

Of course, many of our World War II survivors have received flowers in the years since they were given their Purple Hearts. There was a long good life for many in between, producing generations to carry on that for which their fathers fought. Some are buried in national cemeteries throughout this country where Memorial Day is observed and families visit.

Some of these former survivors have been buried in Arlington National Cemetery in Virginia just outside Washington, DC. Thousands of tourists visit there day after day, standing in solemn silence as they look out over the acres of headstones that remind us of those who fought for our freedom throughout the years. Even the hundreds of workers who leave the Pentagon at the end of each day are quietly moved as they walk down the wide, long stairs that look out over the cemetery.

There are national cemeteries throughout the world, most in such far-off places that families seldom visit. And we cannot forget the unmarked graves of men who were buried where they fell in battle. But they and all others are remembered every Memorial Day when our commander-in-chief lays a wreath on the Tomb of the Unknown Soldier at Arlington. As long as there has been television, we have all been able to watch this solemn occasion.

Memorial Day is a time for *requiescant in pace* wherever the grave is and wherever we are.

Fourth of July

Today it is good to recall that there were many outstanding public service pieces produced during World War II by Young & Rubicam, then and now, one of our top American—now global—advertising agencies. The 1945 Fourth of July broadcast of *Life to the Front* featured "A Strange Sort of Prayer," taken from the agency's public service advertisements. The picture could not be included—radio having no video—but a professional rendition of the compelling words with a musical background gave us a powerful Fourth of July program.

In 2011, in writing the chapter on holidays for *Out for Blood*, I decided to include the 1945 Fourth of July broadcast.. This time readers can see the picture along with the deeply moving words of "A Strange Sort of Prayer."

WELL, GOD, here we are.

You up there. Me down here, with a burning sun, a mess of insects, too much ocean, and other buddies just as lonely as me.

Oh, God, how nice it must be back home, with Germany licked, and the folks humming, and some of the boys all finished with the fighting.

But I guess that wasn't meant for me, was it? And tomorrow and tomorrow I'll still be dodging bullets,

still feeling lost in the middle of the night.

Well, no hard feelings.

I'll go wherever You say, and do whatever You want me to. For You know what's best for me.

But say, if You can only get the people back home to remember me, maybe they'll still bear down. Maybe they'll still send us their blood, still stay on the job, still keep making the stuff we need.

You see, God, I'd like to get home, too.

Young & Rubicam, Inc., 285 Madison Avenue, New York City

A Strange Sort of Prayer.

185

New Year's Day

In 1947, the American Broadcasting Company aired a series called *Our Town Speaks*, featuring the outstanding cities in the country. Boston ranked among them. Henry Lundquist was the writer and producer for ABC on September 13, 1947. After describing the many faces of Boston—educational, historical, medical, and technological—the program climaxed with the following narrative:

> *"We have left the most important item about Boston...or any other city...until the last. It's our people; the ones you've heard called cold blue bloods. Well...it's a fact that the Boston Blood Donor Center, throughout the war, ranked third in the donation of blood to help save our wounded. It turned out to be warm and red after all. And if you had seen the Donor Center on New Year's Day, in 1945, you'd know what sort of hearts Bostonians have. The center expected so few donors it seemed hardly worthwhile to open, despite the urgent overseas need at the time. But the call went out... and the center did the biggest single day's collection in its history. There was nothing cold-blooded about that display."*

Among the New Year's Day donors was Rear Adm. Felix Gygax, USN, commandant of the First Naval District, and a group of Navy personnel serving under him.

Sixty-six years later in 2013, as a nation witnessed the Patriots Day terrorist attack at the end of the Boston Marathon, they were once again reminded of "what sort of hearts Bostonians have." The words Henry Lundquist wrote three generations ago still ring true today. *Boston Strong!*

PART V

ON THE ROAD TO BERLIN

20. FROM AFRICA THROUGH SICILY TO ITALY AND FRANCE

The North African campaign played a major role in World War II. It marked the first steps in the long and painful road to Berlin. Anyone doubting the importance of Africa should read the roster of generals in command: Dwight D. Eisenhower, Omar Bradley, George S. Patton, as well as British and Canadian generals of note. General Erwin Rommel led the Axis troops. Wherever the troops were headed—be it Oran, Algiers, Bizerte, Tunisia, or Casablanca—the Navy was there in force to make sure they got ashore.,.

I had a particular interest in one ship, the USS *Strong* (DD 467), a 2,100-ton destroyer of the *Fletcher* class, named for a Civil War naval hero. She was a New Englander, built at the Bath Iron Works in Bath, Maine, in 1941 and commissioned in the summer of 1942. Her commanding officer, Cmdr. Joseph H. Wellings, was a New Englander, as were many of the crew.

Maybe that's why so many of them came to the Blood Donor Center to give their blood while their ship was at the Charlestown Navy Yard being readied for sea duty. I'll never forget them, especially the large group that came in together one day and delighted everyone in the center at the time. They had such wonderful spirit!

Now they were in action in Africa and I could only hope that the ship would be unscathed—and her men too. I didn't know then that I would be writing about the ship later in the war in the Pacific, where she was sent as soon as her duties at Africa were completed. The *Strong* seemed to be special to me at the time, as she proved to be later in the war.

There was another general on the African scene. Maj. Gen. Norman T. Kirk, surgeon general of the Army, personally went through the Tunisian campaign until the German surrender. When he returned, he gave us the following report on June 7, 1943:

> *"In Tunisia, the wounded had to be carried on an average of 8 to 20 miles through mountains to the first medical stations, and, after that, 600 miles by ambulance to an evacuation hospital. Planes that carried war supplies to the front brought 15,000 men to hospitals, including both battle casualties and the sick. The foremost lifesaver was plasma, the dried blood extract which millions of Americans had been giving to the Red Cross for nearly two years. Plasma saved shock and bleeding and without that many men would have died before they could reach medical care.*

Some of the ambulances carrying the wounded in Africa were driven by members of the American Field Service. One of these drivers, Edgar L. Jones, described the African scene so vividly that it was published in *Vogue* and reprinted in *Reader's Digest* in December 1943. He had come to have great regard for our blood donors at home. This is how he described the wounded, who had such need for their gifts:

> *The final push was on and we had been evacuating casualties since first light that morning. No one at home can imagine what war in the desert is like. None of us have wanted you to know. The wounded at the forward dressing station lay in the hot sun, plagued by flies and stinging gusts of sand. They were exhausted from 72 hours of fighting without sleep but they were too much on*

edge to sleep with the sound of battle so close by. They were inexpressibly thirsty and dirty but the only water we had was the meager pint issued daily to each of us.

It takes a driver about four hours to go fifteen miles when he is carrying patients who involuntarily scream at each jolt of the springs. Hours of grinding through deeply rutted sand, picking your way over boulders, edging into wadis and pulling out again, all the time listening for that raspy intake of breath which means that the patient is still alive and a driver feeling like a murderer every time there's a bad jolt. The blood stains on the bandages grow larger as the man's life seeps slowly out and stains the floor. One wonders how much longer he can hold out.

Edgar Jones wrote that article in answer to another article in *Vogue* that he read when he found a tattered, battered copy of the magazine out in the desert HQ. It was the "case history of a blood donor," and after seeing what the gifts of these blood donors did for his patient, he was moved to write to "Dear Miss Ferguson," the author. He told her that he had been wishing he could say thanks to blood donors everywhere for what they did for his patients.

The combination of the surgeon general's report and that of the ambulance driver gave our donors the urge to give again, and for nondonors to get started.

Although I did not have the privilege of interviewing any of the generals, I did meet with many of the soldiers who were with them both in Africa and Sicily.

One of them was Army PFC James Richardson, who enlisted in Malden, Massachusetts, on March 6, 1942. "I went overseas in September on a troop transport," he said. "We went in on the first wave, and were fighting almost immediately because we received a fiery reception from the enemy. But we felt fortunate because the transport that brought us in was blown up within twenty-four hours of our being put ashore."

When I asked about the loss of life on the transport, he explained, "A submarine came alongside after the first bomb hit and sent a torpedo into the ship. The Navy crew was aboard, of course, and some Army personnel and some troops who had not yet been off-loaded. It was awful. That's why we felt so lucky. It was so close for us."

When I first interviewed Jim Richardson, I noticed a Ranger patch on his uniform. He explained, "I went over with the Ninth Division and fought with them in Africa and Sicily. I volunteered for the Rangers in Sicily and was with them there and at Monte Cassino."

The fighting had been demanding all along the way, but Monte Cassino was beyond all the rest, according to the boys who returned. Historians rank the Battle of Monte Cassino as the worst battle of World War II. It is difficult to understand how one battle can be thus ranked with so many other battles with similar "qualifications."

One day Richardson and a buddy were sitting in an olive grove, talking about olives while waiting for orders to move out on a scouting expedition. They knew about olives because they liked to eat them, but they didn't know that they grew on trees. "I guess I thought they were born in a bottle," said the buddy.

Suddenly they heard shots, and they saw in the distance one of their gunners get hit. "He was down flat," recalled Richardson, "and the enemy fire continued. We just looked at each other and said that we couldn't leave him there. We decided to make a run for it and bring him back out of the line of fire."

These two soldiers made a dash for it and managed to pick up the gunner and struggle back with him to the olive grove while the German machine guns were still firing. Private Richardson received a Silver Star for this act of unselfish bravery. They watched the litter bearers come for their gunner and take him off to an aid station. "A man isn't thinking of bravery under such circumstances," said Richardson. "He just does what he has to do for a fellow soldier. He knows that the man is going to get medical attention. We just couldn't leave him out there to get shot up."

It wasn't long before Jim Richardson was on the receiving end of medical attention himself. As they were searching for machine gun nests, someone called out, "Hey, they got Richardson!" He was badly wounded. Someone called for the litter bearers. As they came running to him, his buddies watched as they lifted him gently onto the stretcher and carried him away to the battalion aid station. But his injury was complicated, and it was determined that he be moved on as soon as possible. He was given plasma while they waited. Then they lifted him onto the upper deck of an ambojeep—a double-decker stretcher on a jeep.

His friend Charlie told the gang about him that night. "He was white and cold and still. The medics described him as being almost gone." But Jim Richardson wasn't gone. He did not regain consciousness on that long trip over the rough roads to the hospital from the aid station, but he did come to long enough to see them giving him plasma before he passed out again.

One bottle, two bottles, three bottles...and still they gave it to him. Operation followed operation and whole blood followed each operation. For seven months, Pvt. Jim Richardson lay in the hospital in Italy, and more than once he said that he shivered in his hospital cot as the Nazi planes came over, dropping death and destruction on some of the hospital tents.

"There was a sort of guilty feeling of relief," he said, "when you knew they landed on tents you figured were far enough away to mean you were out of trouble. Then you got to wondering what poor guys were getting it. Sometimes we heard it was medical personnel...doctors and nurses...sometimes patients...and sometimes we didn't hear anything. We just guessed...and hoped."

That was the end of Private Richardson's active duty for a while. He did not get to Berlin, but he did get home, sure that both plasma and whole blood helped to bring him there. He had great gratitude because he knew how many did not get home from Italy. He was even more grateful when he learned the statistics from Monte Cassino.

Another young soldier, Robert Horrigan, also started out in Africa and ended up in Italy, only his final battle was at Anzio. He came from a large family in Newton, Massachusetts. Of nine children, most were in school. "The rest were in the service," he said. "One was in the Philippines, one was in Germany, and one was a Marine in a hospital in Rhode Island after duty on Palau." I thought of his mother and the worry she must have experienced. What happened to Robert could not have eased her mind.

Private Horrigan had started out in Africa like so many soldiers that I met. He was a replacement in the infantry and had moved over from Africa, through Sicily, and then into Italy. It was springtime here at home in 1944, with the greening of the grass, the leafing of the trees, and the bursting of buds into blossoms, a very pretty time. In the place where Robert Horrigan was over there, all they could see along the thin arc of the Anzio beachhead was the rich brown earth churned up by armored vehicles and the rows of barbed wire that sprang up overnight between the lines.

It was May 17 when our Anzio story begins. It was one in the morning, pitch dark. Six men were crawling along, Indian file, out beyond the front lines. They were headed for outpost duty. It was quiet in the lines as the men edged along, except for the dried-up sticks crackling under them. The guns were never quiet in the distance as the men gained one hundred yards...two hundred yards. They could hear the German voices behind the enemy lines. The six men crawled toward those voices and the six foxholes in the ground that would be their outpost stations—and duty. They kept edging along. The first man made it into his hole; the next man was close when a grenade came over from the enemy lines and got him. Then they got Horrigan, next in the line of defenders edging forward.

Now there were two men to be taken back behind the lines to the litter bearers. Horrigan thought he could walk. His buddy could not; he could not even talk. He would have to be carried. Both were badly wounded, but they all made it back behind the lines where the litter bearers took over. The two wounded men were taken to the battalion aid station. Horrigan was conscious all the way. When he asked what had happened to him, the doctor explained that a thick piece of metal had punctured the left side of his neck and traveled through his body until it came out his right shoulder.

The doctor told the aide to keep plasma going until the ambulance was ready to take the patient on to the hospital. It was about a fifteen-minute ambulance ride to the field hospital, a three-hundred-to-four-hundred-tent hospital with fifty to seventy-five men to a tent. Although they had only a canvas roof over their heads, the doctors in this hospital managed to accomplish things unknown before in any but the most modern metropolitan centers.

After X rays, the doctor couldn't believe the pictures because that piece of metal had missed all the vital spots: windpipe, esophagus, jugular vein, spinal column. His shoulder was shattered so they would operate on that at once, but first he was sent to the plasma tent. He would need plenty. When the operation was completed, medical personnel removed Horrigan by barge to a hospital ship and then on to the big base hospital at Naples.

The doctors still watched Horrigan; he wasn't out of danger yet. In spite of what the X ray showed, the doctors could hardly believe that the piece of metal had really missed everything. The possibility of infection and gangrene concerned them. Finally satisfied, they discharged Private Horrigan. It had been a long ordeal, but it ended when he came home to the States on a transport.

He was now a veteran, having been given a medical discharge. He had served his country from Africa to Anzio on the long road to Berlin. Even if he wasn't there on V-E Day, he had helped his fellow soldiers get there. And now, as a civilian, he was helping us get more donors to assure his buddies who were still fighting that there would be plasma for them if they needed it as he had.

Many soldiers were stopped on their way to Berlin. It happened in Sicily for some. An Army Signal Corps photographer took a picture of one man as he lay on a stretcher in the street, receiving plasma, while three Sicilian women and a child sat in a doorway watching. This picture became famous during the war and ever since. Imagine a mother looking at the picture, like all the rest of us when it first appeared, and then recognizing the face of the wounded soldier as her son. She was a regular blood donor at a Red Cross center on the West Coast. She always knew why she gave blood but never expected to see such intimate proof. We offer this extraordinary picture for our readers to see and for some of you, maybe, to remember.

Wounded in Sicily

I met many other soldiers who had started out in Africa but were wounded in Italy. These survivors praised the outstanding medical care available to them where they fell, crediting plasma with getting them back on their marching feet so quickly. It was their doctors who claimed the importance of our donors, and I was fortunate to interview many of these medics who had labored at the front.

One doctor seemed to know a lot about plasma. It was he who told me about plasma being carried by mule into the mountains of Sicily, when the enemy cut off a battalion aid station. He told me also how plasma went to the Anzio beachhead by LST (a Navy ship that can land tanks, troops and vehicles on a beach) with a high priority or from the sky by parachutes. But his most impressive statement came when he asked me to tell our donors, "There is more to the giving of blood than the element of saving lives. It also permits the surgeon to do more precise surgery which reduces disability, deformity, and infection. Hitherto, this type of surgery would have been too dangerous to undertake. We attempt things now that would never have been attempted before."

This well-informed doctor was Col. Edward D. Churchill of the U.S. Army Medical Corps, commanding surgeon of the Mediterranean Theater of Operations. He was well known in civilian life as the John Homans Professor of Surgery at Harvard Medical School and chief of West Surgical Services at the Massachusetts General Hospital in Boston.

Doctor Churchill possessed impressive credentials in the civilian medical world. When he entered the military world, he quickly acquired equally outstanding credentials as consulting surgeon for the Mediterranean Theater. He even found time to write about the care of the battle wounded. I received a copy of one of his works, *The Surgical Management of the Wounded in the Mediterranean Theater at the Time of the Fall of Rome*, published by J. B. Lippincott Company in September 1944. The doctor wrote at length and in great detail about wound management and the critical need for plasma and whole blood. It was difficult for us at home to envision the enormity of the challenge to get casualties the attention needed to keep them alive and their wounds cared for. What Colonel Churchill wrote provided us with information and inspiration.

"Resuscitation from shock has two goals," he wrote, "first to render the casualty transportable and preserve his life until a hospital can be reached; and second to prepare the casualty to withstand the saving surgical procedures." He continued, "Plasma is used in the divisional area to prepare the wounded for transportation and keep them alive until they can reach a hospital."

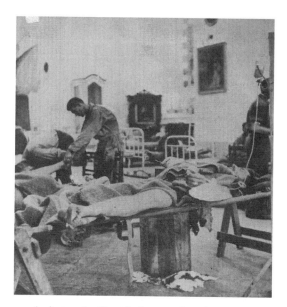

An improvised hospital, somewhere in Europe.

In my interview with Colonel Churchill, he made clear the link that existed between our donors and his doctors. Then the *New York Herald Tribune* carried a piece that underlined that same connection. The heading of the article read, "Uncomplaining wounded of the Italy Drive are rescued by plasma and fast surgery." The piece was filed from the Eighth Evacuation Hospital, 5th Army front, Italy, May 15 (AP):

This is the shock ward of an emergency hospital where blood plasma is stacked like cordwood. All through the day and night, litter bearers have come in from the environs of Santa Maria Infante which our infantry retook yesterday after the Germans had kicked us out. The litter bearers place the wounded on saw horses, such as carpenters use, and when every inch of space is crowded, they spill over into adjoining wards.

You walk down the lengthening rows of white faces and wonder how they can pull through. I followed one case through surgery where eight teams were working around the clock, driving themselves until their eyes were hollow. But they stood there, hour after hour, cheating death, making men whole again.

The number of people on the front who wanted to tell us what they saw there impressed me. They expected us to get their message to the people on the home front. It was a privilege to do so, especially when the expectation came from an Army Medical Corps general serving as the surgeon with the Fifth Army.

Brig. Gen. J. I. Martin wrote, "Blood plasma administered by medical soldiers on the battlefields made it possible to move the wounded men to the surgeons working in tented hospitals just behind the lines." He further stated that "every healthy American at home can actually be with a soldier who has fallen in battle by giving the blood that will start him on the way to health."

Many other battles were fought in the Italian campaign besides those noted. They were all important stops as the Allied troops moved up the Italian peninsula on their way

A field hospital in Italy.

to bring about the fall of Rome and Mussolini. I can't forget one picture of Rome, of a field outside the city where a pitchfork was thrust into the ground and a gun steadied through its handle. From the gun butt hung the "precious plasma." This scene not only shows the extensive use of plasma, but it indicates that there was no time wasted on "fancy fixtures." Speed was of the utmost importance.

The ten-day Casablanca Conference between President Franklin Delano Roosevelt and Prime Minister Winston Churchill took place early in 1943 in Morocco, on the Atlantic coast of North Africa, south of Gibraltar. They had much to discuss: plans for the Italian campaign to be pondered, concern for Germany's production of submarines that were such a menace for the Atlantic convoys, and debates about the timing of the Channel crossing. These were all serious matters, and historians have written much about the conclusions of the conference.

Casablanca was also one of the sites where the Allies first invaded North Africa. After the campaign ended, a soldier who ran for his life across the beach, dodging enemy bullets at Casablanca, remembered it as a place where he thought he was going to die. Many of his comrades lost their lives, while others lay wounded, waiting for the medics to come.

I found a picture in my files of one of those casualties of Casablanca. He was a patient at Walter Reed Army Hospital in Washington, DC. Army Pvt. Henry A. Bauer was receiving his Purple Heart with Lt. Gen. Lesley J. McNair, commanding general of the Army ground forces, looking on. Both men had earned their Purple Hearts in Africa and received plasma there. Private Bauer is in bed at Walter Reed and not sitting up. The private's wounds were presumably not superficial, and that plasma helped get him from Casablanca to Washington.

Today, Casablanca probably means nothing more than a famous Humphrey Bogart movie to most, unless they've read history and know what an important step North Africa was on the road to Berlin.

21. THE MEDICS

The medics of World War II were extraordinary. Doctors, nurses, pharmacist mates in charge of sick bays aboard ships, corpsmen, aides, ward boys, litter bearers—whatever the rank or rating or assignment, their work was remarkable, often truly heroic. If there was a perception that our armed forces awarded comparatively few medals to them, it was probably because they considered their kind of heroics to be routine. "Just doing my job, ma'am" is what they all would say...and mean it.

Sixteen million Americans served in uniform in World War II. The death toll was just over four hundred thousand, of which nearly three hundred thousand were battle fatalities. Chief of Naval Operations Fleet Adm. Ernest J. King, was stoic about this grim statistic when he wrote from the Pacific, "The Pacific War, though thousands of miles away from the shores of the United States, is daily brought directly into many American homes by formal notification of the injury or supreme sacrifice of a member of the family. There is nothing that anyone can do to prevent altogether the tremendous cost of war."

The survival rate among those who were not killed outright, however, was far greater than anyone might have thought possible. It was estimated that ninety-six survived out of every one hundred wounded. Maj. Gen. Norman T. Kirk, surgeongeneral of the Army, presented three reasons for this when he addressed the American

Medical Association House of Delegates in Chicago on June 7, 1943.

"The foremost lifesaver," the general declared, "is plasma, the dried blood extract which millions of Americans have been giving the Red Cross for nearly two years. Plasma saved shock and bleeding, and without that many men would have died before they could have reached medical care. Second in lifesaving was surgery, which cleaned up the wounds to reduce risk of infection. In third place were the sulfa drugs, aiding to minimize infection."

The AMA had always received good press coverage of its meetings. After all, it was the foremost authority on matters medical, so something of significance was expected when they met. Announcement of their speaker for that June event brought greater interest than ever. With the war raging throughout the world and the surgeon general just back from the African front, the media turned out in record numbers. They were so impressed that many of them carried the general's speech in its entirety.

Imagine then, the thrill for our donors when they read their newspapers to find that no less than the surgeon general himself ranked them as the number one lifesavers of our battle wounded. Many donors gave again and again and yet again. Some of the nondonors—the dilettantes, the skeptics, and those who were just plain scared—came forward at last to give. If anyone was counting, the surgeon general netted many a pint of blood for his needy troops. And our donors at home walked a little taller than before.

The November 17, 1943, report of the Office of War Information contained further evidence of the value of plasma and therefore the importance of our donors. This was their first comprehensive survey of the care of war wounded. It was filled with facts and figures. Among the variety of impressive statistics was the following:

"The main reason for saving wounded was:

1. Use of blood plasma to combat shock and hemorrhage.

2. Use of sulfa drugs to combat infection.
3. Quality of medical services which insure prompt treatment."

The survey explained, "Faster treatments and improved Army-Navy Methods for attending the wounded are playing a major role in reducing the number of deaths from wounds."

They further noted, "In the last war, we brought the wounded to the hospital; in this war, we are bringing the hospitals to the wounded."

Sometimes the hospital brought to the front would be nothing more than a tarp thrown over the trees. No matter what the form, it was an important part of a vital medical chain. One of the best descriptions of the Army's setup for caring for its wounded was given us by Ernie Pyle, the noted war correspondent, who wrote for the Scripps-Howard newspapers with a readership of more than 122 million in 310 cities. The folks at home eagerly awaited his columns. The minute that a paper hit the front steps in the morning, someone was ready to grab it up and thumb through its pages for Pyle's dispatch. They needed to know what was going on "over there."

Ernie Pyle had followed the Army through Africa. After the German evacuation to Sicily, he opted to go with the Navy. The vessel he was assigned to was neither a troop transport nor a warship, but she did carry some troops:

> *"Every soldier spent the first few hours aboard in exactly the same way. He took a wonderful shower bath, drank water with ice in it, sat at a table and ate food with real silverware, arranged his personal gear along the bulkhead by his bunk, drank coffee, sat in a real chair, read current magazines, saw a movie after supper, and finally got into a bed with a real mattress. It was too much for most of us and we all kept blubbering our appreciation until finally, I'm*

sure, the Navy must have become sick of our juvenile delight over things that used to be common to all men."

Pyle, as a correspondent duly accredited to the Navy, had intended to stay aboard ship for some time. He rode out the invasion of Sicily, keeping out of everyone's way, watching, recoiling, recording mentally, then writing what he remembered—and could never forget—in intricate, dramatic detail for his column. But he soon had a need to look at what was happening on land, so he hopped a barge going ashore.

Five days later, he was hit by a curious malady, accompanied by a fever that defied diagnosis or treatment, and was put into a hospital where he remained for five days. He never stopped working. From his cot in the corner, he wrote about what he saw and what he heard. From his observations, we learned much about the Army's medical setup for the care of its wounded. He wrote:

Let's take the medical structure for a whole division. A division runs roughly 15,000 men. Almost a thousand of them are medical men. To begin right at the front, three enlisted medical-aid men go along with every company. They give what first-aid they can on the battlefield. Then litter bearers carry the wounded back to a battalion aid station. The battalion aid station is the first of many stops as he is worked to the rear and, ultimately, to a hospital. An aid station is merely where the battalion surgeon and his assistant happen to be. It isn't a tent or anything like that. It's just the surgeon's medical chest and a few stretchers under a tree. Each station is staffed by two doctors and 36 enlisted men. Frequently it is under fire.

A wounded man gets what is immediately necessary, depending on the severity of his wounds. The idea all along the way is to do as little actual surgical work as possible but at each stop merely to keep a man in good enough condition to stand the trip on back to the hospital where there are full facilities for any kind of work. They use morphine and blood plasma copiously at the forward stations to keep sinking men going. The main underlying motive of all front line stations is to get the patients evacuated quickly and to keep the decks clear so that they will always have room for any sudden catastrophic action.

From the battalion aid station, the wounded are taken back by ambulance, jeep, truck or any other means, to a collecting station. The station is a few tents run by five doctors and a hundred enlisted men, anywhere from a quarter of a mile to several miles behind the lines. There is one collecting station for each regiment, making three to a division. All these various crews—the company aid men, the battalion aid station, the collecting station and the clearing station are part of the division. They move with it, work when it fights, and rest when it rests.

The clearing station I lay in was really a small hospital. It consisted of five doctors, one dentist, one chaplain, and sixty enlisted men. It was contained in six big tents and a few little ones for the fluoroscope room, the office and so forth. The station could knock down, move, and set up again in an incredibly short time. They were as proficient as a circus. Once during a rapid advance, my station moved three times in one day.

Behind the clearing stations, the real hospitals began, the first ones usually forty miles or more to the rear of the fighting. These hospitals are separate units. They belong to no division but take patients from everywhere.

The farther back they are, the bigger they get, and in Sicily, patients were evacuated from the hospitals right into hospital ships and taken back to still bigger hospitals in Africa.

In his 1944 book *Brave Men* (Henry Holt and Company), Pyle recalled:

The two main impressions I got from the wounded men were (1) their great spirit and (2) the thoughtful and attentive attitude of the doctors and wardboys toward them. This was especially true of the wardmasters who were responsible for whole tents.

One fellow, with his shattered arm sticking up at right angles, in its metal rack, gobbled chicken-noodle soup which a wardboy fed him while the doctor punched and probed at his other arm to insert the big needle that feeds blood plasma.

These doctors lived a rough-and-tumble life. They slept on the ground, worked ghastly hours, were sometimes under fire, and handled a flow of wounded that would sicken and dishearten a person less immune to it. Time and again as I lay in my tent I heard wounded soldiers discussing among themselves the wonderful treatment they had had at the hands of the medics. They'll get little glory back home when it's all over, but they had some recompense right there in the gratitude of the men they treated.

After Sicily, Pyle moved with the war through Italy, France, and Germany. He crossed the English Channel with the troops on D-Day like many other reporters.

Following V-E Day, he flew to the Pacific Theater of Operations, working there until his prolific pen was silenced when he was killed by a sniper on the island of Ie Shima, near Okinawa.

Ernest Taylor Pyle died in 1945 at age 45, but he lives on through his writing. He received the Pulizter Prize for his dispatches from the battlefront in Europe.

When Ernie Pyle was questioned on the subject of plasma, this is what he wrote: "The doctors asked me at least a dozen times to write about plasma. 'Write lots about it, go clear overboard for it, say that plasma is the outstanding medical discovery of the war.'

"They say that plasma is absolutely magical. They say that scores of thousands who died in the last war could have been saved by it. Thousands have already been saved by it in this war.

"They cite case after case where a wounded man was all but dead and within a few minutes after a plasma injection would be sitting up and talking. These doctors knew. They had seen so much."

Another very important group of medics were the litter bearers. They appeared to be something of a generic lot, unlike doctors, nurses, corpsmen, and ward boys, who were often recognized personally. Certain medics were redheads or blonds, or they spoke with a southern drawl or a midwestern twang. Ernie Pyle even gave their full names and addresses, including street and number. But with the litter bearers, they were just litter bearers.

The doctor could call for litter bearers to remove the stretcher that had been his operating table and have them get the patient moving on toward the next station for further treatment. Or a corpsman would call for litter bearers to lift a casualty out of a foxhole and get him to the doctor in the clearing under the trees. Or reports stated that litter bearers hurried the wounded out to the waiting ambulance, or brought him in to a hospital where they laid him on the floor inside the tent to await his turn.

They bore a heavy burden, these litter bearers, figuratively and literally. The soldiers and marines they carried were usually husky, hefty guys, often dead weight because of their semicomatose condition or, maybe worse still, writhing in pain and shifting their weight on the stretcher. The litter bearers staggered along with their load, stumbling through underbrush and over obstacles, or maybe slogging through muck and mire, not knowing where their next footsteps would fall. Always they were hurrying, often racing death. Their heroism was routine.

And then there were the nurses. They lived up to our high expectations, and in World War II performed more amazingly than even they themselves thought possible. The nurses had heavy duty during the arduous North African campaign.

In the 1940s, our vision of a nurse was an efficient woman in an all-white uniform from her starched cap to her white shoes and stockings. The July 31, 1943, issue of the *Saturday Evening Post* provided a different picture of the nurses in Africa in an article by the popular writer Peter Martin. It was called "Angels in Long Underwear." Much of the material for his story came from interviews with Lt. Col. Bernice M. Wilbur, USA, director of all the Army nurses in North Africa.

Martin explained his title: "When the American nurses first arrived in Africa it was bitter cold. Their blue slacks soon wore out, so they bought men's GI long woolen underwear, men's coveralls and field jackets, men's fatigue hats and men's GI high shoes."

About their work habits, he wrote, "The nurses on duty in the operating tents were supposed to work in shifts, six hours off and six hours on, but it was hard to get them to go off duty—the anesthetists especially. You could drive them away and find them back again in three hours, claiming they had had sufficient sleep, and were fresh, rested and ready to start in all over again."

There were many casualties, including Lt. Gen. Lesley McNair, whom we met earlier with Pvt. Henry Bauer at Walter Reed Army Hospital in Washington. After he was hit, he walked down the side of a hill to a jeep. "The driver drove him back to a first-aid station. He had shell fragments in the back of his head, and the bones of his left shoulder were shattered into small bits. An ambulance took him from the first-aid station to an evacuation hospital and litter bearers carried him into the dressing room," Martin wrote. "An Army surgeon operated on his shoulder. His head was operated upon by still another surgeon and the shell fragments removed."

The Army asked Wilbur to take over the general's care, even returning to the States with him when he was flown home to complete his recuperation. This would be the final step in the recovery path that had started "in the first-aid station where his wounds were dressed and he was given blood plasma. 'It felt as if I had new life put into me,' was the way the general described that emergency treatment."

The general's nurse had something to add. "We've used loads of Red Cross plasma for all kinds of wounds," Wilbur said. "Many of the men receive as much as three pints of plasma during the first few hours and more later on. I've seen them brought in with almost no blood pressure. Five hours later they'd be sitting up. The African campaign hasn't been any skirmish but future ones will be much bigger, and the need for people to donate a pint of blood is greater now than it ever was."

How right she was!

General McNair was not the only high-ranking officer to extol the merits of plasma. Many other generals and admirals did also, although not as recipients.

Anyone who knows anything about the military knows that a primary concern of all commanding officers is the well-being of those in their command. It was not unexpected, therefore, to have these commanders tour the medical facilities in their command. Those who couldn't make the trip could read the detailed reports submitted from each facility. They knew what they were talking about when they released statements about the "miraculous qualities of plasma." Generals Ike Eisenhower, George Patton, Archer Vandergrift, Omar Bradley, Holland "Howlin' Mad" Smith, Hap Arnold, and "Vinegar" Joe Stillwell; Admirals Chester Nimitz and Ernest King; and many, many others released hundreds of such statements.

But for all the effectiveness of these statements—newspaper columns, magazine articles, books, official releases—there was nothing quite like personal contact. We sensed that when we took recipients and witnesses into defense plants and other factories, or to community gatherings in town halls, or to programs in city auditoriums. People were able to see and hear and meet those who had been on the front lines, receiving or watching our donors' blood at work, and that had a greater impact.

The same was true of radio. Listeners heard a frontline story from someone who was there, and it seemed personal. They felt they knew the person, and they were deeply moved—in many cases, moved to become blood donors. This pleased our military guests.

A good example of this was the February 13, 1945, broadcast of *Life to the Front* when we presented a dramatization of a story told to us by an Army doctor from Belmont, a suburb of Boston, home on medical leave. He was the husband of one of our Red Cross volunteers at the center.

The program, a true story with real names of people and places—hence Sgt. Kirby and Anastasia Kirby (no relations) in the script—was called "One a.m. Evacuate." This is a report of Army medics and the crisis with their five-hundred-bed tent hospital as it was flooded by the rising river waters. The following is from the original script.

ANNCR: Today is Belmont Day at *Life to the Front* and we have in our studio audience over 100 blood donors and Red Cross workers from Belmont, many of whom sent their precious pints on their way at 2:30 this afternoon.

In the front row of our audience, waiting to take his place at the microphone later in the program, is a Belmontian who wears the caduceus of the Medical Corps, the gold leaf of a major, the brown-and-green ribbon of the European Theater, and the Purple Heart of a combat casualty. He is Maj. James H. Townsend, whose story of the Army Medical Corps versus the flood-swollen Pisa River in northern Italy is the basis of today's dramatization.

ORGAN: BRIDGE...OMINOUS

REED: It shouldn't be necessary to tell you
                   gentlemen that we've got a problem on
                   our hands. Judging from your boots,
                   you've made contact with the problem
                   already.

TOWNSEND: I haven't even been outside. I just
                   came up from my supply room and I had
                   to slosh through water to get here.

REED: Yes, Major, I'm afraid the Pisa's not
                   content to stay where it belongs. It
                   seems to have joined the ranks of
                   the enemy. We may have to change our
                   plans.

SHACKLEFORD: How fast is it rising, Colonel?

REED: I'm not sure. I just sent Sgt. Kirby
                   out to check. Meanwhile, let's see
                   where we stand. How about you, Colonel
                   Shackleford?

SHACKLEFORD: Well, we've been practicing setting up. I
                   wanted the men to be sure of themselves
                   when we got up to the new location. You
                   never can tell how soon after you land
                   you'll be doing business.

REED: That's true, especially when you're
                   moving toward the front.

21. THE MEDICS

SHACKLEFORD: With the operating tent…I didn't want to take any chances. We've got that all set up now.

REED: Mmm…How about you, Major Townsend?

TOWNSEND: Medicine's in the same boat with surgery, I guess. We've got our ward tents all set up. I figured we'd spend the first part of the ten days practicing setups. Like Colonel Shackleford, I want my men to be sure of themselves.

REED: I know. After being a station hospital in a building, it's not too easy a transition to operate as a mobile tent hospital.

SHACKLEFORD: With ten days to a couple of weeks ahead of us, we thought we'd do a good job.

REED: We'll still do a good job, Colonel. But we'll do it differently, I'm afraid.

SOUND: KNOCK ON DOOR.

REED: That should be Kirby…come in!

SOUND: DOOR OPENING.

REED: Well, Sergeant, what did you find?

KIRBY: Bad news, I'm afraid, sir. River's come up one foot in the last hour.

REED: One foot in an hour...mmmm...

KIRBY: Seems to be rising fast, sir.

REED: Yes...

KIRBY: At that rate, sir...in another hour, she'll be up over the floor.

REED: Then all equipment must be raised. Get it up on boxes or planks...at least six feet off the floor. Pack what you can into boxes, ready to move at short notice. As for the tents and the equipment, you've got to set up out in the fields...

SOUND: TELEPHONE RINGING RECEIVER LIFTED

REED: Colonel Reed.

VOICE: (ON FILTER) Ben, we're in trouble. Can you let me have a hundred of your enlisted men?

REED: What? Who is this?

VOICE: 38th Evac. I need help.

REED: But a hundred men! Colonel, I'd like to help you out...but...we've got problems over here ourselves. I'm in conference with my staff right now. We expect to be flooded out in another hour and we've got to get all our equipment up, including tents out in the fields on practice setups. I'll need every last man I've got.

VOICE: (STILL ON THE FILTER) But, Ben...we're flooded already. The water is two feet deep in the tents and it's still rising.

REED: Two feet in the tents?

VOICE: (FILTER) And I've got patients. We've got to evacuate. I need one hundred more enlisted men to help.

REED: They're on their way, Colonel.

VOICE: (FILTER) Wait a minute, Ben. Our greatest problem is the road.

REED: Where are you evacuating to?

VOICE: (FILTER) Back...about two and a half miles, to higher ground.

REED: The medical supply depot?

VOICE: (FILTER) That's right. But the road is our only means of exit and you can't even see it.

REED: Flooded?

VOICE: (FILTER) Under two feet of water. You can't see it or the fields on either side of it.

REED: Mmm. All right, Colonel, my men will mark the road. They'll leave immediately. Good luck to you!

SOUND: RECEIVER BEING HUNG UP.

REED: We think we've got trouble.

SHACKLEFORD: What is it, Colonel?

REED: The 38th Evacuation Hospital is flooded with two feet of water in the tents already and rising rapidly.

SHACKLEFORD: How many patients have they?

REED: Five hundred….Sgt Kirby, you'll report to the colonel immediately with a detail of 100 enlisted men. Your job is to find the road and mark it. Hop to it.

KIRBY: Yes, sir!

SOUND: SOUND OF DOOR BEING OPENED AND CLOSED
              IN BACK OF FOLLOWING...

REED: Now...our own situation. There isn't
              any time to be lost. I guess that's
              understood by everyone.

CHORUS: Sure is. Definitely. That's right. Yes.
              Etc. Etc.

REED: Better get trucks down into the field to
              pick up your equipment from the tents.
              Get all generators off the floors and
              be sure all the wires are up. This is
              no time to lose our lights. I won't hold
              you any longer. You know what to do.
              That's all.

ORGAN: BRIDGE

BUTSKY: But Sarge!

KIRBY: Listen, Butsky, for the last time...as
              many wooden stakes that we put signs
              on as you can get your hands on. We're
              leaving in a matter of minutes and we're
              taking them with us. Now get going.

BUTSKY: But Sergeant, who cares about the
              signposts? You can't even see the

	road where we're going...and you want signposts? Who cares what street it is!
KIRBY:	Butsky, I've heard the last "but sergeant" from you that you're ever going to say. Do you get me?
BUTSKY:	But...a...(SIGHS) you don't understand. You don't want to understand.
KIRBY:	The stakes are to be driven into the ground on either side of the road.
BUTSKY:	B...(CLEARS THROAT) you can't see the road.
KIRBY:	We're going to find the road...you're going to help. You're going to wade in water up to your waist. You're going to have to surface dive, probably, until your nose touches the road and then you'll come up and say, "Here's where the stake goes," and then you'll dive again...
BUTSKY:	But I can't even swim...
KIRBY:	Then go get the stakes and don't ask any more foolish questions. Here comes the colonel.
REED:	(OFF MIKE) How you coming, Sergeant?

KIRBY: Okay, sir. We're taking along those stakes we use for signs. One of the men is getting them now. Another man is getting out a supply of the white tape we use to mark off minefields...you know...

REED: Good idea...excellent idea.

KIRBY: We can find the road and mark it off with the tape from stake to stake. The headlights of the ambulances and trucks will pick it up easily in the dark.

REED: Good work. That's the greatest hazard at the moment.

KIRBY: That's right, sir. If one wheel goes off the road, the ambulance will probably tip over.

REED: And we can't have that. It's not going to be an easy job, Kirby. And you've got to work fast.

BUTSKY: (FADING ON MIKE) Here they are, Sergeant, but I...I...

KIRBY: (CALLING TO HIM) Put them in the truck, Butsky.

VOICE: (OFF MIKE OUTSIDE) Okay, Sergeant, everyone's aboard.

KIRBY: Well...we're off, sir.

REED: Good luck, Kirby. Get back as soon as
              your job's done there. We may need help
              here.

KIRBY: Yes, sir.

ORGAN: BRIDGE

KIRBY: Okay, Butsky. Pound her in.

BUTSKY: Gee, I'm all wet.

KIRBY: Well, it's the first time I ever heard
              you admit it. This is no time for
              complaints. Take a look in back of you...
              down there in back of the convoy.

              (CALLING OFF) Keep moving with the tape.
              We're making progress, fellows.

VOICE: (OFF MIKE) Are the trucks gaining on us?

KIRBY: (CALLING OFF) No. We're keeping well
              ahead of them. But we can't let up.

Voice: (OFF MIKE) Anyone gone off the road yet?

KIRBY: (CALLING OFF) Not a one. They're coming
              along like a fleet of trucks on a New
              York highway.

BUTSKY: Kind of slow for New York.

KIRBY: Well, you know what I mean.

BUTSKY: But it's not what you said. Gee, I'm soaked.

KIRBY: By the way, did you see what I told you to look at?

BUTSKY: You mean all those guys in the bathrobes wading along behind the trucks?

KIRBY: Do you still feel wet?

BUTSKY: Well, sure. It shuts me up, I guess, but I don't feel no drier.

KIRBY: We're doing all right here. Wonder how they're making out back at headquarters…

ORGAN: BRIDGE

REED: Shackleford…Colonel Shackleford…Hello. Colonel Reed speaking. We'll have to get the hospital out of here. Water's up to the floor now. We start moving tonight for the new site. Get the operating tent out first. That's one tent that's irreplaceable.

SHACKLEFORD: Yes, sir, we've been working on it. X-ray equipment's aboard the truck and all the operating equipment.

REED: How about the other tents?

SHACKLEFORD: Some of them are under five feet of water now. We can't hope to get them up. We've all been working on the operating equipment.

REED: Well, I've got trucks backed into headquarters here. We're under three feet of water, but we're managing to get supplies aboard. I'd like to get your truck from the field down there and my first truck of supplies off from here. We've got all our plasma aboard and some other essentials. I'd like to start the convoy as soon as possible.

ORGAN: BRIDGE

REED: My Lord, Kirby! You look like a drowned rat!

KIRBY: Well, sir, we made it.

REED: Good work, Kirby! Tell me about it.

KIRBY: Our men are all back and have reported in for further assignment.

REED: With the help of those men who've just come back with you, we should be out of here by 4:00 a.m.

KIRBY: Well, the 38th Evac is now setting up temporary quarters in the medical supply depot until morning. It was a tough trip for them but they didn't have a casualty, sir. Not one man was lost.

REED: I'm glad. It was a risky business evacuating all those patients over those roads.

KIRBY: Well, we managed to get the roads marked and keep ahead of the convoy. When we were finished we waded back to help carry in some of the ambulatory patients who were walking. The water was deeper than two feet in places and it was tough on a lot of them. They were completely bushed. But they made it.

REED: Any trouble with the litter cases?

KIRBY: The nurses stuck pretty close to them. They're a swell bunch! They gave up all thought of salvaging their personal belongings and went right along in the ambulances with the patients.

REED:
: I suppose there was a great loss in gear and equipment.

KIRBY:
: Even the quartermaster lost his shirt. But not a life was lost…sir. That's the important point.

ORGAN:
: BRIDGE

ANNCR:
: One of the men who traveled with that convoy at 4:00 a.m. that November day was Maj. James H. Townsend, who is now coming up to the microphone with Anastasia Kirby, and we shall hear what happened when the convoy arrived at its destination.

KIRBY:
: Major Townsend, I'm sure everybody's anxious to know if you arrived safely at the new location.

TOWNSEND:
: We did…without any mishap along the way.

KIRBY:
: How long did it take you to get set up?

TOWNSEND:
: We were taking patients within forty-eight hours.

KIRBY:
: You certainly didn't waste time.

TOWNSEND:
: We couldn't afford to.

KIRBY: Did you have whole blood as well as plasma there?

TOWNSEND: As you know from the story, we had an ample supply of plasma, which we had trucked up through the water. The next day, I drove to the laboratory where the advance blood bank was kept, about 70 miles away, and brought back two dozen pints for immediate use.

KIRBY: What about the future?

TOWNSEND: I made arrangements for a daily allotment of as many bottles as we required.

KIRBY: Was that the daily delivery that's been compared to a milk delivery?

TOWNSEND: We were a little off the beaten track for the daily blood truck that calls at all evacuation and field hospitals, but our mail courier could bring out as much as we needed by jeep.

KIRBY: Incidentally, Major Townsend, where had you been before serving with this hospital?

TOWNSEND: I'd been at a hospital in Naples. You'd be interested to know that there was much plasma used there, for we had a number of navy casualties and, of course, many burn cases.

KIRBY: That is interesting, Major, because we know the importance of plasma for the kind of burn cases the navy suffers. Prior to going overseas, where were you?

TOWNSEND: At the Massachusetts General Hospital.

KIRBY: How long ago was that?

TOWNSEND: Three years ago. I've been overseas twenty-two months and home here on leave one month.

KIRBY: What next for you, Major?

TOWNSEND: I'm a patient at the Cushing General Hospital in Framingham where I was sent from my own hospital in Italy, where I will be returning.

KIRBY: How did you come to be a patient in your own hospital?

TOWNSEND: It was ten days after we arrived at our new location that we caught a little shelling. An evacuation hospital is pretty far forward and sometimes shells come in.

KIRBY: Was the hospital damaged?

TOWNSEND: No serious damage. It splattered shell
            fragments all over the place, tore holes
            in the tents, but no serious damage.

KIRBY: How about casualties?

TOWNSEND: Three. I was one. I was lucky. It just
            got me in the foot.

KIRBY: I don't suppose you had to wait long for
            attention.

TOWNSEND: It was in the middle of the night when
            we were sleeping but the operating
            room was running, of course, and they
            brought me in there where I was imme-
            diately cared for.

KIRBY: On *Life to the Front*, you know, Major,
            the inevitable question is did you
            receive any whole blood or plasma?

TOWNSEND: I did. I didn't suppose that I needed
            any, but when I woke up there was the
            blood bottle attached to my cot and I was
            getting it. It was a comfortable feeling
            to know that it was available and rather
            strange to wonder whose blood it was.

KIRBY: You said that you didn't suppose that
            you needed blood. Why did you get it?

TOWNSEND: It's frequently used, you know, to prevent shock. Even when a person is not in dire need, that's one of its great values: it's a preventative.

KIRBY: Well, Major Townsend, be it a pint of prevention or a pint of cure, we are mainly interested in having the blood there so that you doctors can do what must be done to send us home live and whole men, instead of the sympathy of the War Department.

TOWNSEND: It certainly is important. I wish I might leave a pint of my own with you. I feel I owe it. But I'm told that I must wait 'til I'm out of the hospital.

KIRBY: That's right, Major. But...you know, we don't think you owe a pint half so much as some of our able Bostonians who haven't given one pint yet.

TOWNSEND: Well, it's too bad they can't see what it does for some of their boys in the operating tent.

KIRBY: I guess a few minutes in one of those places would be an inspiration to all of us. Major Townsend, we're very grateful to you for coming to *Life to the Front* today and for telling us the story of the evacuation of your hospital in Italy.

> May we say, "Thank you and good luck to you, sir."

ORGAN: THEME UP AND TO CLOSE

Navy medics did not have to contend with five-hundred-bed tent hospitals. They had hospital ships with that many beds sailing the oceans, standing offshore from raging battles, at the ready. The *Solace, Samaritan, Sanctuary, Relief, Rescue,* and *Tranquility* were a few of the huge floating hospitals, over four hundred feet long, painted white and lit up at night like beacons of hope as they moved through the dark. Navy medics staffed these hospital ships, each carrying from four hundred to eight hundred patients.

They sailed alone with no armament and no support ships accompanying them, protected by decrees passed down from The Hague and the Geneva Convention. Even though the kamikazes violated their protection at Okinawa, they continued to take aboard and treat both Army and Navy casualties that came to them from the fighting fronts.

The Army had a number of smaller hospital ships that performed in a similar manner. All acted with extraordinary courage. And, of course, they all carried ample supplies of plasma and whole blood.

Navy medics staffed all the warships: aircraft carriers, escort carriers, battleships, cruisers, destroyers, and destroyer escorts. Not all ships had a doctor aboard. Some destroyers and destroyer escorts had a warrant pharmacist or a pharmacist's mate first class in charge of sick bay. There were hundreds and hundreds of these ships assembled in the flotilla at Okinawa, but the Navy medics might have been overwhelmed.. The death toll was very high and the casualty list very long, but the medics saved thousands through their dogged determination to do so, their expertise, and the aid of our blood donors

22. THE CHAPLAINS

The chaplains were among the best witnesses for the Blood Donor Service. That's because they worked so closely with the medics and spent so much time with the wounded.

There were over twelve thousand clergymen in uniform as chaplains between 1939 and 1945; 2,934 served in the Navy, ministering to Navy, Marine and Coast Guard. 9,117 wore Army uniforms, following the troops wherever the war took them, including the US Army Air Forces.

They had seen plasma at work; they saw what it could do. That's why they were donors as well as witnesses. They knew.

One Navy chaplain told me that he had more than once been kneeling on one side of a dying sailor, administering Last Rites while a corpsman knelt on the other side administering plasma. He described their elation when the patient opened his eyes and looked up at them with a smile, even if it was a weak one. Neither claimed it was the plasma or the sacrament that brought the man back. They acknowledged the importance of both. When the chaplain came ashore, he became a blood donor. He had watched plasma at work, and he, too, knew.

It was not unusual to see military uniforms in the center. Although a directive from Washington forbade the solicitation of the military, our men in uniform did not need solicitation. They came anyhow because so many of them had seen plasma at the front, and knew what it could do.

There was nothing unusual, therefore, when five naval officers appeared at the center for an afternoon appointment—until a staffer noticed that four of them wore the insignia of the Chaplain Corps on their sleeves. She sent word for me to come immediately because she knew I would be interested in meeting them.

Of the four, two were Protestant ministers; one was a Jewish rabbi and one a Catholic priest. All were from the First Naval District Chaplains Office. All were in Boston following active duty in action somewhere in the world. The senior chaplain was Rabbi Jacob P. Rudin, there after 22 months in the Pacific, including Pearl Harbor, Midway and Canton Island. This was not his first donation but it would be his last. Before he would be eligible for another in two months, he would have reached his sixtieth birthday. Today was a special pint for the chaplain.

Another second-time donor was Lt. (j.g.) Herbert Mueller, Jr., who saw plasma used frequently during his tour of duty at the Chelsea Naval Hospital where both plasma and whole blood were staples.

Lt. Henry J. Beukema carried many pictures of D-Day in his mind. They were difficult to bear, but they would not go away. The ship to which he had been assigned as chaplain was one of the many sunk at the invasion of Normandy. One picture, though, he gladly recalled and described. After he and other survivors of the sinking had been picked up and taken aboard a rescue ship, they listened as an appeal went out over the loudspeakers to all ships around. Some of the ships had an urgent need for plasma. Could any ship that still had a supply send some over to these ships in great need?

Chaplain Beukema described the picture of little boats darting among the big ships on their errands of mercy, delivering lifesaving plasma to the "have-nots" from the "haves." Chaplain Beukema did not have to be told about plasma.

The fourth chaplain in the group was Lt. Cmdr. Henry J. Rotrige, also a repeat donor and one who I had interviewed earlier on a *Life to the Front* broadcast. He had served aboard an escort carrier, the USS Santee (CVE 29), during the Battle of Leyte Gulf.

He said that at one time they had sustained so many casualties on board that they could not handle any more men in sick bay. He was charged with the task of finding a place for the overflow. After rushing throughout the ship, looking for an adequate spot, he finally found one in a bunk room above. From then on, he divided his time between sick bay, the bunk room, and the bridge, which was his battle station.

He gave another example of plasma in action. A TBF Avenger fighter plane was lost over the side returning from a combat mission. This is always an awful moment on a carrier. The pilot was lost, but the gunner and the radioman were able to work themselves free of the wreckage and remain afloat in the water until the destroyer acting as plane guard could come along and pick them up. Both men were badly hurt. Being in the water, even that relatively short time, made matters worse. They were taken to sick bay immediately.

The warrant pharmacist in charge of sick bay felt that the men's serious condition required a doctor. He gave each of the men a unit of plasma and then signaled the escort carrier for the doctor, describing the emergency and what would be needed. The carrier replied, "Doctor on his way." The two ships conducted a personnel transfer by rigging a highline and sending him over on a breeches buoy while the two ships were steaming alongside each other

"We waited anxiously for word of our shipmates," recalled Rotrige. "The first news came when the doctor signaled the carrier to send over more plasma, and that we did. It went over the same way the doctor went over—by breeches buoy."

I was surprised to meet still another chaplain from the Battle of Leyte Gulf, from another escort carrier, USS *St. Lo*. Her chaplain—Lt. Cmdr. Joseph H. Giunta—was on board when she was sunk, but he was rescued by a destroyer escort. I had first heard about the priest from two young naval officers from the ship when we presented them on *Life to the Front* on January 9, 1945. They had been picked up by the same ship that had rescued their chaplain. The destroyer escort carried the division doctor, who went to work on the survivors with a diligence that did not let up. The chaplain was one of his more serious cases because he had been badly wounded and had bled heavily.

The two officers interviewed said that the doctor only occasionally came up to the wardroom for coffee and then went right back down to sick bay to continue his efforts on his casualties. Chaplain Giunta was not doing well, and the doctor worried that he might not make it. On his last trip up to the wardroom, he said he was giving the chaplain more plasma with the hope that it would hold him until they could get him transferred to the hospital ship for surgery that the destroyer could not provide.

The chaplain traveled first to the hospital ship and its specialized care, and then home to recuperate. And finally he stood on the stage of Hovey Auditorium in Waltham, Massachusetts, to speak about the work of the Red Cross Blood Donor Service and the importance of the people at home. He considered himself living proof.

Chaplain Arthur McQuaid also spoke publicly about plasma. He was probably responsible for more pints of blood than anyone. "There is no doubt whatsoever in my mind but that plasma saved my life," he said. This was after he had been critically burned and, in his words, "put ashore on the island of Tulagi to die." Father McQuaid knew personally the importance of plasma. That was why he was willing to spread the word on radio and in person. He was a recipient-witness. He knew.

These chaplains not only helped us at home to get blood to the front, but they helped the medics at the front in getting blood to the wounded. Many a chaplain broke open boxes of plasma on a beach and hung bottles from a tree at a jungle aid station, or from a man's gun jammed into the sand, to assist a medic.

23. D-DAY

D-Day did not need Steven Spielberg to make it spectacular. It was spectacular from the beginning all on its own. From the seed of an idea in a military mind, it blossomed into a full-blown plan on paper for other military minds to pore over and perfect.

Although the final preparations were made in England, with many British military involved, it was an American, Dwight D. Eisenhower, who was in charge. General Eisenhower was not the only one. He had Gen. Omar N. Bradley and Gen. George S. Patton with him. And there were other American, Allied, British, and Canadian officers working diligently until their plan was ready for execution. The departure date was set. They would leave on June 5. But when the day came, the rains came also. Departure was delayed.

All through the night debate raged. Should they wait out the rains if the downpour did not let up? Could they afford to wait? Nature played a part in this plan. They decided to leave on the tide. Any further delay would lose the favorable tide and require waiting days for the next opportunity. Soldiers who wear stars on their shoulders must be prepared to make hard decisions. That was Gen. Eisenhower's burden that night. At 4:00 a.m. he made the call: "We go!"

And they went! Troops, their gear, equipment, and supplies that had been massed in England were standing out of the ports.

In the early morning darkness on June 6, 1944, they crossed the Channel. The English Channel is only twenty-one miles wide at its eastern end where it joins the North Sea near Cherbourg. At its other end 250 miles away, where it joins the Atlantic Ocean, it is two hundred miles wide. Wherever the crossing, the trip was cold and wet and very, very tense for all.

They were destined for beaches along the forty miles of Normandy coast, with the code names Omaha, Juno, Gold, Utah, and Sword. When the landing boats and transports arrived at their assigned beaches, they discharged their passengers to wade the final distance ashore.

At some beaches, the enemy saw them coming. Batteries on the bluff above Omaha Beach were ready to fire on the men as they disembarked. Many never made it to the beach. They were picked off by these guns and dropped in the shallow water through which they had been sloshing ashore. Many drowned in the ever-reddening water, as water lapped over their dead bodies. Some staggered out of the water to fall dead on the sand while other casualties lay waiting for the medics who had traveled with them.

One medical team of five medical corpsmen, a dental officer, and the battalion surgeon landed one hour after H hour. When I interviewed the latter, he told me that "the beach was covered with the bodies of the dead, the dying, and the wounded."

This medical team crawled up and down the beach administering first aid to the casualties, under fire all the time. Capt. Angelo L. Maietta, MC, USA, said he was the only doctor on the beach at the time. He was later awarded the Bronze Star for heroic achievement.

The team moved on, setting up just behind the front lines as the action advanced. "We used plasma for anything and everything. It was a must," said Maietta. "I had my own idea of what was a minimum quantity on hand and I tried never to get below that amount. Fortunately, we had ample stocks in the rear areas where we could send to replenish our dwindling supplies when casualties were heavy. You see, the wounded men had to be in good shape when they arrived in the rear medical area where we sent them for definitive work."

Other medical teams crossed the channel with the troops and were put ashore at intervals along the Normandy coast, ready to work on the wounded wherever they found them. It was obvious where they had been working because of the crushed cartons and empty plasma flasks littering the beach that showed up in pictures sent back by the Army photographers.

D-Day Beachhead

War correspondents who went ashore with the troops on D-Day gave us graphic descriptions of the Normandy beaches. As previously noted, Ernie Pyle's writing was more than popular with the folks at home. They thirsted for his every column. When he wrote about what he saw when he walked the beaches after the action had moved on, he was deeply moved. So were we when we read his words:

Submerged tanks and overturned boats and shell-shattered jeeps and sad little personal belongings were strewn all over those bitter sands. That plus the bodies of soldiers, lying in rows, covered with blankets, the toes of their shoes sticking up in a line as though on drill. And other bodies, uncollected, still sprawling grotesquely in the sand or half hidden in the high grass beyond the beach.

This was not something that people wanted to read but it provided the facts of war—our war, not just theirs over there. Painful as it was, we had to know. It helped ease their hurt when we could tell our people at home that their plasma was there on the beach and all along the road to Berlin. When Gen. Omar Bradley spoke out about the road that he had traveled from Africa on, he gave hope and solace to the folks on the home front with this report:

In the front line medical aid stations, it has been repeatedly shown that the administration of blood plasma has brought casualties out of shock and prepared them for operations which otherwise could not have been performed. Experience in this theater has shown that the use of blood plasma, whole blood and early surgical treatment has saved thousands of lives which otherwise would have been lost.

Those who did not receive plasma because they were killed in action—the lost men of D-Day—were remembered reverently by former comrades who returned for the fiftieth anniversary in 1994 and for the sixtieth in 2004. Those revisiting the scene of the battles stood on the bluff above Omaha Beach, and looked across the rows of white marble grave markers...remembering...and they wept. The sight of those 9,386 headstones in rows across the fields of Colleville-sur-Mer was more than many could bear. Some of the older veterans recalled the verse they memorized in grade school long ago about World War I: "In Flanders fields the poppies blow / Between the crosses, row on row..." And they closed their eyes and shook their heads. As children they had seen only poppies in a field, pretty flowers, not people to be remembered. In 1994 and 2004, they were seeing and understanding very much more and wondering now about the world for which their comrades had died.

Andy Rooney, the self-styled "curmudgeon" of the CBS television program *60 Minutes* and who passed away in 2011, is one of those veterans who returned to Normandy and wept. He had been at D-Day as a private in the Army. Drafted out of college at the end of his junior year at Colgate University, he was assigned to the Army magazine *Stars and Stripes* as a reporter.

In his book *My War*, published in 2005 by Random House, he wrote, "On each visit, I've wept. It's almost impossible to keep back the tears as you look across the rows of crosses and think of the boys under them who died that day."

Andy Rooney's description was this: "Think of taking a drive on a maze of narrow country roads where every farmhouse is an armed fortress, every church steeple a sniper's observation post, where every stone wall conceals infantry with rifles and machine guns, and, where at every curve in a road there may be a tank with an 88 mm gun trained on the curve you're coming around."

One of Rooney's recollections was reminiscent of what Doctor Maietta told me about Christmas Eve 1944 in a makeshift hospital occupying a bombed-out store on the corner of a little street in Arlon, Belgium.

"As many as thirty-five to forty casualties at one time were being treated in that little store while the wind and the snow blew through the papers that were attempting to give shelter where windows should have been. And there were German planes overhead." Then he added, "But we had plenty of plasma, and we used it on the men who were brought in, suffering from concussion, burns, blast wounds, shrapnel wounds, arms and legs torn off."

Plasma was a Christmas present for many that year. The box it came in may not have been wrapped in colorful paper and red ribbon, but there was life inside it for some.

As for the ships that were there in June 1944, we did not know then how many or which they were. Today we find an abundance of statistics to tell that there were four hundred warships and four thousand other vessels. In our work during the war, this lack of ship specifics did not matter. Our donors were well informed that plasma from their blood was in sick bays aboard all warships everywhere and, of course, aboard all of our hospital ships. It was a help, however, for prospective donors to hear reports of interviews with shipboard recipients of plasma following an enemy hit.

One Sailor, John Bunk, was at his battle station aboard the cruiser USS *Boise* when he was hit by a 25-cal. machine gun bullet from a plane. It went in the left side of his neck, just missing the jugular vein, and came out the right side. "It felt like a cigarette burn," he said. "I reached up to flick it off and that's the last thing I remember until I woke up in sickbay two days later." Bunk received two units of plasma at the start. "Without that," he said, "I'm not sure that there would have been a chance for further treatment which I required."

Bunk was not the only recipient-survivor aboard the *Boise* or the other ships that were hit.

One interesting report came from a survivor of a ship sunk at Normandy. Lt. Henry J. Beukema, ChC, USNR, who we met in the last chapter, was the chaplain aboard his ship. When he and his surviving shipmates had been taken aboard the rescue ship, dried off, and checked by the medics, they stood on the deck after the action had moved on. They watched and listened as calls went out over the PA systems of some of the ships. It wasn't "Brother, can you spare a dime?" It was "Captain, can you spare a pint?" There had been so many casualties aboard the ships broadcasting the appeals that they had used up their supply of plasma and needed still more. "It was quite a sight," the chaplain said, "to see the little boats darting among the big ships of the fleet on their errands of mercy, answering the appeals. We watched in a sort of awe after what we all had just been through without major injury."

Many of the ships that crossed the channel on June 6 provided cover for the landings with the destroyers closest to shore, the cruisers next with guns that had a longer range, and the battleships last because their armament could outdistance the rest.

Paratroops from the 82nd and 101st Airborne Divisions were flown in and dropped behind the beachhead lines. These men who dropped out of the sky were not without plasma; it came with them. It was expected that it would be needed and that it should be ready for action with the men flying in.

When the generals led their forces across the Channel, folks at home were unaware of the magnitude of this particular war effort. Today we take instant information for granted. In June 1944, the public was grateful for whatever news they could get. They congregated in large crowds on the sidewalk outside a window that posted a bulletin board with the latest news. Dispatches were taken from the news ticker in the Investment Department on a top floor of the New England Mutual Life Insurance Company's home office.

Then an enlarged copy was made in the Purchasing Department on another floor. Finally the bulletin board made it down to the street floor and into the sidewalk window where it was kept up to date on an hourly basis. This is how the crowd followed the progress of the invasion.

If the people at home had not learned early on June 6 of the enormity of D-Day, they became aware of it when President Franklin Delano Roosevelt asked them to pray with him that night. Many were grateful for the opportunity that seemed to bring them closer to their loved ones at Normandy.

Franklin Roosevelt's D-Day Prayer

June 6, 1944

My fellow Americans: Last night, when I spoke with you about the fall of Rome, I knew at that moment that troops of the United States and our allies were crossing the Channel in another and greater operation. It has come to pass with success thus far.

And so, in this poignant hour, I ask you to join with me in prayer:

Almighty God: Our sons, pride of our Nation, this day have set upon a mighty endeavor, a struggle to preserve our Republic, our religion, and our civilization, and to set free a suffering humanity.

Lead them straight and true; give strength to their arms, stoutness to their hearts, steadfastness in their faith.

They will need Thy blessings. Their road will be long and hard. For the enemy is strong. He may hurl back our forces. Success may not come with rushing speed, but we shall return again and again; and we know that by Thy grace, and by the righteousness of our cause, our sons will triumph.

They will be sore tried, by night and by day, without rest—until the victory is won. The darkness will be rent by noise and flame. Men's souls will be shaken with the violences of war.

They will be sore tried, by night and by day, without rest—until the victory is won. The darkness will be rent by noise and flame. Men's souls will be shaken with the violences of war.

For these men are lately drawn from the ways of peace. They fight not for the lust of conquest. They fight to end conquest. They fight to liberate. They fight to let justice arise, and tolerance and good will among all Thy people. They yearn but for the end of battle, for their return to the haven of home.

Some will never return. Embrace these, Father, and receive them, Thy heroic servants, into Thy kingdom.

And for us at home—fathers, mothers, children, wives, sisters, and brothers of brave men overseas—whose thoughts and prayers are ever with them—help us, Almighty God, to rededicate ourselves in renewed faith in Thee in this hour of great sacrifice.

Many people have urged that I call the Nation into a single day of special prayer. But because the road is long and the desire is great, I ask that our people devote themselves in a continuance of prayer. As we rise to each new day, and again when each da y is spent, let words of prayer be on our lips, invoking Thy help to our efforts.

Give us strength, too—strength in our daily tasks, to redouble the contributions we make in the physical and the material support of our armed forces.

And let our hearts be stout, to wait out the long travail, to bear sorrows that may come, to impart our courage unto our sons wheresoever they may be.

And, O Lord, give us Faith. Give us Faith in Thee; Faith in our sons; Faith in each other; Faith in our united crusade. Let not the keenness of our spirit ever be dulled. Let not the impacts of temporary events, of temporal matters of but fleeting moment—let not these deter us in our unconquerable purpose.

With Thy blessing, we shall prevail over the unholy forces of our enemy. Help us to conquer the apostles of greed and racial arrogancies. Lead us to the saving of our country, and with our sister Nations into a world unity that will spell a sure peace—a peace invulnerable to the schemings of unworthy men. And a peace that will let all of men live in freedom, reaping the just rewards of their honest toil.

Thy will be done, Almighty God.

Amen.

24. A ROUND TRIP: BOSTON TO BOSTON

In addition to plasma, there was also plenty of whole blood for victims of D-Day, pints and pints of it. It was flown from Boston and other East Coast centers to the ETO (European Theater of Operations) Distribution Center and then wherever needed. One of these pints made a round trip—Boston to Boston.

One day a young soldier came to the center to give blood as a payback. Of course he was assured that there was no such thing as a payback for anyone returning from the front. We at home were in his debt, not the other way around. Besides, he was on convalescent leave, not long enough out of the hospital. Pvt. Richard Harvey was disappointed, but he had further business with us. He pulled a little tag out of his pocket, wondering if we might be interested in it. He explained that he had taken it off a bottle of blood that he was being given in a hospital in England. It said "Boston Center" on it.

Interested? We were excited! We wasted no time in tracing the serial number on the tag. We had not far to look. The donor, Mrs. Audrey Woodward, twenty-three, worked around the corner from the center as a secretary in the accounting department of Holtzer Cabot, a company that sent us many donors. I went over to their offices to tell her.

To have a donor meet a recipient of her blood was a first for us and an only! We brought the two together at the center for a private meeting, and then we decided to do a broadcast featuring this very special story.

We were fortunate to have the Hollywood and Broadway

The Donor meets the recipient. Mrs. Audrey Woodward, Richard Harvey with Joseph Hamlin, the chairman of the Metropolitain Boston Chapter of the the Red Cross.

actor, Eddie Nugent, serve as narrator. Mr. Nugent was not only himself a repeat donor, but he always helped us out in broadcasts or other programs when he was playing in Boston. This time he was starring in *The Star Spangled Widow* at the Plymouth Theatre. He was as excited as we were about the story. So was the large studio audience of Holtzer Cabot associates of the donor and Somerville neighbors of the recipient who lived there with his parents, S.Sgt. and Mrs. C. A. Harvey.

Mr. Nugent began the story in early 1943 when Audrey Woodward was in Arkansas getting ready to come to Boston to be near her Navy ensign husband who was stationed aboard a destroyer in the Atlantic. Pvt. Richard Harvey was in Africa where his unit was involved in a major assault against the enemy in North Africa.

During the action, Harvey was injured. It happened as he climbed a hill and was blown off a ledge by an enemy shell. He dropped fifteen feet to the ledge below with fifty pounds of ammunition strapped to his back. Knocked out momentarily, he came to and found that he could stand and walk, although painfully. He decided he could do without medical attention since the battalion was moving on.

Soon they were in the far northern section of Tunis, aptly called the "coffin corner" of the African campaign. The success of the whole campaign hinged on the ability to break through around Mateur. To the north lay Bizerte, southward was the city of Tunis, and straight ahead was Hill 609. The fighting was bitter because Hill 609 was a key position—and the Nazis knew it. On Easter Sunday, April 25, the hill was taken and the Yanks dug in against the counterattacks they knew would be coming. And come they did.

As the enemy regained ground, the Americans' telephone wires became inoperable. They had to be fixed. Harvey raced down the hill from the observation post, through the rain of steel the enemy pointed at Hill 609. He set a new record for himself as he found the break and twisted the shattered ends of the telephone wires together. With a prayer that there were no other breaks, he raced back up the hill to the comparative shelter of the observation post. Now the rest of the outfit was safe. They were no longer shut off. They could be warned of what was about to happen and be ready.

The German counterattack failed, and within a week the Allies took Bizerte and Tunis. The end of the African campaign was in sight. Although Harvey disclaimed any act of heroism, he was recommended for a Silver Star for his work that day on Hill 609.

After Africa came Sicily, and Harvey's division was there. But in the middle of May, the old injury he had sustained so far back on that mountainous ledge caught up with him. Internal injuries do not always show up like external flesh wounds or broken bones. Harvey was in bad shape. He was flown back to a hospital in Africa and operated on. The surgery was clean, neat, and successful...and timely. The required weeks of recuperation were a pleasant interlude in a warring world. It was while he was in the hospital that he was presented with his Silver Star medal for heroism on Hill 609.

"But for every proud and happy moment in a soldier's life, like that one for Harvey," said Mr. Nugent, "there are bitter hours of hardship when he wonders if he will ever again know peace and quiet...peace...that nebulous quality of life and happiness for which men are fighting and dying the whole world over today. In France last summer, there was more than one man who wondered if the awful discord of war would ever cease...the roar of our own guns searching out the enemy...the scream and the blast of the enemy's shells looking for our positions...the endless thunder of planes shuttling overhead, on their missions deep into the enemy's rear."

Eddie Nugent was talking about France in August 1944. Our Private Harvey had rejoined his outfit. Harvey had been with them since June 6 when they went into Normandy at famous Omaha Beach to storm Fortress Europe. Foot by foot at first, and then mile by mile, the division chased a foe that still fought bitterly back. The pace was killing and for Pvt. Richard Harvey it became one of increasing torture as the old injury erupted. At last, in August, it was more than flesh could stand. He was taken out of action and left the war behind.

There followed the evacuation journey to England. He was placed on a flight from that same Omaha Beach, now a bustling port of entry and departure, to a hospital in England. It only took two days from the front lines to that hospital. On such wings does mercy fly.

In September, Richard Harvey lay on the surgeon's table again. This time infection had set in. The incision had to be reopened. Sulfa and penicillin were given in quantity, but first the doctor administered plasma. Then whole blood was required in the delicate postoperative treatment. It was while lying in bed with his arm stretched out to the side, receiving that draught of life, that he noticed the tag hanging from the bottle. With his free arm, he had just enough strength to reach up and tug it off.

At this point, narrator Nugent announced that Private Harvey was in the studio, and he invited him to come to the microphone to help finish the story. Pvt. First Class Richard J. Harvey, U.S. Army, acknowledged Mr. Nugent's introduction and said, "Here's the tag. I pulled it off the bottle when the nurse wasn't looking. I hoped to get home some day and I might show it to them at the Boston Center because that's where it said it came from."

"You didn't yet know who had given the blood?" asked Mr. Nugent.

"No, sir, she was just a serial number."

Mr. Nugent then suggested that the private bring the "serial number" up to the microphone, and Mrs. Audrey Woodward was introduced to the radio and studio audiences.

"Mrs. Woodward, it must be a tremendous thrill for you to stand beside the man who received your pint of blood after taking part in D-Day," commented Mr. Nugent.

"It is," said Woodward. "When they told me, I cried. It was just too much." This special pint of blood was Audrey Woodward's sixth donation, and she was about to become a member of the Gallon Club. "Giving blood makes me feel as though I'm doing something for my husband, but I never expected to learn from the recipient how important it was to him."

"It certainly has to be a great experience for you," said our narrator.

"How do you think I feel?" asked the recipient with a broad smile.

The narrator had a sobering thought. "Those of us who have never come close to losing our lives have little real appreciation, I guess, of what you men must feel to be home and walking around just as though death had never been near you over there."

Private Harvey's response: "There are thousands of men in this war who can honestly feel that their being alive is mighty close to miraculous. When you've been in and out of those hospitals over there and seen the wounded, you can't believe that some of them could ever live."

25. V-E DAY

In a small city in western Massachusetts, a young couple chose May 8, 1945, for their wedding. They didn't have much of a choice, because the groom was a soldier coming home for the first time in three years after serving in Iceland, England, and Germany. Soon he must go back.

The Army planned to commission him as an officer and award him the Purple Heart just before leaving Germany, but he would have to wait three days for the ceremony to take place. After three years, three days were too many, so he left as a happy sergeant without his new ribbon and rank. His bride was a school teacher, home from her job. It was to be a great day for both of them and their families. They just didn't realize how great.

On that special morning, as the bride walked down the church aisle on her father's arm following her bridesmaids and ushers, she heard bells ringing. "For my wedding?" she wondered. "Church bells for me? Can that be?"

As the wedding party came to the altar and the bride still listened to her bells, word spread throughout the congregation—bells were ringing all over town—the war was over in Europe! Germany had surrendered...Hitler was dead! Wedding guests clutched each other's hands and cried...so many of them had family and friends "over there." The groom had three brothers still in Germany.

Before the bride and groom had time to plight their troth, strangers burst into the church, weeping and shaking as they answered the call of the church bells to come give their prayerful thanks. With much distraction, because now everyone knew the good news, the wedding ceremony continued.

Once the last blessing was bestowed and the organ struck up the recessional, the bridal party moved down the aisle only to have to work their way through the crowd to get out of the church and to their cars. Traffic was stalled. Horns honked, church bells still rang, people shouted and ran around the streets. V-E Day was not going unnoticed.

When the wedding party and guests finally moved on to the reception, the bride and groom realized that this was not only their special day; it belonged to all the people in town, indeed all over the world. It would never be just plain May 8; it would always be V-E Day. Celebrations broke out everywhere with nonstop commentaries on radio and headlines in the newspapers. There were quotes from the noted and unsolicited speeches from overjoyed celebrants. Ernest Hemingway told how he led some troops into Paris because he knew the way and they didn't. All the Allied forces in Europe—land, sea, and air—were exuberant. Victory in Europe was theirs, and it had been hard won.

If their exuberance was not total, it was because they knew that some of them would be off to the Pacific soon. World War II was not yet over; the Pacific would now be the new "over there."

Andy Rooney wrote great meaning into his account of V-E Day in *My War*: "There was unrestrained joy—jubilation—in Times Square that all America felt that night, but the reaction of the people of Paris to their liberation had a depth and a poignancy to it that Americans who had never been subjected to a foreign conqueror could not possibly have felt."

The excitement in that small city in the Berkshires in New England—and that in Paris and New York City—was matched by a more subdued observance at the Boston Blood Donor Center. Many donors and workers had loved ones in Europe and an enormous weight lifted from their hearts with this great news.

Time for Life was a weekly broadcast, started when Jack Maloy moved from WEEI to become program director at WCOP, the newly established ABC outlet in Boston, with studios in the Copley Plaza Hotel. Maloy had worked with *Life to the Front* at WEEI and saw its value, and he wanted to do a show on WCOP that would also promote the blood donor program. *Time for Life* featured interviews with various donors at the center. The program on May 8, however, featured some of our volunteer workers whose husbands were Boston-based doctors now serving in uniform in Europe.

Mrs. William V. McDermott Jr. was one of them. Her husband, formerly of the Massachusetts General Hospital, was a captain in the Army Medical Corps at a field hospital in Germany. He knew of his wife's work at the center and wanted her to understand the importance of plasma in his work at the front. According to the information he sent home to her, most of the boys could not get through an operation without plasma.

"I remember one special case of which he wrote," she said. "The man had been very badly wounded and required an immediate operation. He was pulseless, and, of course, they would not operate under such circumstances. The patient took seven units of plasma before the doctors felt that he was in a condition that warranted their attempting surgery."

Another of our volunteers interviewed on this broadcast was the wife of Army Medical Corps Maj. Lamar Souter, head of a mobile surgery in Germany. He wrote her about a special mission requiring fifty volunteers. Their superiors told them they had a fifty-fifty chance of getting through to Bastogne. They were flown in by glider in broad daylight with a fighter escort. When they arrived, they found the casualties so numerous that Doctor Souter said he could think of no description that better suited this sight than that of the Atlanta railroad station in the movie *Gone with the Wind*. According to his report, this mobile surgery unit worked for seventy-two hours without stopping. They used quantities of plasma and whole blood. Then they were flown out. Major Souter was awarded the Silver Star for this mission.

Another of the many missions for this mobile surgery took them into a schoolhouse. A kitchen table was dragged into a classroom and set up on the teacher's platform to serve as the operating table. The last lesson was still on the blackboard.

Mrs. Souter explained that these mobile surgeries did chiefly major surgery, which necessitated the use of quantities of plasma and whole blood. "It was just taken for granted," she said.

It was important that these doctors expect that plasma and whole blood would be there for them as they needed it. It was equally important that we at the Blood Donor Center took nothing for granted as we worked to give the Army and Navy what they needed for these doctors laboring under these extraordinary circumstances to save lives.

We heard about such circumstances from Maj. Gen. Paul R. Hawley, chief surgeon of the ETO, when he said, "Plasma was so vital to the badly wounded that it was even fired in shells to units cut off by the Germans." He further stated that battle experience has proved that innumerable men would have died without plasma and blood transfusions.

As people celebrated V-E Day, many wondered if the end of the war in Europe would make a difference in our need for their donations. On May 9, Mr. Joseph R. Hamlen, chairman of the Boston Metropolitan Chapter of the American Red Cross, made the following announcement on *Life to the Front*:

"For all who have wondered what would happen to Boston's Red Cross Blood Donor Center after V-E Day, I have a significant announcement from Basil O'Connor, National Red Cross chairman. Our Boston Center, which has rated third in the country in requirements and fulfillments, is one of eleven centers to remain open to meet revised requirements of the Army and Navy.

"In Boston, we go on...with a grave responsibility. Air shipments of whole blood will continue to Europe as long as needed for our men wounded prior to the cessation of hostilities. Arrangements are being completed for us to join the whole blood service to the Pacific via naval air transport to Guam.

"Now, more than ever, the Boston Center needs support. We are confident that the good people of this area will carry on as in the past and assure the medical services of the Army and Navy of all the blood they need for our casualties."

On Monday night, May 21, our first shipment of type O donations was rushed by refrigerated truck to a central testing and packing laboratory in New York. From there, it was loaded aboard planes of the Naval Air Transport Service and flown to Guam, the Pacific's Blood Distribution Center. At Guam, based upon requests and requirements, it was forwarded to Army evacuation, Marine field, or Navy base hospitals, or placed aboard ships of the amphibious forces. This new program went into effect as soon as military authorities cabled from Europe that whole blood shipments from the United States were no longer needed over there.

More than two hundred thousand pints of whole blood had been flown to the European Theater of Operations by the Army Transport Command since the whole blood program was inaugurated in 1944. The continuing need for whole blood in the European hospitals would be met by service personnel.

If our shipments of whole blood to the Pacific had gone out only once, it would have been newsworthy and considered a remarkable undertaking. But these shipments would go on night after night, week after week. They became routine. We urged people not to lose sight of the fact that it was still a spectacular achievement that blood be flown from the East Coast of the country to Guam and on to other installations still farther away.

From the vantage point of victory, it is easy to forget the trauma of defeat and the pain and struggle on that long road to Berlin. To remind us, we were made aware of a letter sent by an officer on duty in France that gave us a picture of his hospital there...the shock tent...the pharmacy tent...TENTS!

The shock tent is where the more serious cases go who have to be built up into a state of life again before going to surgery. It looks, under the glare of electric bulbs, of a plumber's idea of a chemist's lab. Every stretcher seems to have a glass jar above it with tubes going down into the arm of a muddy, apparently dying, soldier. Blood and plasma are poured into these men's veins. The way they respond reminds one of the story of Lazarus. It is unbelievable, not only the way it brings men back, but also the expense and organization of getting it to the men. The blood must be flown in refrigerated planes from America. It now, I believe, lands directly in France, then down her roads in refrigerated trucks and kept in electric refrigerators (which you can't buy) in our Pharmacy Tent and comes to the soldier with the original chill still on it. It seems as though all the Army did was to organize a huge Borden's Milk Delivery Service on a gigantic scale by land, air, and sea. Trucks deliver as many pints as you estimate your hospital needs almost daily, wherever you are. We've been bounding over France like a jack rabbit and only once did the blood delivery service lose us on the back lanes."

These hospitals were not mobile hospitals, but they often had to move. Ernie Pyle likened them to a circus, the way they could knock down and set up.

A firsthand description of a casualty brought in to one of these hospitals came from a war correspondent attached to the American armed forces on the battlefront in France. His name was Austen Lake, and before he went overseas, he had shown a great interest in blood plasma and the importance of blood donors. One day he had devoted his entire column to a letter from a naval officer who wrote about the great value of plasma at the front and, therefore, the importance of blood donors at home. Mr. Lake introduced the letter as "a document that requires no floral introduction. It comes from the heart and speaks the universal language of all war-minded Americans." The letter was signed by Lt. j.g. H. W. Lundquist, USNR.

After his longtime interest in the Blood Donor Service, Austen Lake must have been inspired to see plasma in action in France. He wrote a column for the September 20, 1944, *Record American* in Boston:

> *The two litter bearers carried their blanketed burden through the woods and laid it on the grassy floor of the hospital. The lead bearer stripped the covering back from the soldier's face that looked as though carved from marble. The ridges of his nose and his closed eyelids were a violet hue as though smudged with carbon paper. 'Pretty fah gone, ah guess,' said the bearer in a soft southern burr, feeling the wounded man's wrist. 'But he's still gotta li'l pulse.'*
>
> *The Staff Sergeant needed no diagnosis. His months in France had made him an expert in transfusions. Deftly he prepared the plasma...and watched the wounded man's thirsty veins suck eagerly of the lifesaving essence, causing the bubbles to dance in the glass container as the bead dropped steadily to zero. Another bottle and still another while the faint rose tints returned to the soldier's cheeks and the blue smudges on his nose and eyelids faded. His marble pallor had quite gone now and there were answering tremors at the corners of his mouth as the surgeon removed the tourniquet above an ugly, shapeless hole in his thigh and applied an antiseptic solution. 'He'll do,' said the surgeon quietly.*

It would be nearly eight months before V-E Day, but there would be thousands and thousands of casualties, like this man, who would be around for the celebration of victory. As the church bells rang out from coast to coast in the United States, the families of these survivors rejoiced while those whose loved ones were lost found the day very painful. Of course, they were glad for the world and for the survivors, but their own hurt deepened. Such is the raw edge of all victory in war.

Ports of embarkation through which men went off to war were now ports through which men returned. Many had been casualties of battle action but survived because of prompt, dedicated, skillful medical care at the front and the generosity of the people at home who were Red Cross blood donors. The statement of another general, who like so many of our soldiers started out in Africa and was responsible for much of the success on the road to Berlin, was most significant for these donors.

Gen. George S. Patton, Jr., commanding general of the U.S. Third Army, wrote, "In the fighting in Germany just concluded, the death rate of casualties in the United States Army has been the lowest in all military history. While this situation was the result of many factors, it is safe to say that outstanding among them was the ample and steady flow of whole blood and plasma provided by the blood donors in the United States."

PART VI
BACK TO THE PACIFIC

26. THE ISLANDS AND THE SEAS AROUND THEM

Oahu

World War II began and ended on an island in the Pacific. In between, there were major battles on a variety of other islands, some of which President Roosevelt mentioned in his address to the nation on December 8. He didn't group them together, but listed them separately, one after the other: Malaya, Hong Kong, Guam, the Philippines, Wake, and Midway. The geographic location of these islands, attacked within hours of Pearl Harbor, made the intent of the enemy's attacks quite evident. The president's mention of them impressed upon the American people the enormity of the task ahead. The United States would not only have to pick up the shattered pieces of Pearl Harbor, but it would have to retrieve these islands also.

But before the president even scheduled his speech, the military had instituted emergency measures that were underway at Pearl Harbor. All medical personnel had been called to duty on the island. Most did not need a summons; they were on their way already. Their initial attention focused on the dead and the dying—to determine which was which. But first, they had to find them; so many were buried under the rubble left by the Japanese bombs.

Destruction was everywhere. As the smoke cleared, twenty American ships were sunk or damaged, 328 American aircraft were destroyed or damaged, 2,403 Americans were killed, and another 1,178 were wounded.

This is where the Seabees took over, although they weren't the "Seabees" yet. The United States Naval Construction Force began sifting the debris for survivors. Shortly after December 7, they became the Seabees with the motto, "With compassion for others, we build, we fight for peace with freedom."

The chaplains were stretched thin. They blessed the dead and ministered to the dying—and to the next of kin of all. They assisted with funeral arrangements, conducted services, and presided at the burials of the dead.

The remains of some were sent back to the States, where families could have a loved one buried nearby and visit the grave. (Many of the remains would later be interred at the National Memorial Cemetery of the Pacific in Honolulu, known as the Punchbowl.)

Special attention had to be paid to the men entombed in ships that were sunk on December 7, like the USS *Arizona*. Nearly half of the American fatalities on that day were on the *Arizona* (only 333 survived). Chaplains were indeed stretched thin. And they, themselves, were hurting terribly like so many others: physically, psychologically, and spiritually. The disaster of Pearl Harbor was a multifaceted tragedy.

Anxious military leaders hurried to get together and discuss what was to happen next. There were those who believed that the United States should immediately mount a major assault against Japan. Others were convinced that we should move island by island. The latter view prevailed, and the long and tedious trek across the Pacific began as soon as the commander-in-chief approved.

The Geography Lesson

This marked the beginning of a unique geography lesson for the American people. They were faced with islands that they had never heard of before, could not spell, nor pronounce, nor even find on a map—unless you would count a pinpoint in the middle of the ocean. Instead of giving up, many people learned to look for chains. Each chain—the Solomons, Marshalls, Gilberts, Russells, Marianas, New Hebrides, and Philippines—had its individual islands.

An early lesson came on December 7 when some people were surprised to learn that Pearl Harbor and Honolulu were on the island of Oahu, and that the island called Hawaii was actually "the big island," nearly two hundred miles away. The Navy had acquired Pearl Harbor in 1887, a year before annexation, and eventually established a naval station there, with the first vessel arriving in 1903. Then there was Kauai, Maui, Lanai, and Molokai, where Father Damian once devoted his life to the leper colony there. On the little privately owned island of Niihau, the native Hawaiian language was still spoken. And many were surprised to learn that the Hawaiian archipelago stretched 1,600 miles from end to end, and that Midway was one of the Hawaiian Islands.

After the attack on Pearl Harbor, the Japanese left. When they attacked the Philippines at the same time, they occupied the country, and war continued to be waged there. So, people had a lot to learn. If some thought of the Philippines as one big island with Manila as its capital, they were amazed to learn that there are more than seven thousand islands in the Philippine archipelago. Americans would become familiar with the island of Luzon, with Manila, the Bataan Peninsula, and Corregidor—a small island at the tip end of Bataan and the scene of one of the blackest horrors of World War II.

We came to know Leyte mostly through the Battle of Leyte Gulf, said by some historians to be one of the biggest and most dramatic naval battles of this or any war. There were other battles, including some that may be less well known today, but are nevertheless militarily significant.

When the United States started its island-by-island move across the Pacific to Japan, all branches of the armed forces were called to service. Gen. Douglas MacArthur led the Army to the Philippines. Adm. Chester Nimitz moved the Navy toward Wake and Midway.

Wake, Midway, the Coral Sea, and the Philippines

The early weeks of 1942 were not easy. The Navy did not taste victory at sea until spring and then it came with a bitter edge. Wake had been lost (and would not be recovered until 1945), and Midway was attacked. The Battle of the Coral Sea was a strategic victory, but the *Lexington* was lost. The carrier participated in the first sea battle in which the combatants had fought without ever seeing each other.

The loss of any ship at sea is a disaster but the sinking of a carrier is a colossal disaster. It's difficult to envision how it could happen, given the size of a carrier and her built-in protections. If anyone tells you a carrier is the size of a couple of football fields, believe him. It is no exaggeration. A carrier may seem invulnerable, but no ship that goes in harm's way in wartime is invincible.

I talked with many survivors of sinking ships, but it is difficult to imagine the scene with an 888-foot, 48,000 ton carrier with its crew of nearly three thousand men. Nor can one fully appreciate the enormity of the task for the rescue ships—216 *Lexington* crewmen were killed, but 2,735 were rescued.

Lexington abandons ship

Despite the loss of the *Lexington*, Americans did rejoice in their victory at Coral Sea on May 5, 1942. However, that day also brought more tragedy, with the fall of the island of Corregidor in the Philippines. This began the death march for our American prisoners from Bataan north to prisoner-of-war camps. Many of these marchers died of deprivation and torture. Those who survived did so in misery, with a sense of abandonment. On the home front, their families were resentful when they heard that General MacArthur and his family had been evacuated. However, the public did not know that orders had gone out to transport MacArthur by Navy PT boat to the southern Philippine island of Mindanao, where he and his family were flown on a B-17 to Australia. It was a case of orders, not choice.

One month later, the pivotal sea battle of Midway was fought. We lost another carrier, but the Japanese carrier striking force was destroyed, Midway was saved, and the imminent threat to Hawaii was averted. The Battle of Midway, seen today as the Navy's greatest combat achievement at sea, turned the tide in the Pacific forever. But we were a long way from victory over Japan.

The Solomons

The war moved on. The Solomons lay ahead with their many islands. Troops had to be put ashore; the Navy had to get them there and cover their landings.

The island of Tulagi was one of the first to be secured. It was small and took less time than other islands nearby, but it was important because the United States was able to establish an evacuation hospital there. It also provided a safe harbor to which Captain Rosendahl could take his heavily damaged cruiser *Minneapolis* after the Battle of Tassafaronga. Here they were able to make adequate voyage repairs that enabled them to reach Pearl Harbor where the ship could be made more seaworthy for the journey back to the naval shipyard at Mare Island, California.

These battles brought much tragedy for the Navy. One of the worst was the Battle of Savo Island where four fine ships went down under enemy fire: *Astoria, Quincy, Vincennes,* and Australia's *Canberra.* There were other losses in this battle and on the island itself.

The battle of Kula Gulf took place in July 1943, a year after Savo Island. Later that year, a naval officer came back to Boston on well-deserved leave. He was Lt. Colton G. "Chick" Morris, a familiar name and voice to New England radio listeners. Before his sea duty assignment, he had worked at PRO, so it was natural that he would pay a visit to his former colleagues. Lt. Arch Macdonald, with whom he had worked at WBZ, the NBC radio outlet in Boston at the time, conducted an interview with Morris at the PRO radio office that was later broadcast on WBZ. I was invited to join them at the PRO radio office because Chick Morris had been my announcer on an evening program that I did on WBZ before the war. I transcribed an interview with him for use in a future broadcast of *Life to the Front*, when he would be back on active duty. We told the story of the sinking of the cruiser USS *Helena*, where he was the radio officer. We had no idea then that it would be broadcast to mark the end of World War II.

As I always did when I met anyone back from the Pacific, I asked Chick if he had ever seen the USS *Strong* out there. The reader may recall that in 1942, a busload of *Strong* crew members had come to the center as a group to give blood, making an impression on me that I never forgot.

"Seen them?" he said. "We operated with them!"

He explained how they operated with several destroyers that New Englanders built in the Bath Iron Works shipyard in Bath, Maine, part of Destroyer Division 41 in Destroyer Squadron 21. Along with *Strong* were the other ships of the division, *Chevalier*, *Nicholas*, and *O'Bannon*. His ship, the *Helena*, was one of the cruisers that made up the task force.

When he came to the sad facts of the story he told me, "*Strong* distinguished herself in the July battle of Kula Gulf." When he described what happened on July 4, and the rescue operations, I thought of my busload of donors and hoped that the rescue ship had plenty of plasma.

Strong was hit by a "Long Lance" torpedo, and then pounded by Japanese shore batteries on nearby New Georgia Island while *O'Bannon* returned fire. *Chevalier* rescued survivors before *Strong* sank. Many survivors walked to safety over nets thrown from one ship to the other; others had to be carried.

During the rescue operation, the enemy was sighted. "Rescue was cut off immediately and *Chevalier* was ordered to meet the enemy," he said.

Kula Gulf was the scene of much action in July 1943, and he told me that the men of the *Strong* were a special lot. After they lost their ship, they petitioned the Navy to build a new *Strong* and assign the same crew to it.

"The Twenty-first Squadron, under the command of Captain F. X. MacInerney, was tops!" exclaimed the lieutenant.

Bougainville

Many people probably thought the island of Bougainville was named for the colorful flowers on the shrub *Bougainvillea*. In fact, both the plant and the island were named for the French explorer M. Louis Antoine de Bougainville, who named the island for himself in 1768 while circumnavigating the globe.

De Bougainville was not the first explorer to reach the mountainous 3,500-square-mile volcanic island. Portuguese navigator Pedro de Queiros had visited in 1606; Britain's James Cook—whom we remember for his travels in the Sandwich Islands—landed there in 1774. World War II not only gave us a geography lesson in the Pacific, it gave us a little history, too.

I learned from aviators who flew missions from Guadalcanal over Bougainville and Munda that there was great interest in these islands.

Ground forces were at Bougainville, too. Army S.Sgt. Bob McKay flew for four days to get home to Watertown, Massachusetts, for a brief furlough, after serving three years in the Solomons.

If anyone was inclined to still think about Bougainville as just pretty flowers, Bob McKay changed that image. You don't have wounded lined up on the ground waiting for hospital care unless there's been heavy battle action.

"I frequently saw men lying outside the hospital where the aid men had brought them off the ambulance from the front lines. There'd be quite a few of them, and they'd lay them right down there to wait their turn to be taken in and treated. Many of them would get plasma to keep them alive until they could be taken care of. They don't waste much time, you know," McKay said.

Another veteran of Bougainville, Marine Cpl. James Eaton, had served four years in the corps and was a Silver Star and Purple Heart recipient. I learned that he had survived battles on Munda as well as Bougainville. He received plasma on both islands. When he was hit by a Japanese slug, he was treated at the beach hospital on Bougainville. He described the hospital to me as "...consisting of three tents of patients and two tents for supplies, most of which were buried in the sand as a protection from bombs."

He continued, "There were steel stands from which plasma bottles hung. It was standard stuff out there. They were all over the place with bottles dangling from them."

As we discussed the home front, Corporal Eaton said, "It's pretty hard for us who've been out there to believe that people at home have to be sold on the stuff. The way they use plasma...well...all that anyone who hasn't given blood should need is to stick his head in a hospital tent on the beach at Bougainville. He'd give a gallon! I'd guarantee that."

Eaton's enthusiasm for plasma came from what he had seen out there; his gratitude came from receiving it and being a survivor.

The Marines who fought on the island did not visualize Bougainville in the botanical sense. They thought mud, not flowers. When Marines were transported ashore for battle, they knew they might have to disembark before reaching the beach. They hoped there wouldn't be too many yards to wade through the surf—exposed to the enemy—to reach the beachhead, but they took what came. They never expected to have to continue wading even after reaching high ground, as they had to do on Bougainville. They wallowed knee-deep in muck. Sometimes it was waist-deep. They had to eat and sleep and care for their weapons in this unfriendly condition. When rain began to pour down on them, the mud got thicker and deeper.

The medics had to care for the wounded under these terrible conditions and get patients ready to be moved to safety and better-equipped medical care. But the navy corpsmen were grateful for plasma. It was easy to handle and administer, and it held their patients until they could be moved on.

Although it was a small island—like so many others in the South Pacific—Bougainville was far from insignificant. The Japanese considered it very important. One of their top admirals warned, "Japan will topple if Bougainville falls."

Japanese Adm. Matsuji Ijuin had much cause for concern when he and his ships became embroiled with the American fleet on the nights of November 1 and 2 in what the Japanese called the Sea Battle of Bougainville and the Allies called the Battle of Empress Augusta Bay. Rear Adm. Aaron S. "Tip" Merrill was in command of Task Force 39 aboard the cruiser *Montpelier*, with Capt. Arleigh Burke riding his DesRon 23 flagship *Charles Ausburne* (DD 570). Captain Burke concurrently commanded DesRon 23—known as the "Little Beavers"—and one of its two divisions, DesDiv 45.

The Americans won a major victory in the Battle of Empress Augusta Bay, with Burke's "Little Beavers" dealing a heavy blow to the Japanese.

Yap

There could be no problem in pronunciation or spelling with the island Yap, but some people still could not find it on a map. It was small—38.7 square miles—one of the atolls and diminutive islands that make up the Caroline Islands. It did not have the prominence of Guadalcanal or Iwo Jima, but it had its own special significance. Ask any man who fought there, at sea, on land, or in the skies above.

In countless interviews and reports from various war fronts, most have described plasma in the jungle, in a foxhole, on the beach, in big tent hospitals, aboard warships and hospital ships, wherever there were wounded or the expectation of wounded. This letter from an aerial gunner even told of plasma in the skies above the Pacific islands.

S.Sgt. Charles D. Worley wrote back from his war front to a Mr. Cattrell in his hometown of Columbus, Ohio:

> *I am not much of a guy for writing letters but I just had to write you. I get the paper from home and I saw that you are doing your part giving all that blood. All I can say is 'Thanks!' It saved a few of my buddies. We won't take off without plasma on the ship. We have had some pretty rough air battles over Yap and Palau.*
>
> *I know what that plasma does; so do a lot of other Columbus boys. I would like to write to all the Galloners but you see I would have quite a job. And I have a girl to write to.*
>
> *All I can say is 'Keep on doing things like that and we'll promise to beat the hell out of the Japs.*

Many a turret or waist or tail gunner was shot up in an air battle over Yap or one of the other islands and returned to the base trapped in the damaged plane. That's why Staff Sergeant Worley said they never went out without plasma aboard the plane. With a man wounded and trapped on the return trip to their base, another crew member could start the plasma before they even landed. It might be a long wait before the medics and the mechanics could get the injured man free. The minute that the signal was flashed from the damaged plane as it came over the field, the ground crew knew that there was wounded aboard. Plasma would be on its way.

But the casualty was already being stabilized by the plasma they carried on board. As the mechanic worked to free the patient, the medic was ready with another unit of plasma and what medical attention he could get started. They became good at it, this medical-mechanical team. As Worley said, "Yap had a good share of air battles."

Statistics tell us how many people fought in the Pacific, where and when and with what success. Records show how many men were killed and how many wounded, but it's doubtful we shall ever know who remained on the survivor list because of a unit of plasma in one of those shot-up planes over Yap or wherever. The boy from Columbus did not need actual numbers. "Some" was enough to make him grateful.

New Guinea

New Guinea was a major island in the American trek across the Pacific from Pearl Harbor to Japan, but perhaps not as well-known as Guadalcanal, Tarawa and Iwo Jima. It was a vital link in the Japanese plan to isolate Australia and New Zealand, and preserve their newly gained holdings in the resource-rich Dutch East Indies. The Allied campaign to take back New Guinea lasted nearly two years, from January 1943 to December 1944, and the Japanese committed substantial resources to hold on to it.

New Guinea, a large island in the South Pacific, was coveted by the enemy because it is immediately north of Australia. The island is of mixed terrain, with mountains crossed by treacherous trails that posed real danger to our troops climbing there. The medics and their plasma followed. They were always along wherever, whenever. The medics had to set up in the jungle, too. When I interviewed a doctor who had seen duty in New Guinea, he described a challenging job. As we talked about plasma in these setups, I asked him if the medics realized where their plasma came from.

"I do," he assured me, "and I make certain my team does, too." Then he described the scene when they were setting up on one of those jungle clearings.

"We were working fast as always, when four native Papuans appeared carrying a litter piled high with boxes of plasma. My aide in charge of layout pointed to a spot on the ground and called out, 'Over here. Supplies go over here.' I tapped him on the arm. 'That's not supplies,' I said, 'that's people. The plasma in those boxes came from people in the States. It's not a supply. It's people.' My aide said, 'I know, Doc but I forget. We use so much of it, I take it for granted.'"

We agreed that it was fortunate that the native litter bearers did not speak English. Otherwise, they might have dropped the litter and run out of the clearing screaming about "those crazy Americans! They have people in boxes!"

The Navy was present at New Guinea, also. One ship that I followed, the USS *Henley* (DD 391), had

Native plasma bearers

not come to do battle but to rest. She had been at Pearl Harbor on December 7 and in many battles across the Pacific since. When she received orders to put in to New Guinea, the crew was elated; they could surely use a little respite. But it didn't last long. They suddenly were ordered to report immediately to the Bismarck Sea to assist in a fast-developing battle. The men's respite turned to battle stations. After engaging in battle, their orders changed to "Abandon ship!" *Henley*, badly hit, was going down.

I learned about the *Henley* from one of her officers who had been with her since Pearl Harbor. Lt. Joe Grodin of Cambridge, Massachusetts, talked with me after he returned from Cherbourg where he participated in D-Day. After the *Henley*, he joined the crew of the destroyer *O'Brien* for the bombardment of Cherbourg Harbor. It was essential to open up the waterway down to Normandy. But we didn't get into that when we met. We talked about the Bismarck Sea and the *Henley's* ending there.

"We were in the ocean for about seven hours before one of the other destroyers picked us up," he said. "The fighting continued with underwater explosions and many, many internal injuries for survivors. These people were in bad shape. It was in connection with one of these cases that we saw one of the most spectacular jobs done by plasma. The doctors kept giving it to the boys. Most of them would not have had half a chance without it. Internal injuries like that are really tough, but thanks to the prompt and rather lavish administration of blood plasma, those boys came through all right."

27. MOVING TOWARD THE MARIANAS

Tarawa

Tarawa, part of the Gilbert Islands, was a major event in the Pacific war. Although small, the Japanese recognized its strategic location and built a base there. By mid-1943, American military planners had become increasingly concerned about the Marianas. To get to

Victorious Marines leave Tarawa.

Japan, the Americans had to take the heavily defended Marianas first. That meant the Marshalls had to be taken in order to gain their special airfields so long-range bombers could reach Guam and the other Marianas. To gain the Marshalls, the Gilberts had to be taken. It was like dominoes. That's where Tarawa came into the picture.

When historians ranked the Battle of Tarawa as the bloodiest of the Pacific island battles, they found no objection from the men who fought there, but from those who fought on other islands, there was a challenge regarding the use of the superlative. It's not unusual for a man to think his battle is the bloodiest. Wherever, whenever, by whomever fought, every battle was bloody—too bloody. Those same historians were generous with their statistics. They tell us how many ships the Navy had in action at Tarawa, what type of ships and their fate. They wrote of how many Marines landed on the island's shores many became casualties.

Our attention seems to center on the land forces in these island battles. We should not overlook the Navy's huge presence there when we read the statistics prepared by our historians for Tarawa: seventeen aircraft carriers; twelve battleships; eight heavy and four light cruisers; and sixty-six destroyers. And there were thirty-six transports carrying men and supplies ashore. They wrote of how many Marines landed on the island's shores, and how many became casualties—nearly 1,700 Americans killed and more than 2,000 wounded, as well as the 637 Navy men killed when USS *Liscome Bay* was sunk.

A report of the landings said that plasma went in with a high priority, second only to ammunition and other medical supplies. A doctor on a hospital ship told of the double duty of those transports. After the landings were completed and the subsequent fighting underway, the transports stood offshore—waiting—and ready to remove the wounded from the beach. The chief of medicine aboard the hospital ship, Cmdr. Howard P. Sprague, MC, USNR, told me in an interview, "We rendezvoused with the transports to remove the wounded that they had brought out from the beach." As he described the transfer, he explained, "We took the more serious cases, those requiring special surgery."

When asked about the amount of plasma aboard his ship, Sprague told me that they had an adequate supply and "used plenty!" Then he continued, a little boastfully perhaps, but certainly gratefully, "Out of all these critical cases that we handled, only two men died." This was considered a truly remarkable achievement and Commander Sprague gave "the greatest share of credit to the lavish use of plasma." At the end of his tour of duty on the hospital ship, he was transferred to one of the Navy's hospitals in the States. He became Captain Sprague at Chelsea Naval Hospital in Boston.

Hospital ships were something to behold. They were painted completely white and had their lights on day and night to protect them from enemy fire. No one could mistake it for a warship or overlook its conspicuous red cross—the international symbol of peace and aid—prohibiting enemy attack. The doctors on the hospital ships worked hard, with no letup, striving to keep the casualties alive. Their work area was like the exterior of their ship, white and well lit. By contrast, so many other doctors worked by lantern in the jungle or on the beach, as many did at Tarawa.

When those beach doctors looked up to see the big white ship appear on the horizon, their spirits rose and their hearts swelled. They didn't feel quite so alone anymore. They knew that now some of their badly wounded men would get what they needed when they were delivered to the hospital ship.

The Navy transferred another man from Tarawa to Chelsea Naval Hospital. He was Pfc. John Stryhardz, USMC, and he described the beach at Tarawa in an interview at the hospital. He told me how he had been hit by snipers and cared for on the beach. "Before losing consciousness after I had fallen, I saw two corpsmen try to reach me and get hit in the attempt. When I came to, the doctor and another corpsman were working on me. I suppose they were doing other things to me, too, but all I can remember was a bottle hanging from a rifle." It was plasma, of course, and he went on to explain the sensation.

"It was different from anything I have ever known. It was as though I was rising—being lifted right up off the ground. The best thing I can compare it to is being out of breath, and all of a sudden getting your breath back. Half an hour later I was up on my elbow, leaning over on my side, smoking a cigarette and looking around the beach." When I asked him what he saw, he explained, "Poles and rifles all over the place. It looked like a lot of beanpoles in a vegetable garden, only they all had bottles hanging from them and wounded Marines lying on the beach beside them."

There were thousands and thousands of those beanpoles all over the world in World War II—from the beach at Tarawa to a field outside Rome. We'll never know how many men came home survivors because of one of those beanpoles. Our historians' lists did not carry that information.

With Tarawa secured, the United States was able to gain the airfields in the Marshalls and move toward the Marianas. Saipan was finally in sight. Tarawa had achieved its purpose. Like all the other battles in the island trek across the Pacific, it was purpose with a price.

Saipan

Plasma being used on Saipan casualties

With the Gilberts and the Marshalls secured, the Americans could move on the Marianas. Saipan waited on the horizon. This seventy-square-mile island was long and narrow—fourteen miles long by two to five miles wide, with many beaches. No man who fought on Saipan will ever forget Green Beach, White Beach, Red Beach, Black Beach, and Blue Beach.

Amphibious landings are seldom easy, but on Saipan the Marines met heavy resistance, complicating their arrival. In spite of this, the Navy put ashore twenty thousand Marines on Saipan on June 19, 1944.

In addition, the Battle of Saipan was fought on the sea, under the sea, and in the skies above. When the battle was officially over on July 9, the Americans had not only secured the island, but they had put a major dent in Japan's navy and air force. Their pilots could not stand up to ours.

On land, the ground troops found a relentless enemy. The fighting can be best understood through the names the men gave to some of the battle scenes: Hell's Pocket, Death Valley, Purple Heart Ridge. Life was rough for those fighting on Saipan. Many had already gone through battles on other islands such as Guadalcanal, Tulagi, Savo, Florida, Tarawa, Munda, or Bougainville. Their prior experience did not make their lot here any easier. The Battle of Saipan lasted only three weeks, but there was no letup during those bitter days.

There were numbers of Purple Hearts awarded to men who fought at Saipan, some posthumously to their families because they are still out there—buried beneath gravestones bearing no names, just the Marine Corps symbol. The names in this American cemetery are probably long forgotten by most but remembered forever by comrades who left them behind.

One man who lived to wear his Purple Heart was Pvt. Carl Butler, USMC, of Newton, Massachusetts. He went in on the first wave at Guadalcanal, was wounded, given plasma, and evacuated to a hospital in Noumea where he recuperated sufficiently to take part in the initial landings at Tarawa, Saipan, and Tinian. In my interview, he described the landings and the fighting that followed.

It was a painful struggle all the way. When I asked him if the boys out there were ever afraid, he answered quickly.

"You bet your life they were," he said. "Scared to death!" Then he added, "Not of the enemy, because he's inevitable, nor of death because for many of us that's inevitable, too. But we were afraid of being wounded and not getting what we needed to take care of us...afraid of lying out all night suffering. That's where plasma came in, because if you get plasma, you know you stand a chance of being alive in the morning when the litter bearers can come to pick you up. In addition to that, plasma lessens pain."

Of the thousands of Private Butler's fellow casualties at Saipan, a high percentage survived, and there is official evidence that plasma played an important role in that success. Some of that evidence came from a man who was there—one of those veterans of another island before landing on Saipan. We knew of the importance of Carlson's Raiders on Guadalcanal, and here was their leader, Lt. Col. Evans F. Carlson, speaking on national radio over the Mutual Broadcasting System on December 8, 1944, with a firsthand report about Saipan.

I was wounded on the eighth day of the battle for Saipan. The Fourth Marine Division, of which I was a staff officer, had fought its way across the southern portion of the island from west to east and, on this eighth day, we were attacking to the north toward Mount Tapochau. I was with an assault battalion as an observer for the division commander. About a mile north of the jump-off point, the assault units encountered a cross draw which lay at right angles to our line of advance. The draw ended in a sheer cliff on the west. The battalion commander and I sat on the edge of the slope which descended into the draw, watching the progress of the advance elements of the battalion. Suddenly there was a burst of machine-gun fire from a hitherto unobserved cave in the face of the cliff two hundred and fifty yards to left front. The battalion commander's radio operator, Vic Cassaro, dropped with a bullet through his left thigh which broke the bone. While the battalion commander dashed to bring the fire of a 75 mm half-track on the cave, I stooped to assist Hospital Corpsman Campbell to carry Cassaro out of the line of fire. There was another burst of fire and a huge sledgehammer seemed to slug my right arm and left leg, knocking me down. Even as I fell, the thought flashed through my mind, 'Lucky dog! They only got you in the arm and a leg.'

"*Members of the command post personnel leaped to drag both Cassaro and me back out of the line of vision of the offending cave. Friendly hands ripped the garments from the wounded arm and leg, applied tourniquets, and covered the wounds with sterile gauze from the first aid packet which each fighting man carries. Soon we were lifted into a jeep ambulance and trundled half a mile down the reverse slope to the battalion aid station. As we arrived, enemy mortar shells began dropping in the area. The aid station was in an old stable and I can remember lying on a stretcher in that stable, listening to the bursts of mortar shells as they encircled us and thinking that if they couldn't hit me in a vital spot when they could see me, they are certainly not going to do it now.*

A doctor leaned over, examining my wounds and taking my pulse. 'The leg is a flesh wound,' he informed me sympathetically, 'but a bone is shattered in your arm.' Then, turning to a corpsman, he said 'Low pulse, low blood pressure...PLASMA!'

In my years in the service, it has been my lot to participate in many battles. I have seen thousands of men wounded and I have worked with hundreds of them, either administering first aid or assisting in making them more comfortable and safe. In this war, I have seen plasma, the sulfa drugs, and penicillin restore men whose life was ebbing. Always I have wondered what these wounded men were actually thinking and feeling. Now I was one of them. I had not lost consciousness at any time and I was not in any great pain after the first blow of the bullets, for I had received an injection of morphine before reaching the dressing station. Although my mind took in the incidents which occurred about me, I was conscious of no interest in these incidents. I seemed to be a spectator without life or form rather than an actor in this human drama. I was listless and without any desire to move or make any effort. Although I did not realize it, I was suffering from shock and loss of blood. And like so many of the men present on this battle-field, my resistance had been lowered by years of service in the field. My eyes watched the corpsman as he adjusted the plasma container over my head. At the end of the rubber tube there was a hollow needle which he injected into the vein of my left arm. I felt the fluid flow into my vein and suddenly I became conscious of new strength, new life. PLASMA! It was as though I were being fed nourishment which was instantly assimilated, restoring my vigor, sharpening my mind, and integrating me. I knew then what plasma meant to others whom I had seen revived by its use.

In my case, I probably would not have died if plasma had not been available. My wounds were slight as compared with wounds of the abdomen, the chest, or the head. There is no question, however, that plasma increased my chances of living, and it certainly shortened the period of my convalescence by reducing shock and restoring some of the blood that I had lost. I shall be eternally grateful for plasma and eternally indebted to those fellow Americans whose sense of duty and whose desire to assist in saving life induced them to share with me their life blood."

Lieutenant Colonel Carlson had given service to his country before Saipan, earning three Navy Crosses and now a Gold Star from Saipan as well as a second Purple Heart. Sadly, he died in 1947 at the young age of fifty-one.

Almost half a century later, I had a chance to look back on Saipan, Tarawa, and Tinian and other islands out there, when the Naval Institute Press published an article in its November/December issue of *Naval History* magazine, entitled "D-Days Forgotten." We need to be reminded that D day is a generic term applied to all battles, not just a label for Normandy on June 6, 1944.

The story came from author David Gaddis about the anniversary journey of a group of veterans of the war in the Pacific as they returned to the islands where they had fought so long ago. Although these veterans believe that the world has forgotten their D days, it is clear that they, themselves, have not. They lived through the misery of battle and fought through to victory on these islands. These victories, and their remembered comrades, helped bring about the end of World War II.

One visitor was younger than the rest. He walked the rocky shores of the island where his father died. He carried the memory of his father's D day there. It was Father's Day 1994 when Richard DeLuca placed a memorial on the rough earth where his father had been killed. John DeLuca had been a Seabee on Saipan and other islands.

Guam

Guam, the largest of the Marianas, was the last to be rescued. The Japanese attacked it on the same day that they struck Pearl Harbor, and it was an island the enemy did not leave. The months and years between December 7, 1941 and July 1944, were long and painful for the people of Guam. With elation and gratitude they witnessed the arrival of the Marines on July 21.

Members of the 3rd Marine Division landed on the beaches above Agana Bay after the customary offshore bombardment prepared the area for the troops going ashore. But the Japanese were prepared also and offered heavy resistance. The Marines fought on with many casualties and many heroes, not all recognized with medals. That was especially true among the medics, for whom heroism was just routine.

One doctor received two medals—a Purple Heart and a Silver Star—posthumously. They were presented to his wife with a citation that explained what happened. The doctor had been kneeling beside a dying Marine holding a bottle of plasma over his body—watching the faint blush of life coming back into his face—when enemy fire took both that life and that of the doctor as he held the plasma.

With Guam finally secured, the United States lost no time in establishing the Navy Distribution Center for Whole Blood there. The Navy Transport Command was flying in shipments of whole blood from the States. At first it came from the West Coast, and after V-E Day it expanded to whole blood shipments from eleven centers on the East Coast. July 1945 was a beginning for Guam, not an end.

28. THE FINAL PUSH

Iwo Jima

A makeshift field hospital in an Iwo Jima foxhole.

Iwo Jima means rock island, *jima* being the Japanese word for island with plenty of rock there to qualify for *iwo*. A vial of beach "sand," brought back from Iwo long after the war, is so coarse, so sharp, that it feels like crushed rock. One cringes at the thought of corpsmen crawling around on it to reach the wounded, as so many of them had to do.

The island lies in the western Pacific Ocean about four hundred miles from Japan. At five and a half miles long by two and a half miles wide, it is the largest of the Volcanic Islands annexed to Japan in 1887. Mountainous and volcanic in origin, the highest elevation is the extinct volcano, Mount Suribachi, at 546 feet. While no great mountain, it was nevertheless an important and dramatic defense position for the Japanese.

Military strategists had their eyes on Iwo Jima's airfield and considered the island a key stepping-stone to the Japanese mainland. The invasion of Iwo was preceded by sea and air bombardment, but the Japanese had entrenched themselves underground, waiting for the American troops.

Historians of World War II have written at length about Iwo Jima as one of the bloodiest battles of all. The invasion began on February 19, 1945, and was officially ended on March 16, 1945. The Marines lost 4,189 and the Japanese an estimated 20,000. But we took the airfield, allowing our planes to strike Japan's inner defense systems.

We had our own personal history of Iwo Jima in an account of the invasion, sent back by one of our own.

Back in 1942, when Lt. Henry Lundquist finally got through his medical go-round after applying for sea duty—"disqualified, qualified, disqualified, qualified..."—he knew that the paperwork would take time before new orders could be cut for him. He decided to give his assistant a chance for sea duty if he wanted it. Arch Macdonald did want it, so he and Henry discussed at length what duty Arch should request. An applicant might state his choice for duty, but, of course, there was no guarantee he would get it.

How very true! Henry tried to sell Arch on Armed Guard as Bill Schofield had sold him, but Arch was not buying. He was adamant. He wanted no job where he would be responsible for any man's life. He wanted an administrative job anywhere in the war-world where they wanted to send him—at sea, on a ship engaged, or on shore in a war zone.

Finally, Arch applied for sea duty and was accepted. He was ordered to the Amphibious Training School at Coronado Beach, California, to learn the intricacies of ship-to-shore movement integral to amphibious landings on hostile beaches. So much for choice! He put his personal affairs in order, and he and his wife, Jerri, flew to the West Coast. He completed his training and stood by for orders.

They came. Where was he headed? Iwo Jima! This was hardly the hoped-for administrative work that would not burden him with the responsibility for men's lives.

He took fourteen waves of Marines ashore in the February invasion of the island. This is his personal bit of history of Iwo Jima, sent back from the beach to his colleagues at PRO:

Lt. Arch Macdonald interviews
Sgt. Charles F. Kirby Jr.

Hi, you lugs,

…Was pleased as the devil to hear from you. I didn't make the Philippine run but your letter caught up with me just after I had completed another that was really a tough one. Your letter waited for me as a matter of fact. I hadn't received any mail for a month so I guess you can appreciate how I welcomed it after I pulled away from the Nips and their damnable mortar fire.

My officers and men were magnificent and I thank God for the privilege of serving with men like them. And those Marines! Never let anyone talk them down. They are the most courageous guys the Lord ever created. After sharing what I have with them here's one sailor wearing a bit of gold braid that will doff the hat in their presence.

And Hank and Sta—you too Ross—remember this well. I thought I appreciated the full importance of blood plasma back there with you 'apostles.' I didn't.

My job incorporates two phases. I lead the boys to the beach and after I get them in and the beach-head is secured, I direct the 'goods and materials' in to them that they need to carry the battle forward. I have sent gallons of the precious stuff in to them. I've seen what it does for my shipmates—my buddies and for even my own men. My most fervent prayer is one of gratitude for it. I thank God for men and women like yourselves.

"No matter what else I may be called upon to do out here, the one thing in which I pride myself the most is the donations I have been able to make myself. Jerri and I got in an extra pint a piece in San Diego just before I left. So I made it, Hank. I made it 10 before I landed out here.

"Every once in a while I pinch myself and wonder how in 'ell an old radio announcer PRO man ever wound up in this rough-house amphibious deal. The urge to survive is great however and I have learned all the tricks of the trade F-A-S-T. And our Marines are good—very good—teachers.

Remember how we used to discuss our reactions, how we would react under different circumstances? Well, I've found out for myself. I'll respect a man—his weapons—like him—love him—dislike him, even hate him. But never again will I FEAR any man. This business does funny things to a guy. I'm no longer quite the fellar I was. I hope I don't change too much. I want to be the guy my wife, family and friends want me to be but fellas you don't expose yourself to the 'stimuli' that exist out here without 'tightening up.' You have to—to survive.

"I'll never wind up with medals—or many ribbons either. I'm just like a million other guys beside me—but, when the play is on, *somehow or other, thru your faith in God and the men fighting by your side, you find it possible to do what is expected of you. Remember what that Chief said on that 'Men Make the Navy' series? 'Courage is a reservoir.' He's right. Completely right! You have no courage of your own. You draw from the next guy and the next from the next. You borrow from him until the pressure lessens.*

I'm not a particularly religious man but, somehow the only thing to which you can grasp is prayer. When all hell is breaking loose, you find yourself praying and yet damning the enemy. It isn't a sacrilege for the all Knowing Man topside knows what you are thinking.

I was terribly sorry to learn that the skipper's son was in a bad spot. I feel certain that he will come through ok. My kid brother is in India and he describes the country as vast and difficult in which to travel. We didn't hear from him for almost three months. I feel sure that if Neil bailed out, he will turn up again in time. It's tough on the skipper and his family but miracles are wrought a million times over, out this way.

I was interested in your account of what's been happening back there. Good work, fellars! S'help me, I miss it all and each of you. Knowing what I do now, I'd never advise any of you to lead with your chin. I've learned to my sorrow that this is strictly a kids' game...and I'm no kid! Amphibious could never have been intended for men our age. I'm in it up to my ears, however, so I'll stick until the Navy decides that I have finished the job...or it finishes me.

Thanks for your prayers. I can use them to advantage. If it's God's will, I hope some day to return. Who knows! My luck has been good. I've had plenty of close calls but I'm still around—so it may hold. I hope so.

To each and every one of you, my best! Was very happy to hear from you. Write again, please. Till later then...

As ever,

Arch

Lt. Arch J. Macdonald, USNR, came home at the end of the war and returned to broadcasting, where he won an Emmy for his work and, ultimately, the title "Dean of New England Newscasters."

Commander Collier's son, Neil, did not return. His loss in a flight over Burma was mourned by all in the PRO family.

Those hundreds of gallons of plasma, the "precious stuff" that Lieutenant Macdonald shipped ashore, were followed on the beach by Marine Corps Combat Correspondent Sgt. Ralph W. Meyers. He filed this report from Iwo:

> *"Blood is indeed the stuff…the most precious cargo on this island of agony! Medical Corpsmen lie on their backs in foxholes, holding bottles over their heads until their arms ache and grow numb. They sit on careening jeeps and trucks, holding their bottles aloft while wounded leathernecks fight their individual battles for life en route to the rear area.*
>
> *"There are more bottles of blood, whole and plasma, lashed to poles and to up-ended rifle butts at the grim wayside stations on the beaches. The stuff flowing through yellow rubber tubes goes with the men in the Higgins boats to the ships.*
>
> *"And the priceless bottles shine like red and white wine in the white lights of ships' hospitals out there with the fleet. It is a continuous running battle against death for many men, extending from the lines to the ships' operating tables. And the battle is won more often that it is lost."*

The Americans' first success on the island has been immortalized in the picture of the flag raising on Mount Suribachi on February 23, 1945, and in the Marine Corps War Memorial on the edge of Arlington National Cemetery, where a large bronze statue depicts the flag-raising event. It is the impressive work of artist and sculptor Navy Chief Petty Officer Felix de Weldon, based on the photograph taken by Joe Rosenthal of the Associated Press.

Marines on Mount Suribachi.

The famous flag-raising photograph is not the first picture taken there. The original, preserved in the author's files, is shown here along with a notation by Henry Lundquist to his son, many years later.

Ned...this Iwo Suribachi flag raising is one of my most precious pictures. In Feb.1945 while fighting was its hottest and the enemy was still holed up on Suribachi itself, the group in the photo made its way to the top and the picture was taken by a Marine Combat photographer. (The pack radio suggests a major objective was to establish an observation post.) Not too long after the group descended, another group (including, I believe, some of the first group) climbed up again with a larger flag and accompanied by a wire service photographer (my recollection says Rosenthal of the A.P.) who took the famous picture, now immortalized by the statue, etc. But this is the bone-fide real thing. Ask Arch! He was there. He watched it happen.

On the back of the original Marine Corps photo is their caption:

"IWO JIMA'S SURIBACHI RENAMED MOUNT PLASMA."
Photo by the Marine Corps

"This grim faced Marine forms an honor guard for the 5th Division Marines of the 28th regiment as they hoist Old Glory to the top of an improvised flagpole on the summit of Mount Suribachi. So much plasma was used on the rocky slopes of the volcanic mountain that the Leathernecks rechristened it Mount Plasma. Jap snipers, entrenched in the caves, dugouts and natural depressions of the volcano's rocky sides made this conquest one of the bloodiest fights of the war and whole blood and plasma, procured by the American Red Cross, saved the life of many a fighting Marine."

From the surf on the beach to the summit of the mountain, a magnificent chapter in the history of Iwo Jima and the Navy Medical Corps was told in an official Navy Release that explained how the Navy prepared for its Iwo wounded. It was a story of before-the-fact preparation and a report of fulfillment of a most creative plan. It showed the Navy's underlying compassion for its men as well as its practical care of them.

HOLD FOR RELEASE
PRESS AND RADIO
UNTIL 6 p.m. (P.W.T.) MARCH 28, 1945
LST HOSPITAL SHIPS SAVED LIVES AT IWO JIMA

With Amphibious Forces in the Western Pacific- ---Four of the big LSTs at the invasion of Iwo Jima were transformed in record time from instruments of death to instruments of mercy and many of the critically wounded will live as a result of that transformation.

These four ships became floating medical evacuation stations within a few minutes after their amphibious tanks were landed. Remaining close inshore throughout the operation, wounded men were on their operating tables, in some instances, within 20 minutes after they had been hit.

The four ships had been so loaded that all of their tanks would hit the water within seconds after their arrival on the line of departure. These tanks were for the first wave. Navy medical personnel rode to the operation aboard the 'hospital LST's' operating tables, set up in the troop quarters long before the island was sighted, were soon ready. As the last 'water buffalo' rolled down the ramp, cleaning crews went to work, and before the first wave had reached shore, the huge tank decks had been transformed into 150 bed hospital wards.

Whole blood from donors in San Francisco, flown to the Fleet under refrigeration and blood plasma from donors in other American cities, saved scores of lives in these make-shift hospitals afloat.

The work of the doctors on the four ships was under the direction of Captain Robert M. Gillette, Medical Corps, USN.

The story of the first 24 hours after H-hour aboard the first LST was typical of that aboard the other three craft. Huge pontoons, which they had carried on their sides across thousands of miles of ocean, were dropped to form a landing stage alongside for the small boats that would soon bring in the wounded.

The odor of gasoline from the departing amphibious tanks still clung to the ship when the odor of ether started coming from the improvised operating rooms. There had been casualties in that first wave, many of them, and now they were coming back. Some of them were Marines who had ridden to combat on the same ship and had made close friends with crew members. Lieutenant John J. Courtney, Medical Corps, USNR stood on the landing stage and made a quick examination of every wounded man arriving. Lieutenant Courtney was a veteran of Tarawa and these sights were not new.

If there was no doubt that the patient could stand immediate transfer to the better equipped hospital wards aboard the large transports, he was sent on. If there was doubt, his stretcher was placed on a rigid iron framework and swung up and over the LST rail on a crane rigged for that purpose. Its stretcher never paused in its travel down to the tank deck and its adjoining operating room. All cases of chest wounds, head wounds, shock, and excessive bleeding came aboard. Many men were unconscious.

Down in the tank deck and in the operating room, there were doctors who were taking it for the first time: Lieutenant Andrew B. Carson, Medical Corps, USNR; Lieutenant Edwin A. Riemenschneider, Medical Corps, USNR; Lieutenant (junior grade) Gordon S. Leterman, Medical Corps, USNR; and Lieutenant (junior grade) Gordon E. Jones, USNR. Throughout the day and night, these doctors worked on the seemingly endless stream of fractures, mortar and artillery shrapnel, abdominal, head and chest wounds, amputations, flash burns, and every other wound known to combat. There were 34 Navy Corpsmen helping them and every other member of the crew, not otherwise occupied, pitched in. The chaplain, Lieutenant Fred G. Samek, USNR (Chaplain Corps), pitched in and cut splints for fractures. In those first 24 hours, there were approximately 400 wounded men treated on this one LST alone. Of these, only four died while aboard. Several more breathed their last in the small boats on their way out from the blazing beach.

There were sighs of relief from the exhausted doctors when the huge, white, beautifully equipped and staffed hospital ship showed up some 24 hours after the first casualties came pouring in.

Those exhausted doctors who hailed with gratitude the arrival of the hospital ships must have felt privileged, nonetheless, to have worked on those transformed LSTs. They were all a part of a small bit of Navy medical history.

According to the doctors, our donors were, too. One doctor said, "We used thirty-two pints of whole blood in our improvised station and I think we saved sixteen lives. We thanked them silently as we tapped those flasks, and those youngsters on the cots and operating table would have thanked them from the bottom of their hearts had they been able."

Statistics don't usually make for exciting reading, but official details can authenticate facts put forth in a narrative. Lt. Robert R. Brown, USN, in charge of the establishment of the Whole Blood Distribution Center No. 1 at Guam, gave us a few facts to digest:

"14,000 pints of whole blood were used for Iwo Jima, about 7,000 on the battlefields and another 7,000 pints in hospital ships or base hospitals nearby."

"The Marine Corps death toll of 4,189 would have been doubled except for the use of whole blood."

"'Blood donated less than a week before in the United States flowed into the veins of Yanks on Iwo Jima within a half hour after they were wounded."

We heard more about whole blood at work on Iwo Jima from no less than the secretary of the Navy himself. James Forrestal had been appointed undersecretary of the Navy when Congress established the post in 1940 and moved up following the sudden death of Secretary Frank Knox from a heart attack on April 28, 1944. Forrestal was at Iwo for firsthand observation. He was a man who devoted much of his life's work to the betterment of the Navy. That's why we had an aircraft carrier sailing the sea in his honor – the USS *Forrestal*.

When he spoke at the Red Cross Luncheon in New York City on March 21, 1945, he recalled, "I saw whole blood being used on the hospital ship *Samaritan* off Iwo Jima the day after D day there. I found the staff busy with men who had come off the beach a few hours before. Ten days later when I went through the hospital at Honolulu, I saw some of the casualties from Iwo Jima who had been evacuated to Guam and then by air to Honolulu, resting comfortably at the magnificent Naval Hospital at Aiea. Our wounded and sick are being given all of the care and thought that scientific and hospital practice of the country can provide, and the Red Cross is providing its full share in this magnificent accomplishment."

The secretary also paid tribute to "the organization of the NATS—the Naval Air Transportation Service—tasked with getting the lifesaving fluid to its destination with the quality unimpaired." And he reminded us that "whole blood supplements, rather than replaces, the use of plasma, which, as you know, has become one of the foremost lifesavers of the war."

Iwo Jima was an important step toward ending the war in the Pacific. It has been well remembered ever since, not only by survivors but also by the millions who visit the Marine Memorial at Arlington. Blood donors throughout the country learned once more of the powerful value of their gifts through the various official—and personal—reports from Iwo. It was a thrill to hear the comments of the doctor on that transformed LST.

But the blood donors throughout the country in World War II did not need to be told how important they were. They knew. That's why they gave and gave again.

A Postscript to Suribachi

Some sixty years after the Battle of Iwo Jima, obituaries of Iwo veterans appeared in newspapers throughout the country. Some were in an alphabetical column, with an American flag beside the name, followed by facts of birth and death and probably that the man had fought in World War II. If anyone rated an individual column, he was remembered more for his profession, or occupation, or activities in the community, with perhaps a mention that he was a veteran of World War II.

However, one obit of an Iwo veteran, written by Claudia Luther as a special to the *Los Angeles Times*, stretched five columns across a page of the *Boston Globe* on August 24, 2006. The man remembered was Joseph Rosenthal. The son of Russian immigrant parents, he was born in Washington, DC, and, after high school, went to San Francisco to be near his brothers and go to college. Instead he got a job as a reporter-photographer for the *San Francisco News*. When given instructions about his job, he was told to "take this big box, point the end with the glass toward the subject, and press the shutter, and we'll tell you what you did wrong." Quite a beginning for a Pulitzer Prize winner!

After being turned down for military service, he signed with the Associated Press as a combat photographer. He saw duty with the Marines on Guadalcanal and other Pacific islands before arriving on Iwo Jima. When the first flag raising occurred on Mount Suribachi, he was photographing Marines elsewhere on the island and missed the event. When the commander on the ground decided that the flag was too small and should be replaced by a larger one that could be seen from ships at sea and the troops all over the island, he ordered the change. Rosenthal set out to get a picture of one flag coming down and the new one going up. He was not as fit as the Marines scaling the rocky slopes of Suribachi. They were way ahead of him. He missed the flag coming down, but he was able to position himself and his camera for the raising of the new flag. He got his picture, all right—and a Pulitzer Prize for it.

After being developed at Guam, it made its way into professional hands who recognized it as special. From the Associated Press, it went everywhere, even turning up on a stamp for the U.S. Postal Service. When Felix de Weldon saw it, he created a wax model, and it was that from which the Marine Corps War Memorial was created in bronze.

But along with fame came criticism. Some claimed that Rosenthal had staged the second flag raising because he had missed the first. When the facts finally became known, critics understood and withdrew their claims against Rosenthal, but the unfair attitude had hurt.

About a year later, the *Boston Globe* published another obituary—written by Chris Williams of the Associated Press with a dateline of Richfield, Minnesota—that filled a full column from the top of the page to the bottom. The death noted was that of Charles W. Lindberg, one of the Marines who raised the first flag on Mount Suribachi. In an earlier interview, he had described the experience: "I fired my flamethrower into enemy pillboxes at the base of Mount Surabachi and then joined five other Marines fighting their way to the top."

When they made it, "…two of the men found this big long pipe. We tied the flag to it and took it to the highest point we could find and we raised it." Then he described what happened as the American flag waved in the wind. "Down below, the troops started to cheer. The ships' whistles went off. It was just something you would never forget. But it didn't last too long because the enemy started coming out of the caves."

Mr. Lindberg was not present for the second flag raising. He was in combat on another part of the island. Three others from the first flag-raising party were missing also, killed in action. Charles Lindberg was wounded on March 1 and evacuated from the island. In addition to his Purple Heart, he received a Silver Star for bravery at Suribachi. Through the years he had had a hard time convincing people that he had been part of the first flag raising, and he spent many hours speaking in public to raise awareness of the historic event that had been photographed by Sgt. Lou Lowery, a Marine Corps photographer. It is available for viewing but rarely seen.

Okinawa

In early 1945, many people in the States had never heard of Okinawa. They didn't know where it was or what it was. That changed by spring when headlines of all the newspapers shouted "Okinawa!" It was a lead item in the print media and on radio. Ultimately, it became a major chapter in every history of World War II.

Okinawa was the last major campaign of the war. An island of 450 square miles—approximately sixty times the size of Iwo—it was the largest island of the Ryukyu Archipelago. It is located between the East China Sea on the west and the North Pacific Ocean on the east, about 300 miles south of Japan and about 450 miles northwest of Iwo Jima.

The Okinawa campaign followed Iwo Jima by two weeks. The initial air and naval assaults on Okinawa at the beginning of April preceded the amphibious landings. The fighting continued for eighty-two days. With the Okinawa victory, our forces were ready for the final thrust: the mainland of Japan.

Victory in battle is always costly in human life. More than twelve thousand Americans were killed or missing in action and thirty-eight thousand wounded at Okinawa. But we saved more than we lost, and according to official reports, our blood donors contributed to that accomplishment.

The director of the Marine Corps plans and policies division, Brig. Gen. Gerald C. Thomas, wrote of the use of whole blood given by donors at home and administered to Okinawa wounded: "This lifesaving blood practically flowed from one vein into another." Then he had this to add about plasma at Okinawa: "The Navy corpsmen were crawling under intense fire from foxhole to foxhole with vitally needed blood plasma."

An extraordinary follow-up to the general's comment came from a report done at a hospital to which Okinawa casualties were brought. The chief of surgery described the case of a patient recovering from a serious liver injury. He was a pharmacist's mate first class who had been attending to the wounded on the battlefield at Okinawa. He was returning to his battalion post when a mortar shell exploded and hit him in the chest and leg.

"The fragments perforated his diaphragm and liver," said the doctor, "and resulted in a liver abscess with the patient coughing up pieces of liver—he was in bad shape."

When asked about his transfusions, the patient said, "I had five pints of blood on Okinawa before being evacuated and six more after I arrived at the hospital here." The patient was propped up on his hospital cot, his broken leg suspended in a traction splint. He was thin but cheerful and well on the road to recovery.

"I know how much this whole blood can do," he said, "I saw what it did for the wounded on the front—once we gave transfusions all night. Now look what it's done for me. If it wasn't for Red Cross blood donations and penicillin, I wouldn't be here."

Of all the reports from Okinawa, one story came my way about two buddies in the Marine Corps and two blood donors from Brockton, Massachusetts—strangers until they were brought together by the two Marines.

On June 4, 1945, Billy Dugan and his buddy, Butch, went ashore with the 6th Marines on the Oroku Peninsula in southwest Okinawa.

They were told to hit the beach fast and, when they got to the top, to dig in and wait for further orders. As they stormed ashore, they ran into some rugged opposition. There were many casualties. Billy Dugan was one. When Butch saw what had happened to his pal, he started to go for help. Although Billy was hurting—badly—he mustered up enough strength to yell to Butch, "Get down and keep down or you'll be killed!" Butch then called for a corpsman, and when he saw him coming, he moved forward according to orders, but he sure hated to leave his buddy.

Billy was taken to a temporary aid station, then moved to one medical facility after another. Finally he was evacuated to a hospital, and from that hospital he wrote to his mother:

Dear Mom, How are you? I don't know if you have received a telegram yet saying that I had been wounded. Mom, please don't let it worry you. I was shot in the thigh by a Japanese machine gun. However, I am alright. I'm walking around like any person does. So please don't worry. I'm now in an Army hospital quite far from Okinawa. I'm in the Mariana Islands. I was in the first wave that hit that peninsula in south Okinawa. The night before we left for the beach, I asked God for guidance throughout the battle. I guess, Mom, that this was His way of guiding me because I was very lucky to receive such a small wound. I won't see any more action until my division hits another island. When I go back to my outfit again, I'll receive the Purple Heart...most of my outfit will. Well, Mom, that's all for tonight. So long and good luck... please don't worry.

Love, Billy

Billy Dugan said that most of his outfit would receive the Purple Heart. Butch, however, made it ashore safely, and he continued with the attack and establish a 1,200-yard beachhead to control half of Naha Airfield, the best in the Ryukyus.

They rolled on, slowly wiping out enemy forces that were pinned down on the Chinen Peninsula until the Naha Airfield was ours... all ours.

On June 29, in that hospital in the Marianas from which Billy Dugan had written to his mother, he was still recuperating although slowly. He was kibitzing with a soldier in the bed next to him, talking about hospitals. "I hate hospitals," the soldier complained. "I've been in too many. I hate them all."

Billy had a different opinion. "This one is okay," he said. "The view is nice being up on a cliff like this and the air is good." The soldier expressed a longing for some dirty, smelly, noisy city streets back home. As they talked on, a new patient was rolled in with a doctor and an attendant.

"Gee, another one!" said Billy.

"This one looks bad," said the soldier.

Billy sat up to get a better look. He let out a yelp, "Butch!" Then he leaned forward. "Hey, Army, it's Butch! It's my buddy, Butch!" Billy was beside himself. The soldier tried to quiet him down. "Wait 'til the doctor goes. They're giving him blood. We should be quiet 'til they're through. He doesn't look good."

Billy sat back until the doctor left, then tapped the aide's arm. "Will he make it? I know him. We've been through a lot together. He's my buddy and he's an all right guy. Will he be okay?"

"He has a critical need for another operation; that's why he's here but we didn't think he could get through it when he came in." The aide had been fingering Butch's pulse. "He's coming around. I think he's got a chance now. You can relax, Marine; your buddy will probably make it."

"It's the blood," said the soldier, all knowingly. "I've seen it before, lots of times, and I've had it, too."

"We use a lot of it," said the aide. "It comes from the States. People give it back home."

"My father's given sixteen pints to the Red Cross," said Billy.

"That's where it comes from. The Navy flies it in," the aide added.

"Sixteen pints?" The soldier was wide-eyed. "That's two gallons. Wow! What a guy your father must be. You sure must be proud of him."

"I am," said Billy. "Didn't your father give blood?"

"Nah," said Army, "my old man don't do that kind of stuff."

"Is that a tag on the bottle?" asked Billy.

"Yes," replied the aide, ripping it off. "It's where it comes from." He read it: "Boston Blood Donor Center."

"No kidding!" exclaimed Billy. "That's where I come from." He took the tag that the nurse passed to him. "Is this a name on the tag?"

"Yes," replied the aide, reading the tag, "James A. Hunt. Know him?"

"No," said Billy, "but my father might."

"Hey look," said the soldier, "the guy opened his eyes."

"Butch! Butch! It's me Billy, Billy Dugan, your old buddy."

Butch's eyes had closed again, but now they opened wide as he looked at Billy. "I been so worried about you, kid. You all right?"

"I'm swell," said Billy, glowing. "And you will be, too, now that you've got some good Boston blood in you. And I'm going to find out who this Hunt guy is so he can know about you."

That night, Billy Dugan wrote home again.

> *Dear Mom, Well here I am again. Sorry I didn't write the other day but I've learned a new card game and that's all that I've been doing. One of the casualties that came in yesterday was in my platoon. He got blood that came from the Boston Red Cross. The donor's name was Mr. James T. Hunt. So if Dad should ever run across Mr. Hunt, he can tell him that his blood was given to one of my buddies. They're going to sew up my leg tomorrow. We had a USO show today...Love, Billy*

There was no time wasted in following up on Billy Dugan's letter. His father arrived at the Brockton Chapter of the American Red Cross the next day.

Of course they had records. And Brockton had something to record. Nine visits to Brockton by Boston's Mobile Unit resulted in 12,430 pints of blood for plasma. The Brockton Red Cross Blood Donor Committee sent a dozen busloads of type O donors to Boston for donations for whole blood, over five hundred pints of it, for shipment to the European Theater at first, and then to the Pacific Theater after V-E Day.

According to the record, Mr. James T. Hunt had given nine pints of blood for plasma and two for whole blood and was already scheduled for his twelfth donation.

The pint of blood that Butch received in the hospital in the Marianas on June 29, 1945, was given by Mr. Hunt in Boston on June 14 when he and thirty-five Brockton donors chose that way to celebrate Flag Day.

It was time to find Mr. Hunt and let him know what had happened to his Flag Day gift. Of course the news was a surprise.

Donors never expected to know just where their blood went, much less who received it. The personal connection made it even more important. He was thrilled and deeply grateful to the young Marine for his thoughtfulness in writing home to his parents about this special pint of blood. He also had thanks for Mr. Dugan and the Brockton Red Cross for tracking him down. Everyone was thrilled by the connection and deeply moved by the description of Billy Dugan watching the Hunt blood flow into Butch's veins until Butch came to.

Mr. Hunt had already taken satisfaction from the ten pints he had given for plasma that could not be traced but made him a part of the great romance of the war in giving—maybe life itself—to a wounded stranger somewhere in the war world far away.

The culmination of this Okinawa story came when *Life to the Front* broadcast a dramatization of the Billy Dugan story before a large Brockton audience in the studio. And they had a chance to meet two of their fellow donors and Brockton neighbors, James T. Hunt and Francis G. Dugan, after they were introduced to the radio audience.

We might call this the result of joint operations: the American Red Cross working for the Army and Navy, the Navy Air Transport Service flying the blood from the States to Guam and then to that Army hospital in the Marianas, and finally, two Marines completing the saga.

People were well aware that the Army and Marine ground forces were not alone at Okinawa. The Navy was there in force from the beginning, covering the landings of the troops and supporting their subsequent advances. One of the largest flotillas ever assembled was there at Okinawa. And American planes protected all on land and sea from the skies above.

The enemy was in the air, also, with their infamous kamikazes. Although their air corps was depleted, they used what they had left to fly suicide missions. The pilot's orders were to hit to destroy and that meant his plane and himself. Not all reached their objectives. Most were taken out by the ships they targeted, shot down by our planes or other ships, or missed their target altogether.

The captain of one U.S. Navy ship wrote a detailed report of living with enemy planes for just one day. The ship was the USS *Tawakoni*; the commanding officer was Lt. Cmdr. Clarence L. Foushee; the date April 6, 1945. They were at Okinawa.

Just as we were turning to clear the anchorage, an enemy plane came in without warning, and crashed between us and a landing craft anchored in the next berth. He had missed his mark and we again went to battle stations. Twelve minutes later we took another enemy plane under fire, and, with the assistance of a few other ships in the anchorage, shot it down. That success made us quite proud and, I'm afraid, a bit cocky. About another hour later, we spotted another enemy plane and promptly took it under fire. We crippled this one, and, with the help of two other ships, shot it down also. And a few minutes later, we took a third plane under fire, but we were not so successful and it continued on its way. Then we sighted numerous planes flying low over the water. The air seemed full of them and there was no doubt in anyone's mind that they were enemy planes. But this time we were outside the vessel's port, rolling around the anchorage area and we were all alone. Once, just once, after seeing all those planes, the thought occurred to me to turn back and rejoin the other ships. But it was only a fleeting thought. That is something that is not done in the best of navies. And so we went on!

"*The enemy saw that we were all alone and we must have looked like an easy target to them. First we noticed five planes on our starboard bow, all heading for us, then we saw two more on our port beam, all coming toward us. They dove and made feints and passes at us. For some reason, they were not firing at us or, if they were, we did not notice it. We were too busy firing at them. It was like a cat playing with a mouse. Slowly, stealthfully, and surely, two of the planes peeled off and dropped astern of us. During all this time, we were going through evasive maneuvers. Their idea was for the ten planes over us to keep us busy so that we would not be able to take on the two that dropped astern of us and they could come up for the kill. Because we were given Divine Guidance, we saw the first of those two as it started in for our stern. Our guns took it under fire and the gunners kept the projectiles pouring into it, but it kept coming. It looked like that plane was certainly going to crash into our stern. And, to make matters worse, just about that time, enemy shore batteries on a nearby island, took us under fire. Our guns kept roaring and that plane kept coming in. Just before it reached our stern, something happened to it or the pilot. The plane suddenly changed its course and tilted upward and headed for our pilot house. It came over us between the top of the pilot house and the top of the mainmast. Just then, I swung the ship hard to starboard and the plane crashed into the water, about 50 feet off our port bow. As it hit the water, the bomb it was carrying exploded and scattered pieces of the plane and gasoline all over topside. We looked astern and saw a second plane heading in for us. This one we promptly took under fire and shot it down before it got near us. But there were still planes over us and we were still firing at them. And then, what seemed like a miracle to us, happened. A flight of our own planes came in driving the remaining planes away from us, and shooting down several of them and the remaining planes away from us and shooting down several of them. The action was over! During the two hours of the attack, which was like an eternity, we had engaged fifteen planes, actually taken five of them under direct fire. Of these five, we had, with the assistance of other ships shot down three and, alone, without assistance brought down two more."*

The Allies lost ships, planes, and men—to suicide bombers. Historians have written much about that action at Okinawa.

Lieutenant Commander Foushee wrote his report aboard his ship on the day it happened. It is personal. It is special.

The statistics seem to be coldly impersonal: eighty-eight destroyers (DD) and thirty destroyer escorts (DE) were damaged and twelve destroyer types were sunk at Okinawa. In 1953, the Naval Institute Press published Theodore Roscoe's book *United States Navy Destroyer Operations in World War II*. In it, the author filled out the details of that brief statistic of those 113 ships, and it became anything but cold and impersonal.

Roscoe listed every damaged ship—DD and DE—by name; the commanding officer of that ship—his full name and rank and whether he was USN or USNR (there was a high percentage of reserves in command of those ships); the date of the damage to the ship; and the extent of the damage: major, medium, or minor. Most were major.

The last column was headed "Casualties" and was divided into those killed and those wounded. There was an asterisk after some listings of the wounded. It read, "some fatally." In fact, the Navy had more casualties than the Army or Marine Corps, and it suffered more killed (4,907) than wounded (4,874), largely because of the kamikazes. No longer is that statistic of eighty-eight destroyers and thirty destroyer escorts cold or impersonal. The names of those ships and the names of their captains give us a sense of reality of what happened at Okinawa. One senses the pain of the captains who lost so many men and of that of other survivors aboard those damaged ships. The strong bond that develops among shipmates intensifies such pain.

I had a personal connection with the Navy at Okinawa. In June 1939, I shared godparent duties with Herb Howard, a teenager who had just graduated from Boston Latin School and was headed for Harvard in the fall. The baby being baptized was his nephew, the firstborn of his sister, a lifelong friend of the godmother. The baby was christened John Howard Engler—known today as Doctor Jack

Engler, an eminent psychologist, author of many books, and teacher at Harvard Medical School. His parents were Leslie Winfred Engler and Doris Howard Engler.

Herb graduated from Harvard in February 1943 in an accelerated program, moving on to Midshipman School at Columbia from which he was graduated and commissioned Ensign Herbert Warren Howard Jr., USNR. He received orders to the submarine base in Miami, Florida, and went on to the Navy's gunnery school in Washington, DC. After further training in Norfolk, Virginia, he joined the newly commissioned USS *Bowers* (DE 657) out of San Francisco. When the ship joined the fleet, she steamed out into the Pacific and into troubled waters, including the Battle of Leyte Gulf. The ship pulled through that encounter and, eventually, was ordered to Okinawa.

When she was assigned to antisubmarine screen duty six miles north of Ie Shima, she ran into trouble on April 16. At dawn the ship shot down one attacking Japanese plane. Then at 9:30 a.m., two more planes came in, flying low and fast. *Bowers* maneuvered radically to avoid the planes as they split to attack the escort.

The first plane came in dead ahead but the ship's guns brought it down. The second passed over the ship as her port guns came to bear. Despite the heavy gunfire, the kamikaze regained altitude, turned, and came in from a forty-five-degree angle forward. It crashed into *Bowers*'s flying bridge, spraying high-octane gasoline over the bridge and pilot house. The plane's bomb penetrated the pilot house and continued down through the ship for twenty feet before it exploded and sprayed the deck with fragments. Firefighting parties brought the flames under control in about forty-five minutes.

Referring to Theodore Roscoe's details of destroyer escorts at Okinawa, he categorized the USS *Bowers*'s damage as "major" and describes the scene: "Destroyer escort *Bowers* came out of the suicide crash with half her crew lying on deck dead or injured."

Referring again to Roscoe, we learn that the USS *Bowers* lost forty-eight men on that April 16 morning. Lieutenant Howard was one of them. April 16 was his twenty-fourth birthday. He was on the flying bridge with the captain when the kamikaze came at them. Fifty-nine were injured, including the commanding officer, Lt. Cmdr. C. F. Highfield.

The dreaded "missing in action" message is devastating to all parents as it was to the Howards. They reached out for more information and turned to the Lieutenant and Mrs. Lundquist for help. There were no details available at the time. All that could be offered was consolation and condolence, both limp substitutes. But within a matter of a few weeks, there was something substantive for these stricken parents: long, personal letters from the captain and the surviving officers of the *Bowers*, written while the battle of Okinawa continued.

There was another letter in the collection of papers, entrusted to me by Ellen Engler See, granddaughter of Mr. and Mrs. Herbert W. Howard Sr. It was from the lieutenant's mother to his sister. It might have been written by many another mother of a son lost in war.

Dear Dor and Les,

It is very difficult for me to write at this time. Herb's very words were: "You must face facts." The letters speak for themselves. No intelligent naval officers would write these words if they were not sure. The plane hit where Herb was standing. There is no doubt. We must adjust our minds to it and the sooner we begin the better for everyone. I will try very hard to fight for the sake of those who are living and love me. After the first awful blow, Dad has been wonderful. He is trying very hard not to think too much about it. We must all do that and think that he is away.

As far as Herb is concerned, he is happy and out of all struggle...We thank God that he went quickly with no suffering and, as he said, it was a wonderful way to go. We can always think of him as being young and gay and gallant and brave and that everyone loved him and that he had the respect of all with whom he came in contact. His card was up; the time had come, he did his job well and in his short life dispensed much happiness...

I am so happy that Les was with you when you got the letters. I took it alone and did not tell Dad until after dinner that night... Herb would want us to be very brave and strong. He asked before he left that, if anything happened to him, we would not go to pieces after it. He seemed to face it all and went just the way he predicted and the way he wanted, if he had to go.

I am glad that you are going away and that Les is going with you for two weeks. That will be a great help. I am all right when Dad is home. The hours alone are hard but I must steel myself to be cold if possible. It is most awful to be a sentimental person like us. When boys reach maturity, the parents must give them up but it is so hard to release the strings of childhood. Instead of giving Herb up to a wife, we gave him up to God and someday we shall see him again.

Be brave as he would want you to be.

Love, Mother

There were other passages in this mother's letter, describing lengthy and frequent conversations with other mothers of lost sons. Some of these sons had once been childhood playmates and later college classmates and now were MIAs.

One son had been returned home to his parents in a flag-draped casket, accompanied by his commanding officer.

Another had been assigned to a military hospital near his home so that his family might assist in his tedious and painful and dubious recovery. Sometimes there is a sweetness to be found in death.

Still another mother could not attend to her own sorrow because of her concern for her daughter, who was overwhelmed by the loss of her brother who had been her best friend.

Mothers carry a heavy burden in wartime, as do all parents. It is such a blessing for them when they have each other for shared strength.

The Navy's casualty statistics at Okinawa were very high: 1,455 men killed or missing in action, 34 ships sunk and 368 damaged. *Bowers* was one.

Billy Dugan and Butch were not listed with the Navy's casualties. They were counted, along with their Army ward mate, among the 36,000 wounded Army soldiers and Marines on the ground.

In spite of these losses, many more survived—both ships and people. The pain of the folks at home was eased considerably when our donors were assured—officially—that their blood had helped keep the survivor rate so high. Of course, one would never suggest that any survivor cane through Okinawa unscathed. But both men and ships stood ready to "carry on." And that they did, so many, so valiantly.

We had a chance to follow a ship that did "carry on." She was the USS *Henry A. Wiley*, originally built as a destroyer (DD 749), then converted and commissioned as a destroyer minelayer (DM-29). She was relatively new to the war, built in 1944 by the Bethlehem Steel Company in Staten Island, New York, and commissioned in the Brooklyn Navy Yard on August 31 of that year. After a shakedown cruise, she returned to the Navy yard to be readied for war. There she received orders to the Pacific Fleet. As she departed New York, she passed Ambrose Light for the last time for a long time and began her voyage around the world to the Pacific.

Her introduction to the war scene was Iwo Jima. Almost immediately after her arrival there, she received an urgent radio request from Marines on the beach. Would the captain of the *Wiley* bring his ship as close to shore as possible in order to blast out the Japanese holed up on Mount Suribachi, ready for a suicide counterattack against the Marines who had planted the Stars and Stripes on top of the mountain? The Marines were intent on securing the area, and they needed help. *Wiley* did her job and the Marines prevailed. That was February 20-21. After the destroyer moved away from shore, there were other demands for her services until orders came through to proceed north to Okinawa.

The Okinawa campaign began April 1, but *Wiley* was there early. She was a minelayer, although she never laid a mine at Okinawa. On March 28, she used her equipment and training in support of the minesweepers making the waters safe for the amphibious landings on April 1st. The ship also served as radar-picket for the larger ships, the cruisers and battleships. She had been ordered to assist in rescue operations for the USS *Luce* (DD 522), which was sinking after being set afire by one of these enemy bombers. Their ship could have been taken out by a kamikaze that had her as its target.

It was the habit of other kamikazes to retreat behind a cloud and wait for rescue efforts to get underway after another plane's hit, and then move in for another attack. That happened at the *Luce* assist. There were 186 *Luce* survivors—fifty-seven of them severely wounded and thirty-seven with minor wounds. As she was busy helping *Luce*, *Wiley* also came under attack by suicide boats and planes that had been waiting to pounce on ships providing assistance. One suffered a near miss and went into the ship's wake. That was close...too close. *Wiley* splashed another approaching plane, and still another. The men of *Wiley* were holding their own.

When another enemy plane came at them—so fast and so close—the *Wiley* crew worried whether they could get it before it got them. Suddenly, a Corsair from Marine Fighter Squadron VMF 323 dove out of the sky. The pilot swooped down over the ship's deck and took out the kamikaze before it could take out the *Wiley*. The crew watched this courageous and breathtaking maneuver with awe and admiration...and trepidation...and gratitude. They sent a "Well done!" to the pilot. In fact, the crew never forgot him. Indeed they adopted him as one of their own: a lifesaver.

During the Okinawa campaign, *Henry A. Wiley* expended nearly five thousand rounds of 5-inch and antiaircraft ammunition, destroying fifteen Japanese planes, as well as rescuing *Luce* survivors. For her actions off Okinawa, *Henry A. Wiley* received the Presidential Unit Citation.

The ship continued her hazardous operations at Okinawa until the campaign ended in June. Ultimately, she was attached to the Second Fleet and finally received orders to return to the United States for overhaul. On January 17, 1946, she flew her Homeward Bound Pennant and sailed past her flagship, rendering honors. Signal flags sent a message, "Well Done," but the men of the *Wiley* were impressed by the message their commanding officer received from Commander Minesweepers, Pacific Fleet Rear Adm. A. D. Struble: "CoMinPac commends you for a job well done and all MinPac will long remember the important part you had in the many Pacific operations. Goodbye, Good Luck, and Smooth Sailing."

After the war ended, the men of the *Wiley* did not lose touch with their ship, their shipmates, or their adopted Marine, Captain Robert F. Muse, USMCR. When they held a reunion, they invited him to come. He brought his wife, a former WAVE who had spent the war years decoding messages for the Navy at First Naval District headquarters in Boston. She is remembered as a blood donor who came to the Boston Center with a group of WAVES from headquarters and was photographed by a Boston newspaper.

When a future reunion was held in Boston, the Muses—now Robert F. Muse, Esq., and his wife, the Honorable Judge Mary Beatty Muse—played host to the group. "What an experience!" reported the visitors, "especially the police escort through the streets of Boston to visit the USS *Constitution*." It was a real thrill—a moment to remember—for the men of the *Wiley* to be received aboard "Old Ironsides."

When I interviewed Robert Muse in 2005, he made light of his contribution on May 4, 1945. But that's not the way the men of the *Wiley* felt, as exemplified in 2003 when Marine Fighter Squadron VMF 323 observed the sixtieth anniversary of its existence. A plaque was prepared and delivered to Miramar in San Diego for presentation at the banquet on August 1. It read:

> *To: Marine Fighter Squadron VMF 323*
> *From: USS Henry A. Wiley DM-29*
> *On the occasion of your 60th reunion, we congratulate you on your many years of valorous service to our country. We are forever grateful for your role of protecting radar picket ships at Okinawa, especially on the morning of May 4, 1945, when you helped our ship survive a fierce kamikaze attack.*

In addition, many *Wiley* men sent personal notes to the reunion organizer to be presented to Bob Muse that night, remembering May 4, 1945. Bob's reply to the men of the *Wiley*: "Words cannot express my gratitude to each of you for your kind consideration and thoughtfulness in taking the time to send the beautiful letters which were presented to me at our banquet...there were eight of us who were pilots and we watched with great pride the honor bestowed on our commander General George Axell, a great man, a compassionate man, deeply involved in the lives of his 'Fighter Pilots.'"

When the USS *Henry A. Wiley* was sold in 1972 and broken up for scrap, the spirit of that ship lived on in her men. It would live unbroken through her last man—whomever he might be. These destroyer men were fortunate to have able, generous shipmates who planned and managed reunions for them. There were many reunions throughout the years and across the country and many regular attendees.

The talent and dedication of their scribe, Bill Zinzow, who published frequent newsletters, contributed to the success of their reunions and kept the men in touch with each other and kept the spirit of the *Wiley* alive.

Although they had procured a bottle of fine cognac to be put aside and passed along for a "Last Man's Toast," they had a change of heart and mind when it came time for their sixtieth and probably last reunion. The bottle of cognac was too much for one man to drink alone. He—whomever he was going to be—should have the company of shipmates. And so the bottle was brought to the banquet, and at each *Wiley* man's place was a little cognac glass with a picture on it of the ship, its name, and the date, September 2005.

The "Last Man's Toast" was the climax of the evening, and an emotional time it was. Delivered by Bill Tucker, it brought the men of the *Wiley* to their feet with glasses raised:

"Shipmates, let's drink a toast—a toast to the honor of each and every last man of us who ever stood watch; paced the decks; and went to GQ aboard the USS *Henry A. Wiley*. And to the memory of our esteemed captain, Paul Bjarnason, and to the memory of all our glorious reunions, and to the support and participation of our wives and families.

"Shipmates, gentlemen all, since you don't drink cognac 'down the hatch,' we'll play a few strains of an old Civil War dirge entitled 'The Vacant Chair.' And, as we savor and sip this very finest of brandies, take these moments to reflect on Bill's words and our great good fortune in having been assigned to the *Henry A. Wiley*."

The Corsair pilot was with them that night. Even to the Last Man's Toast, they remembered. The *Wiley* is an example of some of the beauty that came out of the horror of Okinawa.

In November 2012, Bob Muse's long, full life came to an end. Before he died, he penned a statement for his daughter to read at his funeral. He recalled the May 4 mission that he flew at Okinawa as a Marine Corsair pilot to save the *Wiley* and her men from the kamikaze that was trying to take them out. He appreciated the fact that the mission saved so many, but he never forgot the face of the kamikaze pilot, and he prayed for him every day of his life.

PART VII
THE ARMY AIR FORCES

29. A SALUTE TO ITS HISTORY: AUGUST 1

August 1, 1945, was Air Force Day, a time to recall something of the history of this great and powerful branch of the U.S. Army: our Army Air Forces.

The U.S. government purchased its first plane from the Wright Brothers in 1909. There was much dickering in the beginning when the government stated the details of its terms. "The plane must fly 125 miles from a given point and return."

"But, sir," said the Wright Brothers' representative, "we have just established a new world's record...ninety-five miles including all turns in two hours, eighteen minutes, and thirty-five seconds."

Although the government did not wish to minimize the importance of the record, they were compelled to stick to the terms of their paper, accepting nothing else. So the Wright Brothers went back to their drawing board, to the airfield, and the skies. They tried and failed, and tried again and failed again. But on July 30, 1909, they fulfilled all the conditions set by the U.S. government. There followed an exchange of money and one plane. The Wright Brothers were paid $25,000 plus a $5,000 bonus.

In 1914 there were sixteen officers and seventy-seven enlisted men in what was known then as the aviation section of the Signal Corps. By November 11, 1918, the service had grown to 18,000 officers and 135,000 enlisted men.

At first the pilots carried only a revolver or a rifle, occasionally a few bombs. After a while, machine guns were added. That was in the days of World War I, when the first American squadron, the Escadrille Lafayette—with seven American aviators—won first honors over Verdun in the days when pilot Eddie Rickenbacker held the unofficial title of the Ace of Aces because of his twenty-five attested victories.

By January 1941 the Army Air Corps announced it would expand to 54 groups to include 16,000 officers, 15,000 aviation cadets, and 187,000 enlisted men. Not long after this 54-group plan was set aside in favor of a new 84-group plan involving an eventual strength of over 400,000 men. (The Army Air Corps became the Army Air Forces in June 1941.)

By World War II, many people knew all about the Army Air Corps. They could recognize planes and knew their specifications and armament. People at home in August 1945 knew what their Air Force had been doing for them, and they had profound respect and gratitude for it.

Now it was time, on this Air Force birthday, for the people to tell the Air Force what they, the people at home, had been doing for their flying forces all over the war world. We reminded them of a statement made by their own commanding general, Hap Arnold: "The blood of volunteer American donors, flown and shipped throughout the world, has saved the lives of thousands of our fighting men. I can think of no finer gift that anyone at home can make than a donation of a pint of blood for our men engaged in our great final drive against Japan."

Sometimes it's effective to tell a story with another story. That's what we did about the Air Force. We presented a dramatization of a story told to us by one of their own, an Air Force pilot. It was part of the *Life to the Front* broadcast, and it went like this on August 1, 1945:

SOUND: PLANE FADING IN...HOLD, INCREASING VOLUME

VOICES: AD LIB IN GENERAL CONFUSION

SOUND: PLANE MOTORS FROM INSIDE...MACHINE GUN
                FIRE FROM PLANE...OCCASIONAL SOUND OF
                ENEMY FIGHTERS CONTINUE THROUGHOUT THE
                FOLLOWING

SOUND: CLICK OF INTER-PHONE

PILOT: (ON FILTER THROUGHOUT) Pilot to top
                turret.

TOP TURRET: Top turret. Go ahead.

PILOT: What's going on up there? I haven't
                heard from you for quite a while.

TOP TURRET: Not a thing overhead, skipper. Everything
                that's been coming in has either been
                from the same altitude or below. Just
                haven't seen a thing above us.

PILOT: Okay! Let's hope it stays that way. We've
                got enough trouble as it is.

GUNNER: (ON FILTER) Tail gunner to pilot.

PILOT: Pilot to tail...go ahead.

GUNNER: (ON FILTER) Three MEs coming in at 7
                o'clock and coming fast.

PILOT: Okay! On your toes in the waist and belly turret.

TOP TURRET: Oh-oh! Top turret to pilot!

PILOT: Pilot to top, go ahead.

TOP TURRET: Flight of five more coming down out of the sun at three o'clock.

PILOT: Okay, Mac, you and the right waist gunner handle them.

TOP TURRET: Roger. (TO HIMSELF) Oh brother! Look at them come!

SOUND: PLANES DIVING AND FIRING FAINT MACHINE GUNS FIRING IN SHORT BURSTS OF FIRE

TOP TURRET: Hey! I got one. He's a flamer.

PILOT: Nice going. How about the other four?

TOP TURRET: One of them overshot. The other three are just coming in.

PILOT: Okay! Hope your luck is as good on these.

SOUND: PLANES DIVING IN (SAME AS ABOVE) ENDING IN MINOR EXPLOSION.

PILOT: Pilot to top turret. (PAUSE) Pilot to top turret...

VOICE: (ON FILTER) Waist to pilot. Top turret's been hit bad. I'll go have a look at him as soon as it's clear here.

ORGAN: BRIDGE

NARRATOR: Meanwhile, back at the base, the ground crew awaits the return of the mission— the way they do every day—pacing back and forth, watching the sky and counting.

SOUND: PLANE COMING IN FOR A LANDING CIRCLING OVER THE FIELD

BURNS: That makes five that are back. Six more to come. Hope they can land all right. Looks like they got shot up a bit.

AID: How some of these fellows get back is beyond me. So long's they've got a wing on each side of them, they seem to make it.

BURNS: Yuh, but I don't breathe until they're all set down. Hey! They're firing a flare. (CALLING) Hey, Doc! Wounded aboard! Come on, gang, let's go!

AID: Some poor devil got it again.

VOICES: AD LIB OFF MIKE (AS THOUGH RUNNING TO THE PLANE)

SOUND: PLANE LANDING

BURNS: What have you got?

SOUND: PLANE DOOR BEING OPENED

PILOT: (OFF MIKE) It's Mac, top turret gunner. He got it bad and he's trapped.

DOC: Can we get in to him?

PILOT: Yuh, I think so, Doc, but you can't get him out until they cut away whatever's got him pinned down.

DOC: Okay, mechanics, you take over and I'll try to keep out of your way. Burns, break open a couple of units of plasma and crawl in with them just as soon as you've got them ready. I'll see what I can do for Mac, meanwhile.

BURNS: Okay, Doc, I'll be in on your heels.

ORGAN: BRIDGE

NARRATOR: Time passes. Not just a matter of minutes but hours. Finally the doctor gives the word. Okay, men, lift him out.

MAC: (WEAKLY) Thanks, Doc.

DOC: Don't thank me, son. You did a lot yourself. It's been four long hours. You did well to stick it out.

MAC: Whatever you gave me, Doc, it sure saw me through. I didn't think I'd live when we landed.

DOC: Then you can thank the people at home who donated blood because it was plasma that I gave you.

ORGAN: CLIMACTIC BRIDGE

The program was a success. The Air Force was a popular branch of the service. Some of our donors felt that the Air Force birthday warranted a suitable present, so they gave another pint of blood. Others realized that it was time they got about giving. They'd always wanted to give. This time they would do it. They would call next week and make an appointment for later in the month. But they were too late. They missed out on that wonderful experience of being a part of the great romance that connected the people at home with the wounded abroad.

30. ITS ORDERS TO TINIAN: AUGUST 6

In July, a high-level meeting had convened in Potsdam, Germany. President Harry Truman represented the United States; Prime Minister Winston Churchill and his successor, Clement Attlee, represented Great Britain; and Premier Joseph Stalin represented the USSR.

Their first order of business was to implement decisions made previously at Yalta regarding the aftermath in Europe of Hitler's surrender in Berlin in May. They had much to consider and action to be taken.

They were concerned, too, about the war in the Pacific. It had to come to an end. It had to be *brought* to an end. They knew Japan's resources were depleted. She could no longer defend herself, much less wage aggressive warfare, always Japan's intention.

On July 26, members of the Potsdam Conference decided to issue an ultimatum, known as the Potsdam Declaration. It gave the Japanese government a choice between unconditional surrender and total annihilation. The ultimatum was delivered.

Japan made no reply.

On August 2, the Potsdam Conference concluded its deliberations, and the members went home to their various countries. Still no response from Japan. Another day went by and yet another.

Finally, the matter was put before President Truman. He asked for facts and figures. What was the statistical expectation of American casualties if the invasion of Japan went forward? The answer: at least a half a million Americans alone. He asked about Japanese casualties and was given the similarly sobering statistics. The war with Japan would drag on for months. That was enough information for President Truman. There was an alternative, he was told. He sent the order to the Air Force to fly a mission over the industrial city of Hiroshima on August 6. The weapon was an atomic bomb.

Unbelievably, even after the destruction of Hiroshima, Japan still did not reply to the Potsdam ultimatum. Truman authorized a second mission. A B-29 Superfortress from Tinian in the Marianas was ordered to drop a second atomic bomb on another Japanese industrial city, Nagasaki.

The delay in Japanese response came from friction in the palace. Emperor Hirohito leaned toward surrender, but his military advisers wanted to continue the war and were considering a coup d'etat. Matters finally come to a head.

The Allies' peace offer, issued in the Potsdam Declaration in July, was acknowledged and the Japanese accepted surrender. But it was not unconditional. They asked to be allowed to keep their emperor. Such permission was granted. The war in the Pacific was over, 1,331 days since the attack on Pearl Harbor.

PART VIII

V-J DAY

31. THE ALLIED FLEET SAILS IN BLACKOUT

During this time, the U.S. Navy and ships of the Allies were steaming steadily and in blackout toward Japan's mainland. They all knew where they were going and why. Automatic electronic announcements had not been invented yet, so the long-awaited news of the war's end was passed with immediacy from ship to ship. The first ship to get the news canceled its blackout and all its lights went on. Then one ship after another picked up the cue and lit up. It was like a light display at Christmas.

It was a sight never to be forgotten, as described to me in 2007 by a Marine who was aboard one of the escort carriers in the Pacific in August 1945. "Those lit-up ships dotting the Pacific had great meaning for the Navy and the Marines aboard." His carrier was the USS *Puget Sound* (CVE-113), part of a small task force in the vast Pacific Fleet. She had been recently commissioned in Tacoma, Washington, but many of the men were not at all new to the war, and they were well aware that they were headed into harm's way.

Part of Chaplain J. B. O'Malley's commissioning prayer that day is remembered by those who heard it.

Deign, O Lord, to hear our supplications and bless this ship and all who sail in it. Extend to us Thy right hand as Thou didst to Peter walking upon the water, that we may be preserved from the perils of wind and storm and from the violence of the enemy. Give us the strength we need to fight injustice in every form so that, as decent men, we may live decently in a decent world.

These small carriers proved to be an asset to the fleet because they could maneuver closer to the beach to launch air strikes in support of the amphibious assault. They carried two squadrons of Marine fliers. One squadron on the *Puget Sound* was VMTB 454 flying the TBM-3E Avenger torpedo bomber.

The veteran Marine telling me this story in 2007 is my brother, Bud. He didn't get to Tokyo Bay in time for the signing of the surrender, but when the ship did get there, it was not for an amphibious attack as originally expected. Instead they made a peaceful port call. And when VMTB 454 flew missions over Saipan, Guam, and Midway, they were not dropping bombs. More port calls followed, including a week anchored off Hong Kong, a stop at Luzon, and Manila for Christmas, before heading home across the Pacific. For Charles F. Kirby Jr., it was the end of his four-year tour of duty in the Marines and back home and to college.

32. ABOARD THE *MISSOURI* IN TOKYO BAY

Other ships made it in time and anchored in Tokyo Bay, watching and listening on September 2, 1945, as admirals and generals and other high-ranking officers were rendered honors aboard the battleship USS *Missouri* (BB-63).

With the principals on deck and official papers and pens in place, formalities began with an opening speech by Supreme Commander of the Allied Forces Gen. Douglas MacArthur, U.S. Army.

An official photograph of General MacArthur at the signing table shows dozens of uniformed personnel lined up, shoulder to shoulder, witnessing. There is a similarity about them. They are in khakis, no jackets, open shirts, no ribbons, mostly with embroidered visors on their hats. Some could be recognized if you knew who to look for, with many famous names in the lineup. If you looked carefully, you might identify the insignia on the collars of most. Representatives from Australia, Canada, China, France, Great Britain, the Netherlands, New Zealand, and the USSR signed on behalf of their countries.

Other Americans participating in the signing were Fleet Adm. Chester W. Nimitz, USN, Adm. William F. Halsey, USN, and Gen. Richard K. Sutherland, USA. Hundreds of sailors from the battleship's crew were unofficial witnesses, occupying every available topside space.

When we broaden the picture of General MacArthur signing, we see the official Japanese contingent standing together, facing the table and the instrument of surrender. Foreign Minister Mamoru Shigemitsu and Gen. Yoshijiro Umezu wore top hats, tails, and white gloves. With them were other members in full uniform with aiguillettes, ribbons, and polished boots. They were grim.

Facing the Japanese group, standing behind General MacArthur, were two men whose presence must have brought tears to the eyes of their war-hardened colleagues. They were Lt. Gen. Jonathan M. Wainwright, USA, and Lt. Gen. Sir Arthur E. Percival of the British Army. Both men had been released from Japanese prison camps.

It is likely that there was also a sameness under those khaki shirts, in the hearts of the men standing there. They must all have felt a profound and burning gratitude for the end of the war. Many of them had been through the worst of battles, lost colleagues, close friends, shipmates, and relatives. Some were survivors of that dreaded command to abandon ship and had watched so many of their men go down with their beloved ship.

Emotions must have been strong in their chests. The journey from the "Day of Infamy" at Pearl Harbor had been long and painful and costly. Now it was over. World War II had come to an end.

USS Missouri at Tokyo Bay.

At the conclusion of the formalities of the signing, and brief remarks by General MacArthur, a flight of one hundred planes swept over the *Missouri* and her sister ships anchored in Tokyo Bay. The planes were meant to be symbols of Allied power. Perhaps they could also be seen as symbolic of birds, warplanes as doves bringing peace—at last!

PART IX

THE END

33. THE WARTIME BLOOD DONOR SERVICE CONCLUDES ITS MISSION

When the war in the Pacific came to an end, the American Red Cross Wartime Blood Donor Service came to an end as well, and the Boston Center closed its doors for good.

The American Red Cross had entered into a contract with the Army and Navy to collect blood from volunteer donors for the exclusive and extensive use of the armed forces. The Red Cross opened thirty-five centers throughout the country, and the Army and Navy set a quota for each. Boston's started at three thousand pints a week, increased to five thousand, and for most of the war years rose to six thousand pints a week.

The majority of the blood taken was sent to a laboratory for processing into plasma, then shipped wherever the Army and Navy directed. Eventually, the blood of many type O donors was flown as whole blood directly to Europe by the Army's Air Transport Command and, after V-E Day, to the Pacific by Naval Air Transport Service—or NATS—planes. From the beginning, plasma—and later whole blood—was credited by the surgeons general of the Army and Navy as being the greatest lifesaver of World War II.

The wartime Blood Donor Service was no simple operation, but complex and far-reaching. The abrupt closing of centers through-out the country was complicated because laboratories, shipping programs, and mobile units booked well in advance. So many cancellations—so many notifications! This exciting date in history that brought about such a welcome relief to the troops on the fighting fronts—and their families—brought about drastic changes in the lives of many on the home front. Hundreds of volunteers had put in long, dedicated hours at the center, many on a daily basis. For the medical, technical, shipping, clerical, and administrative personnel, some found hardship in suddenly being out of work.

The elation over the war's end far outshone the shadows of anyone's distress. The disappointment felt by donors who were booked for an eighth or a sixteenth pint to give them membership in the coveted Gallon or Two-Gallon Club disappeared in the joy of fighting's end.

A letter, dated September 15, 1945, from Joseph R. Hamlen, chairman of the Boston Metropolitan Chapter of the American Red Cross, stated the situation quite simply:

"The mission of the Boston Blood Donor Center to the armed forces was completed the evening of August 14 with President Truman's historic announcement that the war was over."

34. *LIFE TO THE FRONT* IS BROADCAST FOR THE LAST TIME

Life to the Front was planned in advance, but with the war ending, it faced cancellation. That meant disappointment for those donors who expected to be in the studio audience for these upcoming broadcasts. In addition, the situation required a hurried preparation of an important final program for the series.

The final broadcast.

Invited to participate in this culminating broadcast were Alan R. Morse, chairman of the Red Cross Blood Donor Service Committee of Boston; Harold E. Fellows, general manager of WEEI; and Cmdr. Neil Rex Collier, USNR, commanding officer of the Public Information Office of the First Naval District (formerly the Public Relations Office).

It was a day of tribute and thanks. Mr. Morse acknowledged with deep gratitude the generosity of WEEI and the Columbia Broadcasting System in sponsoring *Life to the Front* for more than three years. The center had evidence, he said, of more listeners than they could count who gave their blood and who gave their time as workers because of an interview they had heard on the series.

Mr. Fellows noted that it had been a privilege to work with us and for "the station and CBS to carry such a tremendously valuable weekly public service feature." Then he mentioned his pride in his staff, who gave not only their professional assistance to the program but their blood as repeat donors. He cited his secretary, Florence Mitchell, as a fifteen-pint donor.

Turning to Commander Collier, Mr. Morse recognized the outstanding professional assistance of his office in the production of *Life to the Front* from its beginning. He recalled that it was Commander Collier who introduced Navy Chaplain McQuaid to the Boston Center, resulting in a most productive and rewarding association. The Red Cross was not only aware of the Navy's generosity but most grateful for it.

It seemed appropriate to conclude this special program with an interview, as we had done so many times in past broadcasts. This time we were not out for blood. This time we had a last chance to tell the public how special their donations throughout the war years had been. That had always been a secondary intention behind *Life to the Front*: to give donors the satisfaction of learning how important they were to the wounded and the medics whose job it was to keep those wounded men alive.

Our final interview was actually transcribed months earlier at Navy headquarters when the interviewee, Lt. Colton G. Morris, USNR, radio officer on the USS Helena (CL 50), which had gone down in Kula Gulf on July 6, 1943, was in town on leave..

The interview:

KIRBY: Well,   Chick, it's been a long time since you and I sat on either side of a microphone.

MORRIS: Three years to be exact.

Lt. j, g. Colton G. Morris

KIRBY: And since then you've become Navy Lt. Colton G. Morris and sailed halfway round the world and back.

MORRIS: Just like in the storybooks.

KIRBY   Can you say that and mean it, after what you've been through?

MORRIS: No. Reading about adventure and disaster in a book in a nice warm, comfortable chair is one thing. Living through it in a cold, wet, and oily sea, with explosions, fire, debris all around you...not to mention death...well...that's something else.

KIRBY: I expect it is, Chick, very different... and something that those of us at home can never really appreciate, never completely understand.

MORRIS: Well, there are just three things you can be when it's all over. You can be a survivor, a casualty, or a mortality. Every sinking has all three and the *Helena* had her share of each. I was lucky to be on the survivors' list.

KIRBY: We were mighty glad to hear about that. When the news broke about the *Helena* being sunk in the Solomons, everyone was reminding everyone that Chick Morris was her radio officer, and we were very anxious.

MORRIS: As I said, I was lucky.

KIRBY: What was the ship's mission?

MORRIS: We were ordered to move in on Kula Gulf and intercept the so-called Tokyo Express reported ready to steam toward New Georgia Island for the purpose of reinforcing the Jap garrison just off the Munda airfield.

KIRBY: And that became the Battle of Kula Gulf...a major engagement, right?

MORRIS: Oh yes, and the crew and the ship were keyed for battle. Down in the wardroom and all over the ship, men and officers gathered in circles to discuss the oncoming battle and, as usual, pick up the tune, "Just before the Battle, Mother." They nearly always sang it.

KIRBY: What happened in the battle?

MORRIS: We had the misfortune to bear the brunt of a daring torpedo attack. The ship leaped at least five feet straight up in the air. Our fire and the torpedo crossed courses so we scored a hit. But we were done.

KIRBY: Did the call come immediately to abandon ship?

MORRIS: Yes, and I rushed back to my room to salvage some valuable papers. There was nothing there but water. That part of the ship was gone. I just walked off into water. Only problem—somebody walked off behind me and stepped on my head as I came up with a mouthful of oil. Fortunately, I had my hat on and that saved me. No concussion but he pushed me down under again.

KIRBY: How long were you in the water before you were rescued?

MORRIS: Four hours.

KIRBY: With the battle still going on around you?

MORRIS: It raged with all its fury. Torpedoes actually slid beneath us and set up waves that filled us with still more oil. All around us, shells were breaking, some exploding in the water. A few of them exploded near enough to make us think it was all over.

KIRBY: How did you hang on for four hours with all this going on around you?

MORRIS: We alternately sang, prayed, and just tried to keep calm. I did not see one man of our entire complement fail to display the courage Americans back home could be proud of. We even managed a little humor when we came upon a shipmate struggling in the water and the boys would pick up a chant, "Imagine meeting you here!"

KIRBY: You were in the dark, weren't you, because this was a night battle, wasn't it?

MORRIS: Yes, and that was a problem because we couldn't tell which were our ships in the dark. We finally decided to take a chance on one we thought was ours. But we took a vote on whether or not

to approach them. It was agreed and we
boosted up the communications officer
who used a flashlight that we cleaned
up for him to signal HELP-50. Then we
waited, scarcely breathing. Suddenly,
there came a return message, blinking
in the blackness: "Friendly ship. Come
alongside."

KIRBY:

I'm sure you didn't waste any time
in doing just that! Did you have any
trouble getting aboard? Were there any
wounded among you?

MORRIS:

Yes, there were, but we did not know
how bad they were until we were aboard
the destroyer. The men seemed to tough
it out in the water. But the corpsmen
could tell and took the serious cases
right into sick bay and gave them plasma
immediately to bring them out of shock
and keep them going until the medics
could assess their cases.

KIRBY:

Do the boys really know about plasma
and where it comes from?

MORRIS:

They know all right. And they are very
grateful.

KIRBY:

What do you think they would say to the
people at home if they had a chance?

MORRIS: Some of them would say, "Thanks for my life." Or maybe just, "Keep it coming. We don't mind fighting, but give us a chance if we get hit."

KIRBY: They really count on us, don't they? It makes us sort of a lifeline behind the front line.

MORRIS: That's right. And in that front line are some of the greatest guys in the world. Every fellow out there goes into battle every day, knowing full well that he may never come out of it...that he may never live to enjoy the peace for which he is fighting. You see he's really not fighting for himself. He's fighting for the people at home and for their future.

This interview with Lieutenant Morris gave us a glimpse of what V-J Day meant: no more raging battles in the Pacific, no more sunken cruisers or other ships, no more sailors torpedoed into a briny death, no more survivors hanging on to a raft in turbulent seas for hours...and so much more "no more!" V-J Day meant that the war in the Pacific was over. World War II had come to an end. This was certainly a cause for jubilation. The troops would be coming home.

Our donors joined in the celebration, but they had a personal satisfaction also. They knew that many of those returning were survivors because plasma or whole blood—or both—helped bring them home.

The generosity of these donors can be traced for generations into the future. They were indeed part of a great romance, and their children are, too, because many of these children are alive today because the life of a father or grandfather was saved by the blood of one of these donors.

35. A PERSONAL FINALE

Planning and writing *Life to the Front* had been demanding, but my many interviews with medics, chaplains, and the wounded who survived battle action on fighting fronts all over the world provided great inspiration, their words to be deeply appreciated and forever remembered.

My responsibilities at the center were also demanding, but there, too, was inspiration on a daily basis. It came from thousands of donors and their impressive backgrounds that can never be forgotten. Looking back on this experience, I am reminded of what Chaplain Arthur McQuaid said in our final meeting before his return to active duty, following his medical leave.

When I thanked him for all that he had done for us, he said, "Don't thank me. I thank you." Then he added what I am remembering now: "You worked me hard," he said to me, "but it was worthwhile and I thank you for it!"

THE END

AN EPILOGUE

Lt. Henry Lundquist applied for sea duty but was turned down because of his eyes. He took a week's leave and reported to a local optometrist who specialized in a regimen of exercise and treatment to stimulate a person's vision. When he returned, he passed easily. When he reapplied for sea duty, he was subjected to another physical by a new doctor who decided that he had a heart murmur and was not qualified for sea duty. He was ordered to Chelsea Naval Hospital to be "surveyed out of the Navy." This was a shock.

He had argued with the examining doctor that his murmur was functional, not organic, and known to exist for a long time. His argument was not accepted, so he was off to Chelsea. There he requested and received an appointment with a ranking doctor whom he knew. This doctor happened to be an eminent Boston heart specialist. He examined the lieutenant and found no problem with his heart. He was now qualified for sea duty. His orders had him still attached to the hospital, but he went back to PRO immediately where he had work waiting for him.

He knew that it would take time for his orders to be reprocessed and catch up with him, so he gave up on sea duty for a while and offered his assistant, Lt. j.g. Arch Macdonald, a chance for sea duty if he wanted it. Arch did. When nothing happened to Lieutenant Lundquist's application for sea duty, he decided to get married. His wife always considered herself a substitute for Armed Guard, which is what the lieutenant wanted for sea duty.

After the war, Henry Lundquist returned to broadcasting at WCOP and later WBZ in Boston. He taught writing for broadcasting at Boston University for sixteen years. He retired as the director for public information at the Massachusetts Department of Public Works in 1974.

Bill Schofield returned to his newspaper after the war but remained in the reserves. He authored many books and magazine articles besides his editorial work on the paper. He will always be remembered as the founder of Boston's famous Freedom Trail. As Captain Schofield, he delivered the Fourth of July address aboard "Old Ironsides" for our country's bicentennial celebration.

Both continued to be involved with the Navy after the war. In 1949, along with Cmdr. Tom Horgan of the Associated Press (formerly of PRO), they founded the Navy's Public Affairs Reserve Unit in Boston.

In 1999, Lundquist was honored as its surviving founder by NAVINFO 101 when that unit celebrated "Fifty Years of Navy Public Affairs Excellence." He spoke to the celebrants that evening at the Kennedy Library in Boston and was presented with a framed tribute to "Founding father, LCDR Hank Lundquist with great respect from Naval Reserve Navy Information Bureau New England 101." In October 2003, our producer became the late Henry W. Lundquist. Looking back to the war days of August 1942, when he was learning—without indoctrination—how to be a naval officer, he could never have foreseen the many years of life that lay ahead.

**

Charles F. Kirby Jr. came home and attended the University of California at Los Angeles, graduating in 1949. He had a career in marketing and sales, retiring in 1986 as executive vice president for apple juice producer Tree Top in Washington State. He passed away in 2010.

The Browns and the Kirbys (Joe E, Lillian, Bud, Charles Sr., and Kathrine Brown) celebrate Bud's graduation from UCLA.

**

Chaplain McQuaid remained on active duty after the war, achieving the rank of captain and serving as csenior chaplain for the Atlantic FleetDestroyer Force. Upon his retirement he returned to parish work.

**

Some of the facts regarding incidents discussed in this book became clearer after the war, and in some cases, related stories became known.

When I interviewd Lt. Joe Groden for *Life to the Front*, he described the value of plasma in saving the lives of his wounded shipmates on USS *Henley* (DD 391) when it was sunk at the Bismarck Sea,. In 2005, I talked with him again, and he told me the extraordinary story of the *Henley* when they were at Pearl Harbor on December 7, 1941.

He had the midwatch, from midnight to 0400. When he got off of his watch he left instructions to be called at 0800. But at 0755 he was awakened by a blaring alarm calling the crew to general quarters. He threw on some clothes and ran out to see what was happening. He found a young Sailor quaking as he explained how he had made a mistake, intending to call the crew to breakfast. Joe Groden knew this was an error, and when the ship next to them inquired about the general alarm, he told the Sailor to tell them it was a drill. But then the men on deck could see aircraft attacking other ships in the harbor. At first, they all thought the planes were friendly and participating in some sort of practice. But it soon became obvious that the planes with the big red "meatballs" were not American. They were able to make the ship ready for sea and fight back. Both the commanding officer and executive officer were still ashore, but they were brought aboard later in the morning. This following report discusses the *Henley*'s actions at Pearl Harbor.

From: Commanding Officer, USS *Henley* (DD 391)
To: Commander-in-Chief, United States Pacific Fleet

Subject: Offensive measures during air raid on Pearl Harbor, T.H., December 7, 1941

Reference: (a) CinC, Pac.Flt. dispatch 102102 Dec., 1941.

1. At 0755 December 7, 1941, the following conditions existed aboard this vessel:
   1. Through error of the gangway watch in calling crew to quarters for muster at 0755 the GENERAL ALARM was sounded instead of the gas alarm which was customary.
   2. As a result of (a) above, the crew and officers on board were "on the move."
   3. All of the crew were in the general vicinity of the fantail and they saw first torpedo plane attack on the *Utah.*
   4. The upper handling room on 5" gun No. 2 still had ready service ammunition (25 rounds) stored there due to a material casualty of the lower ammunition hoist for that gun. The ammunition was so placed during the preceding operating period. Repairs were to have been undertaken on this day.
   5. No awnings were spread.
   6. None of the armament, other than the hoist mentioned in (d) above, was out of commission.

2. Upon realization that torpedoes dropped from planes aimed at the *Utah* did not constitute a target practice, the crew proceeded to their battle stations while the general alarm sounded for a second time. The "Rising Sun" emblem was plainly visible about the center of the fuselage of the black planes. Members of the repair party proceeded to set material condition "Affirm" in accordance with ship doctrine. Word was sent to the engine room to make immediate preparations for getting underway. By the time this word arrived, lube oil pumps had already been started and the fire room had been instructed to open by-passes and get up steam.

3. The time required to fire the first gun is not known exactly, but the 5″ gun No. 2, mentioned in the first paragraph, was one of the first, if not the first, medium caliber gun to fire. Early targets were light bombers in irregular formation at an altitude of about 17,000 feet on an apparently steady northerly course, approaching from seaward and passing over Ford Island. The majority of attacking planes were all east of Ford Island. At 0830 this vessel was underway from Buoy X-11. While slipping the chain to the buoy a large bomb intended for the nest struck the water about 150 yards on the port bow. After clearing the nest a signal, "submarine in harbor" was received. The *MacDonough*, directly ahead, proceeded to make a depth charge attack and then cleared channel at high speed. This vessel

was the third ship to sortie. After rounding
Hospital Point the ship was subjected to a
strafing attack by a light bomber coming up
from astern showing five distinct sources of
machine gun fire from the plane. This plane
was taken under fire by .50 caliber machine
guns at close range. Machine Gun No. 2 is
given credit for bringing down this plane for
as it passed ahead of the ship; smoke and
flames issued from the fuselage and the plane
was seen to crash offshore. A few minutes
later, while this ship was still in the channel another light bomber approaching from
the starboard hand, flying about 2000 feet
altitude was taken under fire jointly with
a destroyer in Sector No. 1. A close burst
forced this plane into a dive from which he
was unable to pull out and this plane like-
wise crashed at sea. Upon arriving at the sea
buoys, this vessel proceeded to the outer
edge of Sector 2 and thence to Sector 3 to
patrol the area as ordered. While enroute
through sector 2 a fairly certain sound contact was made, close aboard to port. Sound
contact was lost bearing abeam distant about
200 yards. After a hard left turn two depth
charges were dropped. No visible surface results were apparent. About 1030 a visual signal from the *Trever* reported that the *Henley*
Captain and Executive Officer were aboard
that vessel. About 1130, permission was obtained to pick up the Captain and the *Trever*
was closed. While the *Trever* was steaming at

five knots to stream her magnetic sweep this vessel took position ahead and streamed a life raft on a long piece of manila line. The Captain and the Executive Officer, Lieutenant H.G. Corey, U.S. Navy, jumped from the *Trever* and got aboard the life raft, then aboard the *Henley.*

4. LOSSES—DAMAGE: No losses or injuries were experienced with any personnel. The only damage occurring to the ship was the result of strafing attack in the channel. During this attack three machine gun bullets struck and penetrated the director shield. No other damage resulted. The forecastle shows evidence at several places where bullets ricocheted from the deck. Considerable difficulty was experienced with the control circuit relays from the QCB equipment. These kept coming open as a result of gun fire. These relays were gagged to keep them in. When an opportunity was available relays were adjusted so as not to open so freely.

5. DISTINGUISHED CONDUCT OF PERSONNEL: All enlisted personnel conducted themselves in a manner which left absolutely nothing to be desired. Chief Machinist's Mate, W.H. Fiddler, F-4-D, U.S.N., while preparing to muster the engineering department, saw the first torpedoes launched and proceeded to make preparations for getting underway without further orders. G.T. Dukes, BM2c., U.S.N., gun captain gun No. 2, had his gun loaded with

a projectile set with dive bombing fuse setting and pointed at the attacking aircraft
before phone communication was established
with the director. He reported ready to com-
mence firing, awaiting only orders to do so.
D.J. Seely, GM3c., U.S.N., gunner for machine
gun No. 2. is credited with the bringing
down of the plane making the strafing attack. Chief Quartermaster M.O. Nelson, U.S.N.,
rendered invaluable assistance in piloting
clear of the harbor. He performed his duties
in a calm, collected, and highly efficient
manner. During the sortie and the three
days at sea afterwards, M.H. Tapley, RM1c.,
U.S.N., worked day and night almost continu-
ously to keep the radio and sound equipment
in excellent material condition and rendered
valuable assistance in communications. All
five of the ship's reserve officers were on
board and performed the duties formerly assigned to regular officers in a highly efficient manner. Lieutenant F.E. Fleck, Jr.,
U.S.N., was commanding officer of the *Henley*
at the time the air raid commenced. The manner in which he got the ship underway and
fought the enemy during the sortie of the
Henley is worthy of special commendation.
The seamanlike manner in which he picked up
his Captain and Executive Officer at sea is
greatly appreciated.

**

When Red Sox owner Tom Yawkey thanked me in May 1944 for the courtesy I showed him at the center, I did not know then that the season pass enclosed would be my claim to fame in a college dormitory at Marquette University many years later. There were many Red Sox enthusiasts among my son's friends as he boasted that his mother had a season pass to Fenway Park and that she was on Mr. Yawkey's private list, mentioning the number of her pass. Every year, come opening game, they would ask, "Did she get it?" Each year they had to know what her number was. Their curiosity went on even after graduation when they had gone their varied and distant ways.

When the boasting son met up with old pals over the years and around the world, he was again asked the number of her pass. When one of the most ardent baseball fans came to the change of command of his old classmate, Capt. Carl I. Lundquist, USN, his first question to the captain's mother was "Do you still get your Red Sox pass?"

"No, it ceased with Mr. Yawkey's death in 1976," I said. The next question brought some satisfaction when that classmate, Andy Curtin, asked, "What was the number of your last pass?" I said, "Five."

What a great claim to fame for a mother, because she was just doing her privileged job those many years ago before she became a mom.

**

Neither Henry nor I met Arleigh Burke during the war, but some thirty years later our son, Carl, did at an annual Surface Warfare Party in Washington. When Admiral Burke noticed Carl Lundquist's Swedish name, he told him that he, too, was Swedish, not Irish as so many people thought. When his grandfather came to this country in 1857, he was afraid no one would be able to pronounce his name, Bjorkgren, so it was changed to Burke when he entered this country.

Admiral Burke and Lieutenant Commander Lundquist did not talk Navy in this meeting; they talked Sweden. They found that both of their grandfathers had come from Gothenburg. Arleigh Burke had visited the city, and he described it with great pleasure. When he found that neither Carl nor his father had ever been there, he urged a sentimental journey to their ancestral homeland.

Carl met Admiral Burke again when Arleigh Burke Hall was dedicated at SWOS and Carl, stationed there as director of Surface Department Head Training, had the pleasure of moving his office into those beautiful new quarters.

At the time of the building dedication, Carl could not have foreseen another connection to Arleigh Burke, but it happened in 1994 when Captain Lundquist took command of Destroyer Squadron 21, the "Rampant Lions." There was always a special kinship between DesRon 21 and DesRon 23. Both had been born in the Solomons campaign in 1943; the "Rampant Lions" were in the command of Captain F. X. McInerney at Kula Gulf while Captain Arleigh Burke commanded the "Little Beavers" at Bougainville.

In 1949, Arleigh Burke became the youngest non-wartime admiral at the age of forty-nine. His service to his country extended from 1923

Admiral Arleigh Burke

to 1961. Besides serving at sea in wartime, he held the position of chief of naval operations in Washington. He died on January 1, 1996, at age ninety-four. Grandfather Bjorkgren should have been very proud of his Burke boy.

**

After the war ended, the islands of Micronesia became part of the Trust Territory of the Pacific Islands, and the United States was assigned by the United Nations to be the trustee and administrator and therefore responsible for their security. That called for periodic visits by Navy ships, and in 1977 the surveillance mission was assigned to the USS *Tawakoni* (ATF 114), an oceangoing tug that served during World War II (her kamikaze attack at Okinawa is recalled by her commanding officer in chapter 28 . If you were to ask what a fleet tug did for the Navy, expect a long answer. Towing, diving, and salvage are only generalities of fleet tug duties.

In November 1977, *Tawakoni* added the Trust Territorial visitations to her schedule. *Tawakoni*'s orders listed islands to be visited: Tobi, Helen Reef, Merrir, Puluanna, Sonsoral, Angaur, Peleliu, Koror, Kayangel, Ngulu, Yap, Ulithi, Fais, Sorol, Eauripick, Wolei, and Guam.

Ensign Edward H. Lundquist, USN, was the operations officer who would make the visit on each island. *Tawakoni* was his first sea duty. He had chosen this service at commissioning because of the far-flung places this kind of ship might go—and *Tawakoni* did go!

His uniform of the day for these special visits was shorts and sneakers to get him over the coral heads and in to the shore, but, of course, he wore his cap and his uniform shirt with its insignia on its collar tabs. He carried a bag of "handclasp" materials including an American flag, which he had added at the last minute. He would present these items to the chief on each island visited.

When the official party found the chief on Woleai and presented the gifts, the chief fingered the flag and asked, "What is it?"

"It is a flag," he was told. "What is a flag? What's it for? What do I do with it?"

Ensign Lundquist explained that it was an American flag. "It is a symbol of our country. You fly it from a flagpole. It means my country will protect you."

He wasn't sure that the chief understood. He returned to the ship and told his division chief, Senior Chief Quartermaster Dan Kerins, about the exchange with the flag. He later recalled, "I never felt so inadequate about explaining something."

Ensign Lundquist and Chief Rinfl.

About a year and a half later, he received a telephone call from his former *Tawakoni* shipmate who had since been transferred to another ship that happened to be engaged in the Trust Territorial Surveillance Operation. "Remember that chief on Woleai who wondered what to do with the flag you gave him? Well, guess what? Your flag is flying high over the island from a sixty-foot-tall flagpole."

After a series of eventful island visits that November in 1977, *Tawakoni* came to Yap. But the ship could not get into the channel due to a combination of weather and scheduling. A small boat came out of the lagoon with a bag containing one piece of mail, and *Tawakoni* continued on her duties.

In December, *Tawakoni* was back in her home port of Pearl Harbor. Ensign Lundquist booked a flight from Honolulu to Boston. He was coming home for Christmas. After he arrived and settled in, he unpacked his presents—he brought many—and put them under the Christmas tree. There was one special package with his father's name on it. On Christmas Eve, it was a family custom to unwrap one present each after midnight mass. The rest came in the morning around the tree. When Ned handed his father his special package, Henry opened it to find a large American flag with a card: "To My CHIEF." It was the flag left over from Yap. Instead of flying over the island in the Pacific, it flies high between two tall and ancient oak trees in the Lundquist backyard in Newton, Massachusetts. It is hoisted aloft by ropes especially rigged by the ensign's chief.

**

Looking back from 2014 to 1994, we find still another Lundquist connection with the Pacific islands.

The island of Peleliu is little known in the world today, but it is well remembered by the U.S. Navy. This island of just five square miles in the western Pacific, today part of the Republic of Palau, is well known as the site of the World War II Battle of Peleliu that commenced on December 15, 1944.

Some historians claim that the battle should never have been fought, that it was not necessary and could have been bypassed as part of the island-hopping Pacific campaign. But don't tell that to the men who fought there or their families. There were 1,794 killed in the battle on the U.S. side and 8,010 wounded or missing. The medics went with the troops, of course, and plasma as always. Our blood donors at home had the satisfaction of knowing that some of those wounded remained alive because of their plasma.

The Navy remembered the battle when it commissioned the escort carrier USS *Palau* (CVE 124) in 1946, and later the amphibious assault ship USS *Peleliu* (LHA 5), commissioned May 3, 1980 and still serving in the fleet. As is the Navy's custom, all new members going aboard a ship must go through a period of indoctrination. On the LHA 5 it was the movie, "Battle of Peleliu." When the ship sailed past her namesake, she stopped for a visit. The crew invited the islanders out to see the ship, and enjoy a movie and refreshments. They ferried them back and forth with the ship's boats and helicopters. Crew members were allowed to visit the island and were awed at the untouched (by law) relics of one of the war's bloodiest battles.

The ship's engineer officer, Commander Carl Lundquist, went ashore and climbed Bloody Nose Ridge alone, silently gazing at shattered helmets, overgrown vehicles and dismembered tanks. He took pictures until a heavy tropical shower poured down as if in protest, drenching the camera and ruining the pictures.

**

There are countless records of what happened where in World War II: how many troops went ashore, how many ships sunk, how many bombs dropped, but there is no complete record of how many lives were saved by the administration of blood and blood plasma. Only a few of the donors and a few of the recipients are chronicled in this book, and we can never adequately thank or honor all those who gave the gift of life or received it on the battlefront and lived to come home.

ABOUT THE AUTHOR

Anastasia Kirby served as assistant director of the Red Cross wartime Blood Donor Center of Boston during World War II.

In collaboration with Lt. Henry W. Lundquist, USNR, radio officer of the Public Relations Office of the First Naval District and blood donor officer for the headquarters, she created and wrote a radio series called *Life to the Front*. It was broadcast weekly through the Columbia Broadcasting System's New England outlet, WEEI in Boston.

Out for Blood, her book about World War II, completed in 2014, combines her experiences with both the blood donors and the survivors whom she interviewed on her broadcasts.

Before and after the war, she wrote for print, broadcast, and performance. Her Christmas book for children, *A Dream of Christmas Eve*, published in 1937 and reissued for a fiftieth anniversary in 1987, is still sought by new generations.

A collection of character sketches, which she writes for her own performances, has been featured on radio, television, and stage.

She has owned a bookstore, lectured on books, and served as Book Fair radio editor.

Although essentially a creative writer, she has been tapped for historic pieces, such as *A Newton Sampler* for the 1973 bicentennial of the city of Newton, Massachusetts, and *The Chapel Speaks* for the restoration for Emmanuel College's historic chapel.

She received a bachelor of arts degree from Emmanuel College in 1935 and a doctor of humane letters, *honora causa*, in 2005.

In 1944 she married Lieutenant Lundquist in a formal Navy wedding. They had three children, two sons who are retired Navy captains and a daughter who is an artist-musician-educator.

Before her husband's death in 2003, they divided their time between two old houses in Massachusetts: an 1857 in Newton and an 1830 in Harwich on Cape Cod.

With *Out for Blood* complete, she is now turning her attention to two works in progress, a novel and another Christmas book.

INDEX

Made in the USA
San Bernardino, CA
19 August 2014